I0820238

EAST NASHVILLE SKYLINE

The Gary Hartman Series in Texas Music
Sponsored by the Center for Texas Music History,
Texas State University
Jason Mellard, General Editor

i could see there being a god
but i am certain there's not a todd snider
i could prove it

—Todd Snider
Hendersonville, TN
March 23, 2025

East Nashville Skyline

The Songwriting Legacy of Todd Snider

BRIAN T. ATKINSON

Forewords by Ramblin' Jack Elliott, Loretta Lynn, and Richard Lewis

TEXAS A&M UNIVERSITY PRESS • *College Station*

First edition

This paper meets the requirements of ANSI/NISO Z39.48–1992 (Permanence of Paper).
Binding materials have been chosen for durability.

Library of Congress Cataloging-in-Publication Data

Names: Atkinson, Brian T., author. | Elliott, Jack, 1931– writer of foreword. | Lynn, Loretta, writer of foreword. | Lewis, Richard, 1947–2024, writer of foreword.
Title: East Nashville skyline: the songwriting legacy of Todd Snider / Brian T. Atkinson; forewords by Ramblin' Jack Elliott, Loretta Lynn, Richard Lewis.
Other titles: Gary Hartman series in Texas music.
Description: First edition. | College Station: Texas A&M University Press, [2025] | Series: The Gary Hartman series in Texas music | Includes bibliographical references and index.
Identifiers: LCCN 2025022226 | ISBN 9781648433245 (cloth) | ISBN 9781648433252 (ebook)
Subjects: LCSH: Snider, Todd. | Lyricists—United States—Biography. | Singers—United States—Biography. | LCGFT: Biographies.
Classification: LCC ML420.S6729 A85 2025 | DDC 782.42164092 [B]—dc23/eng/20250516
LC record available at https://lccn.loc.gov/2025022226

For the kid

who finally summoned

enough courage

to sign up for

Songwriters Night

this week

"East Nashville Skyline"

Watching TV just makes me sad
Too many people treating people too bad
There's no hope
My old lady she's sure gonna be mad
Just spent the last fifty bucks we had
Spent the last sixty bucks we had on Mad Dog

East Nashville skyline
Crossing over to a state of mind
Leaving all our troubles way behind
That old Cumberland River
East Nashville skyline
Discount cigarettes, liquor, and wine
Anywhere, any time
We deliver

I'm still mad about the Slow Bar
I guess that's just the way things are
Something good comes along, then it's gone
It's kind of like the Phoenix Radio
We used to listen
Then where did it go?
It went off the air so that more Sheryl Crow
Could come on . . . come on

East Nashville skyline
Crossing over to a state of mind
Leaving all our troubles way behind
That old Cumberland River
East Nashville skyline
Discount cigarettes, liquor, and wine

Anywhere, any time
We deliver

Crossing the river we play them our songs
They're probably right
When they say we're all wrong
For these days
So much for money, so much for big
Who needs the trouble
Man, there's always a gig
At the cafe, the Radio Cafe

East Nashville skyline
Crossing over to a state of mind
Leaving all our troubles way behind
That old Cumberland River
East Nashville skyline
Discount cigarettes, liquor, and wine
Anywhere, any time
We deliver

TODD SNIDER, "EAST NASHVILLE SKYLINE,"
FROM *PEACE, LOVE, AND ANARCHY (RARITIES,*
B-SIDES AND DEMOS, VOL. I)
SHAD-N-FROYD-A MUSIC, 2007

Contents

Galleries of images follow pages 54 and 140.

Foreword

Todd Snider really speaks to the country's youth in their own language. He keeps them moving in the right direction and does so much good. Todd also is a very good musician who has great rhythm. I love the way he plays guitar and banjo. We did a tour together riding his bus, and I really enjoyed our time together. I hope we do another tour someday. We have young people who want to know what's happening in the world and need to communicate. Language is the most important part of a song—way more important than the melody and musical accompaniment—and it's always changing and being enriched by newly invented words. The music is just a vehicle. The way Todd embodies Woody Guthrie's legacy is very important. The song travels along as cargo, and you're the driver. Todd drives very well.

Ramblin' Jack Elliott
Marshall, California

Foreword

I have never been a cowriter. Well, not a good one anyway. I'm not knocking cowriting, but it just wasn't my cup of tea. [The Wilburn Brothers'] Teddy Wilburn was one of the very few I could share song ideas with. [Sometimes] he would give me an idea, and we could write a great song. My son-in-law Mark Marchetti, who is married to my twin daughter Peggy and is also a great songwriter himself, called one time and asked if he could bring his good friend Todd over to meet me. I said, "Well, sure." Now, understand I didn't have a clue who Todd was. You know, some friends come from the most odd pairings.

I am proud to call Todd my friend now.

Loretta Lynn
Hurricane Mills, Tennessee

Foreword

East Nashville Skyline: The Songwriting Legacy of Todd Snider is well overdue. Todd Snider deserves a book. Why wait for someone to be dead? Write about him now. Todd's already a legend. Anyone who knows and loves him admires him. He is totally down-home and beloved by his fellow singers. There are too many good things about him that scream for a book. Very cool. I had to write my own memoir because no one was coming around to write a biography. I repeat the word "authenticity" when I talk about Todd because there's not much around today.

Todd is authentic.

I so love that Todd always pushes the envelope. I thought he was a genius before I even met him. He was going through a bad time the other day, and I said, "You're Todd fucking Snider. Let it go, man. You're one of the greats. You're always striving for more. One percent of the people who start out doing this get to where you are." I'm a father figure to him in a way. I'm a fucked-up father, but I do love the guy. *East Nashville Skyline: The Songwriting Legacy of Todd Snider* will help people know Todd better.

Todd Snider. What a great subject for a book.

Richard Lewis
Los Angeles, California

Acknowledgments

Thank you first and foremost to my old buddy David Lechler, who sat me down one day in his condo at 16th and Larimer in Denver more than a quarter century ago. His eyes twinkled with discovery as he pulled a disc off the rack. "You gotta hear this," Lechler said and handed me *Songs for the Daily Planet*. "Todd Snider. Trust me. You'll dig this." He was right. I'm pretty sure we were in the audience for the songs recorded in Boulder on Todd's live album *Near Truths and Hotel Rooms* a few years later. I called my friend Jodee as this book started rolling along and asked if she remembered us talking about Todd back in the day. "Dude," she said. "You and Lechler always talked about him. We saw Todd every time he came to town."

As always, very special thanks to **The Gary Hartman Series in Texas Music**, Thom Lemmons and everyone at Texas A&M University Press, and series editor Jason Mellard for making this idea a reality. Special thanks to Jenni Finlay, who spent more time passing information between Todd and me than Todd and I spent talking to each other. Jenni was essential in this book's development. Thank you to my parents, Ted and Ruthanne Atkinson, who have supported even my wildest dares and dreams. Additionally, big thanks to the countless Todd Snider friends and followers within these pages—most notably, Scott Beckwith, Elizabeth Cook, Stacie Huckeba, Jack Ingram, Richard Lewis, Mark Marchetti, Steve Poltz, Chad Staehly, and Anita Webb—who went miles above and beyond by opening doors and minds.

Biggest thank you to Todd Snider for jumping in headfirst and swimming along as this book came together. I expected maybe one hour-long interview with Todd, but we ended up racking up more than a dozen hours over six interviews (not to mention countless follow-up calls and emails), which often started before five o'clock in the morning and always wrapped after dawn. Todd's generosity and honesty throughout greatly improved material in this book. In fact, I want to encourage readers to take the time to read the notes at the end of the book, because Todd frequently made comments and recounted memories about the people and events that simply did not fit the narrative in the main text. A unique feature of doing a book like this on a living artist is getting the chance to hear what the artist thinks about what others think about them. And Todd's comments are—like everything else about him—authentic and completely uncensored.

Additionally, a huge thank you to all the singer-songwriters, players, and industry veterans who offered their time to talk about Todd. Some I wished to interview remained unavailable despite several requests, but nearly everyone jumped at the chance—and several flagged me down on their own hoping to further boost Todd's shooting star. All these conversations during the COVID-19 pandemic's first year made the otherwise monotonous time fly.

EAST NASHVILLE SKYLINE

Prologue

Todd Snider

I grew up in Raleigh Hills in Portland, Oregon. My dad was wealthy until I was in ninth grade, but then he went bankrupt. He was in construction. Everybody suspected he was involved with something unethical, and he liked that they thought that. There was all this weird talk in my youth that reminded me of [the popular HBO series] *The Sopranos*. I found out the main heroin dealer in Portland had taken over Beaverton, which is the little town I grew up in. Those guys were drifting around in my neighborhood. My dad liked it. They were like this West Coast, Republican, strip bar, cocaine version of *The Sopranos*. Cocaine got my dad when he was probably forty. He lost his connection to the man and moved to Houston when I was fifteen.

We were weird. My brother and sister wore Polo shirts. My dad drove a Mercedes and had a horrible reputation. I grew up around sports like the World Football League because my dad was one of the investors when they started the league. I got to meet [Winnipeg Blue Bombers running back] Rufus "Roadrunner" Ferguson. Then my dad brought in this kid when I was in the ninth grade. He played football for Oregon State. He wanted this kid to be our trainer because he needed a place to crash. The kid brought Lynyrd Skynyrd into the house. That was the end of sports for me. My dad thought Skynyrd were homos because of their hair. He certainly wasn't ready for who came next: Mick Jagger. Then I found Jim Morrison my sophomore year in high school, moved out when I was sixteen, and decided to be a problem.

Mike Snider

Our parents married young and weren't educated. Our dad was a developer and builder who was full of shit. We lived in a nice neighborhood but were the outsider public high school kids who were into all sports. I enjoyed the shit out of our childhood. Our parents were fun. Dad was a little crazy. Todd and I were a year and a half apart but very close. He was my best friend growing up. We shared friends, but he hung around with mine more than I hung out with his. Todd was always funny. Sports was a bigger deal for me, but we both played them. We all were into the same music. We did a little drinking when we got older. Magical time. We had a ranch style house with a swimming pool where everybody hung out. We threw parties and had boys spend the night. Our house was welcoming. Todd was tough in high school. He didn't take any shit. He was a leader and the class clown.

Todd was quick-witted and smart. I thought he would become a comedian or a sports broadcaster. He was different and always having fun, so everybody liked to hang around him. He still makes me laugh today. I think he played football because that's what kids did, but I was a better athlete. Todd was a very competitive guy and worked pretty hard at it, but I don't think he ever took it seriously. He was stronger and tougher than I was and did everything very well, but football was never a priority. I think that was because I was older, and he had to follow me around. He started games as a linebacker, but then the quarterback got hurt and he played quarterback. Todd always has been a pretty rebellious kid who pushed the envelope. He was naturally smarter than me. He didn't take risks like jumping off a building, but he took pride in naturally being different. Todd has always marched to the beat of his own drummer but fought to conform in high school. Then he said, "Fuck it."

Introduction

Todd Snider lives poetry in motion. He wakes up before every crack, dusts himself off, and follows the next song. His imagination corners him around every bend. Snider is a marvel and a mystery, true romance that evaporates every time a new idea sparks his fancy. He lives and will die for the song. Snider will not think twice. He creates at any cost. You think you understand what makes Todd Snider tick? Give up. He doesn't understand himself. However: He trusts. He trusts his instincts. He trusts his every move. He believes. Snider said the words in a song many years ago: He believes everything. He honestly does. Snider believes everything and nothing at the same time, yet he has faith in himself even when no one else does.

His faith builds confidence. Confidence enables security. Security allows truth. Todd Snider tells the truth. He tells the truth about everything. Literally everything. He will bullshit you about everything and never tell you a single lie because everything he says is true. Everything he says is true to him, and he speaks his truth without hesitation. You know that song that says you know a man's lying because you see his mouth moving? You know Todd Snider is speaking his truth—and straight from the heart—when you see his mouth moving. He wastes no one's time even when he wastes everyone's time. Snider says he doesn't care. The man cares. He cares enough not to bullshit you. He says nothing affects him, but everything does.

Everything affects him.

Todd Snider feels the earth's every turn underneath his bare feet.

He absorbs all our missteps. Then he humanizes them in a song so we can all relate. You know the people in his songs. They are you. They are him. They are everyone under the sun. Todd Snider writes for the everyman because he is one. He's an everyman with burning curiosity. He understands that all we have in this earthly world are questions. We have no answers no matter who we ask in the sky. Snider has songs called "In the Beginning" and "If Tomorrow Never Comes." They ask those questions and answer nothing. His albums *Agnostic Hymns & Stoner Fables* and *The First Agnostic Church of Hope and Wonder* deliver his philosophy. After all, Todd Snider is a philosopher who signed up for the most thankless job in the world. He asks questions even though he knows there's no right answer. There's never any answer at all. Only truths. His truths. Our truths. Todd Snider belongs here to deliver the truths he's discovered along the way.

Now, let's back up and start at the beginning.

Todd Snider writes songs.

He writes songs with unmatched clarity. Rattles words with wild wonder. After all, the tatterdemalion troubadour, a rakish raconteur and kaleidoscopic drug enthusiast whose tumultuous subterranean lifestyle fuels his creative consequence, fortifies his workaday narratives with combustible curiosity. Results pay dividends. "Todd is as poetic a writer as anybody," legendary songwriter Kris Kristofferson says, "but words don't seem crafted with him. They come out naturally and move you emotionally in the direction he wants, but without you feeling conscious of it."[1] "Todd Snider is a flat-out musical genius," echoes country music legend Loretta Lynn. "I've been around a pretty good while, and there are a very few singer-songwriters who I would say that about. Todd is one of them."[2]

Snider, a longtime East Nashville, Tennessee, resident, born October 11, 1966, in Beaverton, Oregon, but raised as a songwriter in San Marcos, Texas, has earned equal measures critical acclaim and widespread popularity over the past three decades. A keen eye guides the journey. "Todd is always listening and observing," longtime *Houston Chronicle* music writer Andrew Dansby says. "'Talking Seattle Grunge Rock Blues' [from his 1994 debut album, *Songs for the Daily Planet*] should be a really dated song—and in some ways it is—but you can substitute current [specifics] to make it just as funny because of how he processes things. Also, Todd is very good at channeling what makes somebody feel elevated within a small circle. He paints the little details right so people seem huge in that circle like with [his friend Skip Litz] in 'Play a Train Song' [from his masterwork *East Nashville Skyline* a decade later]."[3] "A smoking, long black Cadillac, the engine's winding down / He'd park it up on the sidewalk like he owned the whole damn town," Snider sings on "Play a Train Song." "I'd hear him talking to some chick through a thick ghost of smoke / Through a thicker haze of Southern Comfort and Coke / Say, 'Girl, you're hotter than the hinges hanging off the gates of hell / Don't be afraid to turn to me, babe if he don't treat you well' / And by 'he' he meant me, so I laughed and shook his hand / He laughed a little louder as he yelled up at the band / 'Play a Train Song, pour me one more round / Make them leave my boots on / When they lay me into the ground.'" "I earned 'Play a Train Song' by loving Skip and hardly wrote those lines," Snider explains. "The details were there: Skip had a black Cadillac, and he parked the car on the sidewalk."[4]

East Nashville Skyline lifted Snider's trajectory from lovable loser ("Age Like Wine," "Tillamook County Jail") to living legend ("Iron Mike's Main Man's Last Request," "The Ballad of the Kingsmen"). So much so that an entire emergent songwriter counterculture followed Snider and his seamless song cycle to East Nashville around the millennium's turn. "Songwriters will always find Todd," Americana music beacon Jason Isbell says. "He does a certain thing that nobody does, and I don't say that lightly. Everything has been done a thousand times before, but Todd is so smart and good at making everything seem natural. John Prine is probably the closest comparison, but John was more ethereal. There was something more psychedelic about John's images, but Todd has always been a far more psychedelic person than John was."[5]

Snider informed his craft by splitting pages with the best early on. "My first songwriting mentor was Kent Finlay, who was a songwriter and owned Cheatham Street Warehouse in San Marcos, Texas," he says. "Kent's songs are as good as Townes Van Zandt, Guy Clark, and anyone we call a poet. Kent told me, 'You can be Hunter Thompson, John Prine, or Jerry Jeff Walker, but songwriting has to become a drug.' We listened to the main three songwriters all the time: Shel Silverstein, Kris Kristofferson, and Billy Joe Shaver." "Todd Snider is absolutely the best there is," the late Finlay said in *Kent Finlay, Dreamer: The Musical Legacy of Cheatham Street Warehouse*. "We're both better writers when we write together. Todd's mind works with great ideas and songs."[6]

Several have turned heads over the past thirty years. Hitmakers including Mark Chesnutt ("Trouble") and Gary Allen ("Alright Guy") as well as superstars Garth Brooks (the recorded but unreleased "Alright Guy") and Tom Jones ("Talking Reality Television Blues") have tipped hats toward his songwriting. "['Talking Reality Television Blues'] shows television's power is to remind us how wonderful, crazy, and inventive we are," Jones says, "but also how scary the reality it reflects can be."[7] "The whole key to songwriting is opening your heart and showing people what's in there,"

Snider says. "Show people you're a sweet and soulful man and a grateful human being. I am grateful when I wake up every day and remember that I don't have a job. No bad can happen from there."[8] Snider capitalizes on his freedoms by relentlessly studying fellow craftsmen. He seeks out new music daily—folk and funk, rap and rock, soul and swamp, and everything between—as he further sharpens his skills. He eases his own catalog back and forth between straight rock 'n' roll (1996's *Step Right Up*) through poignant story songs (2004's *East Nashville Skyline* and 2009's *The Excitement Plan)* and mystical folklore (2008's *Peace Queer*). Singular songwriting weaves together the fabric (2019's *Cash Cabin Sessions, Vol. 3*). Snider backs every vibrant vignette ("Rose City," "Tension") with Technicolor narratives ("Easy Money," "East Nashville Skyline," and "Can't Complain") and biting sociopolitical commentary ("Conservative Christian, Right-Wing Republican, Straight, White, American Males," and "L. W. D. (Little White Dick)").

Snider's protagonists frequently fall flat over and again ("Long Year," "Tillamook County Jail") yet grip bootstraps with hurricane force ("Looking for a Job"). They laugh easily at their own shortcomings ("Greencastle Blues") but always deliver heart ("Waco Moon"). "Todd writes with class, empathy, and humor," explains singular songwriter Hayes Carll. "You don't see many people getting pissed off at Todd's views even though they may be wildly different. He has a sense of humor onstage and off, and the way he incorporates that into his songs rarely gets old."[9] "Todd's fans know he's speaking the real truth with no bullshit," the late iconic comedian Richard Lewis says. "He whittles down the fat on his brilliantly funny stories. Todd takes those spoken word parts between the songs as seriously as his music. He likes his role as a preacher."[10]

Snider's legendary storytelling in concert has drawn as much attention—if not more—than the songs themselves. Witness *Near Truths and Hotel Rooms* (2003), *Todd Snider Live: The Storyteller* (2011), and *Live: Return of the Storyteller* (2022). Crowds multiply exponentially for his marquee monologues. Snider's finest—rambling diatribes about blue-collar country singer K. K. Rider, a NASCAR racer Bill Elliott lookalike, and the tale about The Devil's Backbone Tavern in Central Texas are among the more popular—mirror the seeming looseness in songs like "Doublewide Blues," "The Devil You Know," and "The Ballad of the Kingsmen." Not a syllable moves by happenstance. "I type out and edit the stories I tell for songs like 'The Ballad of the Devil's Backbone Tavern' [and 'If Tomorrow

Never Comes'],” Snider admits. “I started approaching them like songs and kept my antennae open for more.”

His “Eighteen Minutes Speech” foreshadowed upcoming between-song speeches for years. “Don't stop me if you've heard this,” Snider would say. “This is for that friend you dragged out. If you've never heard me play before, my name is Todd Snider, and I've been driving around this great country of ours for almost fifteen years now. I make this shit up and sing it for anybody who will listen to it. Some of the songs are sad, some are funny. Some are short, some will seem like they go on for as many as eighteen minutes. Sometimes I may talk for as many as eighteen minutes in between a particular song.”

“I came up with the ‘Eighteen Minutes Speech’ in the late nineties,” Snider says. “John Prine had shown me how to write a show, and I got this idea so that I could play, and sing, and talk all at one time from muscle memory. I discovered that eighteen minutes would go by after I played ‘Can't Complain’ and ‘Long Year’ and talked between songs. I would have had time to check the temperature of the room, get dialed into the frequency, and give myself to it. Calibrating a house used to take five to ten minutes. Then I wouldn't have to think anymore. The show would become more like a meditation or trance, but I don't need that trick anymore. I've let go of the part of myself that isn't on because it seemed off. Now the set list tends to indicate more what won't happen.”

Such fearlessness allows focus. Snider effectively tells stories around a campfire during his shows. His words are intimate and familiar. Songs join your fabric. “The things Todd talks about lyrically are very conversational,” Isbell says, “but his songs open like an onion. You just get more meaning once you start laughing.” “Todd is like French cooking,” explains top-tier producer Don Was (Bob Dylan, Rolling Stones). “All the ingredients are seemingly contradictory, but what comes out is really delicious anyway. He's funny and as deep as you can be with songs—maybe within the same sentence—and makes it seem so nonchalant as he hits on the essence of life. He plays with time, place, and humor, seriousness, optimism, and pessimism at the same time.”[11]

Snider's deceptively carefree “tipsy gypsy” persona resonates above all. “I don't want to have big, lofty ambitions that I would have to write down, but they sneak in sometimes,” he explains. “My biggest thing was the notion that I could impact others the way others had impacted me. I'm mostly in this to be a gypsy and travel, but the thought that you can help one person is a big reason, too. I don't try to do that, but I think it would be cool if it happened. That would make me feel really good, but I mostly feel good about still making up songs and wanting to play them. I ask the older people who write songs and travel around, 'Do you still love it?' Because I do. I still love doing this."

Verse: Cheatham Street Warehouse

THE SAN MARCOS YEARS

Todd Snider passes through Northern California on his way from Oregon to Central Texas as a teenager. Snider eyes songwriting as a life and lifestyle but has no blueprint as a guide. Enter Kent Finlay. Snider lands on the couch of the songwriter and owner of Cheatham Street Warehouse one night around fall 1987. He stays nearly three years. The sage spirit teaches him about living life outside the box and writing songs for a living. "Meeting Kent was a big thing for Todd," says his brother, Mike Snider. "Todd played an open-mic night at Cheatham Street Warehouse and found someone who could teach him and who acknowledged that he was a writer." "Dad liked Todd from the get-go," echoes the mentor's daughter, Jenni Finlay. "He knew how to grow Todd as a songwriter."

Snider immediately starts writing songs. He never stops.

Todd Snider

I met Kent Finlay when I still wanted to be a problem and live a chaotic life. My brother was in San Marcos, and my dad was in Austin. My brother told me about Stevie Ray and Jimmie Vaughan, but I was really into lyrics. I saw Jerry Jeff Walker playing solo at Gruene Hall [in New Braunfels, Texas] before I met Kent around 1986. What he was doing seemed doable for a guy who wanted to be a lyricist. I was with [Snider's friend] Trog [referenced in his song "The Ballad of the Devil's Backbone Tavern"] that night. I had left home when I was a sophomore in high school and was really into Hunter Thompson. A million light bulbs went off when I saw Jerry Jeff Walker.

Jerry Jeff made me feel the lifestyle was romantic. I had just seen it as a sadness and weakness before that night. Now I thought I would always be rambling and scrambling. Gambling? I'm in. Drinking? In. Sex? In.

That other stuff? Not in. My dad identified with gypsy culture. He worked in car sales for the king of the gypsies before I was born and was German and dark-skinned. My dad liked to think he was a gypsy in the way that some people like to think they're Indians. I saw the gypsy song man in these wild boots with these wild stories with Jerry Jeff Walker. I was like, "I'm doing that now. I'm living on this Trog guy's couch now. I don't have a car. I'm just shucking and jiving."

I would do any job at Gruene Hall from being Jerry Jeff's roadie to the door guy and loved it. I realized that the small concert is my thing. I started having an obsession with four-hundred-seat shows. They don't even tell you those exist growing up in Oregon. Now I know that Ramblin' Jack Elliott was playing the Aladdin Theater [in Portland] when I was growing up. I imagined that they would never ask me to leave when I was staying at Trog's if I could sing later. Finding another sofa felt looming. Bells went off. Who doesn't want to give a ride to the guy who sings all these songs? Who doesn't want to let him crash? I realized that before I met Kent. I didn't even have a song. I knew a couple chords from the guys around me, but I had massive visions of grandeur at night.

I bought a guitar the very next day for sixty bucks and quickly made up my first song in San Marcos called "Bus Tub Stew." I was a busboy at Pepper's [at the Falls in San Marcos] and had been writing abstractly like, "Ride the snake down the highway." Meeting Kent changed my opinion about Jim Morrison being a poet. Kent was singing linear songs about needing a ride and a place to stay. Well, I needed a ride and a place to stay. I had an epiphany that I could write about the life I was living. I stopped writing, "The silver shadows . . ." and started writing, "I pick up busboy food," which was a very Texan way to write and a big thing when I got into linear songs. They came easy. You play a couple chords and sing the truth. I sang a song for the Martin Brothers one night they were playing at Pepper's and Bubba dared me to play "Bus Tub Stew." The fucking house came down.[1]

I immediately had a new focus. I was serious about writing Mark Twain-like rock 'n' roll, but I also was a mainstream listener who knew Jim Croce and Jimmy Buffett and thought I was like them. I was couch surfing and hitchhiking already and was terrible with girls. I already was leaning into anything with alcohol and any other negative influences. My dad had been a bullshitter to the detriment of others, but I saw Jerry Jeff as a bullshitter to their enjoyment. I still think Jerry Jeff embodies something bigger than music. Townes Van Zandt followed his footsteps. Some people argue that his lifestyle choice is negative, but I'm not one. Ramblin' Jack talks about developing the craft of a gypsy as a lifestyle first and then as art second.

Kent was a tether to that reality. He had this real ethic that said, "You don't know that that homeless guy is unhappy. You don't know why he's there. He may be thrilled." Kent made me feel like he was standing up for me. I wasn't going to college and didn't have a plan. Kent thought you were already living the John Belushi and Hunter S. Thompson life if you could write about it. Kent had seen the reality, though. There was a difference to split between having a good time and destroying yourself to become an artist. I always felt like being an artist was accepting that you wouldn't be part of anything constructive.

Kris Kristofferson's song "The Pilgrim, Chapter 33" is the one that really hooked me. "See him wasted on the sidewalk in his jacket and his jeans / Wearing yesterday's misfortunes like a smile." I look back on that and think, "What a crazy thing for Kent to have fed a young kid, and look how long it lasted." "Never knowing if believing is a blessing or a curse / Or if the going up was worth the coming down." I was with Bob Schneider one time watching John Mellencamp play. He was like, "That is a grown man hitting a box with strings tied to it and yelling at the rest of these people." "I know," I said. "Don't tell anyone, but what a weird thing for an adult to do."[2]

Mike Snider

I remember listening to music at Kent Finlay's Cheatham Street Warehouse. I was into Stevie Ray Vaughan and was learning to play blues guitar, but I wasn't into [lyrics] as much as Todd. He was into Billy Joe Shaver. Kent Finlay taught him about songs, song structure, chords, and how songs are written. Todd knew nothing about that. He was faking it by listening to others. Kent actually sat down and taught him. Todd had found someone who did this for a living and thought he was good. Todd has taken songwriting very seriously since then.

Kent and Todd were attached at the hip for a very long time. Todd spent his time at Kent's house and Cheatham Street. He would repeat everything Kent said to me and still does. Of course, Kent and Todd didn't always agree. That's for sure. Todd thought Kent was wrong many times because Kent's thing wasn't exactly what Todd wanted. Same with [Todd's next mentor in Memphis] Keith Sykes. He eventually would fight with them, Jimmy Buffett, and [Oh Boy Records President] Al Bunetta, but I don't think he ever fought with John Prine. Todd was his own thing. Kent didn't like when Todd got a certain amount of success regionally.

Todd wrote his first song in one night. We had been partying and doing cocaine, but I had to work the next night and went to bed. I had taught Todd how to play the G, C, and D chords. He fumbled through learning those at nine at night. I came out the next morning, and Todd was still up. He had written "Bus Tub Stew" and played it for me. He played it live soon after. Todd always was nervous that people wouldn't like his shows. He was always trying out new things, scrapping things, and was crazy writing new stuff at that point. I don't remember him playing long sets in San Marcos. He would crush them in three songs. He would go in, tell stories, make people laugh, and leave. Mic drop.[3]

Mike Snider is Todd Snider's older brother. He works with Christian music recording artists for the William Morris Endeavour agency in Nashville.

Kent Finlay

Todd was a teenager when he started coming to Songwriters Night at Cheatham Street Warehouse. He came in with this gorgeous mahogany brown Takamine guitar that he got for Christmas around 1986. He had a smart, witty humor and was a good bullshitter even then, which was what sold his songs. There was one called "Fat Chicks on Mopeds" and a protest song called "Stand Up If You're Eighteen" that he wrote because the drinking age was raised from eighteen to nineteen. "Bus Tub Stew" was a funny song. I told Todd I could help him write songs, and he ended up moving in. We wrote every day.

The first song we wrote together was called "This Old Guitar." That one has really stuck with me: "Popped a Dr. Pepper and drifted away / Hopped up on a toolbox, and I began to play." Todd had that hunger. I would point out what was good with songwriters like Kris Kristofferson and Shel Silverstein and [interpreters like] Bobby Bare every day. Kristofferson was a great influence on both Todd and me. He wrote great alliteration and those incredible rhymes. I taught Todd to drink Jack Daniel's the night we worked on a song called "Who Says It's Lonely at the Top." I'm not sure who brought the song to the table—probably Jack Daniel's—but we definitely were channeling Bobby Bare and Shel Silverstein.

Todd has so many great songs that have knocked me for a loop. "Long Year" was one. Sometimes the really funny ones do the same. Funny songs are harder to write than something really serious. Of course, Todd wrote "Waco Moon" when Billy Joe Shaver's son, Eddy, died [on December 31, 2000]. That song will knock you out and make you cry every time you hear it. Writing with Todd is like writing with myself. He knows what I'm thinking. I know what he's thinking. Todd Snider is like a brother and a son.[4]

Kent Finlay (1938–2015) was a singer-songwriter and owner of Cheatham Street Warehouse in San Marcos, Texas. Kent Finlay, Dreamer: The Musical Legacy of Cheatham Street Warehouse, *tells his story.*

Jenni Finlay

"Fat Chicks on Mopeds" and "Bus Tub Stew" were funny songs, but Dad taught Todd how to write clever-funny and not quirky-funny words and phrases. Todd wrote "Happy Hour Hero" about his dad pretty soon after. "Happy Hour Hero" describes those old men who sit at the bar there every night. Todd was inspired to write the song by real guys at this weekly gig he, john Arthur martinez, my dad, and I would play at Katy Station in San Marcos, Texas. Those guys he describes in the song always say they're so busy. They say they're about to fly out for some important business trip and have the busted Rolex to prove how big time they supposedly were. Of course, they're always right back at the bar at five o'clock the next day.

I was about seven years old when Todd started crashing at our house. It wasn't unusual for me to wake up and find another songwriter sleeping on the couch in those days. Dad welcomed anybody and everybody who was writing their own original songs and offered a place to eat and sleep, but Todd was different. All the songwriters who would come around were from the area, but Todd was from Portland, and he talked like someone we had never heard. He would say stuff like, "Slap me some skin." My brother, Sterling, and I were like, "Wow. What does that mean?" Todd taught us all these other cool catchphrases that he had brought in from the West Coast. He was so funny and cool—easily the coolest person we knew. Dad saw great potential in Todd when he brought him home, and Todd ended up living with us for about three years.

Todd slept on our camping air mattress in the music room where Dad kept his electric Roland piano. We lived in a house Dad built way out in the country. The house itself had a personality of its own. Dad could pretty much fix it if something broke. He repaired our band van's alternator with a part off a broken dishwasher one time, which blew the mechanic's mind when it broke down again a couple years later. Anyway, because the way the house was wired—and I still don't know exactly why this happened—whenever the landline phone would ring, even though the phone in the music room's ringer was off, that Roland piano would make this guttural buzz that Todd would put in a song decades later. Dad taught Todd how to make his songs better. Todd really studied like a serious student. Dad taught him to do charts and lyrics and played him Bobby Bare, Kris Kristofferson, and Shel Silverstein songs.

Also, Dad would instruct Todd to do certain things and was very peculiar and specific with his lessons. He would have Todd walk to the oak tree and back. The oak tree is a significant place on our property. We had one hundred acres, and the oak tree was the halfway point. Todd had to walk fifty acres slowly and think about what his next song would be. Those lessons obviously resonated. Todd still walks out the front door today when he has a song idea and doesn't come back until he writes it. Dad and Todd were always writing. Todd even wrote a song with my mother called "Songwriter's Prayer."[5]

Jenni Finlay manages singer-songwriter James McMurtry and owns Jenni Finlay Promotions. She co-owns Eight 30 Records, Barefoot Recording, and Catfish Concerts with the author.

Diana Finlay Hendricks

Todd and I wrote "Songwriter's Prayer" one afternoon when he was experiencing what may have been his first songwriting dry spell. Todd was writing good songs every day and batting them out of the park every time. He was nineteen or twenty with a quirky sense of humor that belied his age. Todd wrote about low-hanging fruit for a songwriter and waiter living in a college town like fat chicks on mopeds and bus tub stew, but he also wrote really brilliant satire about current events and finding hypocrisy in the moral majority.

We had stacks of yellow legal pads in every room of the house, and the quest became to fill the notebooks with songs, lines, and ideas once one started. Todd was hanging around the kitchen and coming up with nothing the day we wrote "Songwriter's Prayer." We began to play around with a songwriter's prayer, and [the words] just flowed. There was no shining star in the east or struggle to climb a mountain. We just went back and forth and line for line. I had tossed lines into songs and edited them for Kent and others who were around the house, but I guess Todd was the only person who ever gave me cowriting credit. I'm glad it was Todd if I was going to have one cowrite with someone.[6]

Diana Finlay Hendricks is the author of Delbert McClinton: One of the Fortunate Few. *She is a San Marcos-based freelance writer and photographer.*

Jenni Finlay

Dad and Todd were trying to write a Shel Silverstein song for Bobby Bare when they wrote "Who Says It's Lonely at the Top." Dad brought a bottle of whiskey, a Sprite, and a cup of ice into the music room that night. He wanted to teach Todd how to drink Jack Daniel's properly. He put everything down. Then he took the Sprite away. "Son," he said. "This is how you do it." They wrote differently. Dad would make up songs out of his head. Todd writes what he knows. He picks up stuff from television and people watching. Todd would write the first line. Then Dad would write the second line. I know exactly who wrote which lines in [the Finlay and Snider cowrite] "Statistician's Blues" [from 2002's *New Connection*]. "They say 65 percent of all statistics are made up right there on the spot" came off the bathroom wall at Cheatham. Dad saw that.

Todd was so many things to Dad—a brother, a son, and a co-conspirator. They ran around together. Everybody knew that Todd was Dad's favorite. Nobody could mess with that. Dad would drop everything anytime Todd would show up. Dad would always call and say, "What are you working on?" That was his big deal. He always wanted Todd to be writing. All the other songwriters understood they could never be Todd to my dad. Todd was his favorite cowriter. Dad once said, "It's like I'm writing with myself when I write with Todd." Todd probably had written a hundred songs by the time he left for Memphis because he had been studying under my dad so much. I remember the first great song I got to witness. I was sitting way up on a palate leaning up against the wall in the music room.

The song was called "This Old Guitar," which was one of my favorites. Getting to watch the process was almost as beautiful as the song. I remember when they were working on the lines, "I popped a Dr. Pepper and I drifted away / Hopped up on a toolbox, and I began to play." They came up with some great lines for the choruses like the beginning of the first one, "You know me and this guitar have seen brighter days / Wrote better songs and traveled so far / You know we traveled far / Now all its strings are rusted, all my dreams are busted / He said, Son, there are no more songs left in this old guitar." Then they ended with, "So I sat beneath the moon tonight just picking to the stars / Mister, there was one more song left in this old guitar." Then Todd wrote "Stand Up If You're Eighteen" and a beautiful song called "I'm Gonna Rest in Peace." I don't know if these songs are even around anymore.

My mother made live-in songwriters have a job to earn their keep at our house like washing the dishes, shoveling the ashes out of our enormous fireplace, sweeping the porch, setting up the guitars, or cutting the grass. Todd's job was driving Sterling to his weekly Cub Scout meetings, which could explain a lot about my brother today. Todd had a big, faded 1969 Buick LeSabre called "the Peach" with a CB radio connected to an outside speaker that could blast all over San Marcos. He left San Marcos for Memphis in the Peach, but the car broke down somewhere around Waxahachie. The car might still be right there in its tracks. If anyone finds it, they should put a plaque on that thing—or maybe some cool graffiti. We never found out how Todd actually got to Memphis.

Pretty sure he doesn't know either.[7]

Scott Beckwith

I crossed paths with Todd was when I was playing with Sleepy LaBeef at Raven's on Sixth Street in Austin in the late eighties. Kent and Jenni Finlay were playing inside, and we were playing outside. I heard Kent singing a song called "Reaching for the Stars" and related to the lyric, "Reaching for the stars and working for the door." I talked with Kent for a brief second. "Come back tomorrow if you like songs," Kent said. "We have a big songwriter thing going on," which was his songwriter showcase outdoors at Raven's. We were staying over in town that weekend, so I came back the next day. All these great songwriters in that scene were playing: Terry Warren, john Arthur martinez, Olin Murrell, Kent, and Todd. Todd was a guy my age singing great songs and having a great time.

I asked him if it was cheap to live in Austin. Todd said it was super cheap. "I'll tell you what," he said, "that guy over there has his finger on the pulse of the whole songwriter scene in Austin. His name's Kent." Todd was talking about the guy who I had met the night before. So, the first time I met Todd he pointed me to Kent as I'm sure he had done with many other people. Todd was staying at Kent's house but also was sharing an apartment down by Pepper's at the Falls across from where everybody lays out in the sun in San Marcos. Todd was very encouraging to me and others in the scene no matter how young and green. He definitely was the best songwriter of us—even in his raw state. The guy obviously had something going on.

I moved down from Massachusetts later that year and immediately hooked into the scene. I went to songwriter nights at Katy Station that Todd was doing and would go over to the apartment that Todd shared with rugby guys. I would play him my new song and just talk about things. He said, "You're every bit as good a songwriter as I am." Which isn't true, but he was very encouraging. "Why hasn't he made it?" I asked about Kent. "Kent's gonna make it through somebody else," he said. "He's more interested in helping other people." He did. Todd turned out to be that guy—among many others in their own way. I ended up being the guy staying at the Finlays right after Todd left and was camping out on the floor in the songwriter room.[8]

Scott Beckwith is a Wimberley, Texas-based songwriter, author, and owner of Birdsong Guitars. His latest book is Together by Choice: A Year in the Lives of Forming Intentional Community Circle *(2023).*

Todd Snider

I agree with the Charles Bukowski quote, "Some people never go crazy. What truly horrible lives they must lead." I saw madness as a natural thing even as a young person as opposed to getting your shit together. Kent's last song was "We Never Jumped That Train." I was like, "Kent, I did. I jumped a lot. I made an ass out of myself." He wrote these amazing songs without ever really jumping off the rope swing too far. That's not a put-down to him either. There are people who create huge bodies of work without hurting a million other people. Kent was one. He didn't have to go get arrested to write a song about being arrested. I remember thinking, Kent, I wish you would have jumped on that train with me just one time, but he felt like out here in the train is where I was getting the crappy songs. I know. That chips away at the perfection.[9]

Scott Beckwith

Kent's marching orders were to do whatever it takes to get the song. You write every day. You should write these lyrics in your own blood. Don't waste time with extra words. Simmer them down. Todd has lived that way ever since. There were some hardcore Kent Finlay songwriting devotees who found that path as almost a religious experience. I'm sure Terri Hendrix sat across the desk from Kent a few times. We devotees stayed on the floor and had jobs around the house. Todd found the track to destiny with Kent. Kent always spoke very highly of Todd [after he left for Memphis]. Todd had come in and totally became this great writer right off the bat. He had his own great presence. Todd walks into a room and the energy changes.[10]

Terri Hendrix

Todd told me about Cheatham Street Warehouse. Kent Finlay appealed to me because he never booked artists based on their beer sales. Kent cared about the people who came into his building as long as they respected the songwriter. He loved lyrics, thought about every word he wrote, and created a magical atmosphere in a venue that was all about the songs. Todd and I both had jobs at Pepper's at the Falls. Todd was a busboy and a waiter who was only there because he had to earn money. His head was really into the songs by the time he arrived. He was already starting to get a following and was getting ready to launch his career.[11]

Pioneering independent artist Terri Hendrix has released nineteen albums on her own record label and founded the Own Your Own Universe nonprofit arts center in Martindale, Texas.

Scott Beckwith

Todd and Kent's cowrites like "You Bring the Condoms, I'll Bring the Wine" and "Bubba Sunday" were legendary around San Marcos. Fantastic works. Kent was my guru, but Todd was a big influence on me because I related to him as a peer my age. He entertained people and had a great time. His songs already were better than anybody else from the time I met him. The people in the circle Kent were nurturing and showcasing were all good, but Todd even young and green was something special. Obviously, it takes a long time for someone's serious songs to develop. He couldn't have written "Long Year" back then, but he could write the hell out of "Fat Chicks on Mopeds" with the same level of craft as a Kristofferson song.

Kent's biggest lesson was to write every day. Writing twenty songs in a week isn't easy, but it is doable if songwriting is a way of life and not a hobby. You fit everything else in around your time with a pen and a notebook. Joining Kent was like joining a Cosa Nostra. You could have called us a "cosa notebook." You go through the ceremony, and then you are in. Now you write every day. Nothing got by Todd. You can tell by listening to the words in his early songs. No opportunity got by him either. He got arrested one time for not having on his seat belt and went to jail. He came out with "Hays County Jail," which was a great song and Todd in a nutshell. The situation easily could have been diffused, but then there would be no song.[12]

Kent was a songwriter's songwriter. I wouldn't be surprised if Kent let that seat belt thing happen [so Todd would find a song]. I don't think either of them had any regrets about Todd going to jail. That happened before I got there and already was the Todd Snider lore that was starting to build when I showed up. Then when Todd got his marching orders he hopped into a ratty old '69 Buick named the Peach. That thing blows up halfway to Memphis, and he keeps going. Again, Todd in a nutshell. He knew the next song was in Memphis. His car blows up? He would just start walking if he had to walk.

Sundance Records in San Marcos had posters for *Songs for the Daily Planet* when the album came out. *Songs for the Daily Planet* was playing on their stereo, and everyone was buzzing. One customer bought the album on cassette and said he thought Todd was the voice of a generation. Todd put into words what many felt and the irony of those lyrics, "My generation should be proud . . ." "Talkin' Seattle Grunge Rock Blues" was everywhere. In fact, the song saved my life two times. I heard it on the radio once while waiting for a job interview that would have negatively changed my life. I looked at what I was doing when the song came on and went, "Nah." Left. Then I was stocking shelves another time on the overnight shift. Todd came on the radio. I was like, "What the fuck am I doing?" Bailed. "What would Todd do?" Not this.[13]

Greg Ellis

Todd hadn't even written his first song when he came to Sundance Records for the first time. He just came in and looked around. [Sundance owner] Bobby Barnard and I would play him singer-songwriter records. We started talking and he was very excited about everything. He was eighteen years old and had loads of positive energy. He later had a well-put-together talking blues called "Fat Chicks on Mopeds." "Bubba Sunday" was more ambitious. Those two really stuck out in my mind.[14]

Greg Ellis owned Sundance Records in San Marcos for several years. He currently owns Groover's Paradise Records in Austin.

Jimmy Collins

I met Todd when he was cooking gravy in the kitchen at Pepper's. I'll never forget how unbelievably dirty he was. He got up onstage and sang "Bus Tub Stew." The first verse and chorus were incredible. I drove out to Kent Finlay's house after seeing that and said, "Kent, you have to hear this young guy Todd Snider." Todd started going out to Kent's house in Martindale right away. Kent was a sponge. He would observe what Todd was doing and helped him form a song from it. I can assure you that Todd knew nothing about songwriting back then. Period. Kent did. Kent and Todd became quite an item for a long, long time. Todd has a heart that would blow people's minds. Everything he does is about putting that heart in a song. Songs are his babies. Kent brought out that motivation.

Todd was scary brilliant. He would write these songs even before *The Daily Planet* so he could play places. Kent, Todd, and I would play at Katy Station down the street. I remember the first time Todd made $300 at a gig. He was like a kid in a candy store. I knew Todd was a star. He had a big following that went into Austin and would knock your head off. Same later at the Daily Planet in Memphis. Todd had learned so much from Kent. He wrote a lot of those early songs staying at my house in Nashville. My brother Chad Collins and Mark Maynard had a lot to do with it. They tried to keep Todd in line. Hell, you can't keep Todd in line. That's what makes him a star.[15]

Jimmy Collins is a singer-songwriter based in Nashville. He owns Flying C Records.

Todd Snider

Kent helped me see the fundamental underlying thing. I felt like a bum with no future, but he had this freedom of spirit and expression and was doing performance art. Music was one of his tools. He didn't stop. He never got offstage, and I loved him for it. His life was a seventy-eight-year cosmic joke that he saw early on. I thought I was living at the will of others like a permanent guest, but Jerry Jeff sang about what I was living, romanticized it, and made me feel like a superhero without any ties by being a songwriter.[16]

john Arthur martinez

I met Todd at Songwriters Night at Cheatham Street Warehouse. We connected as songwriters. Also, he gave me responses to songs I had written. Kent really liked my song "Canta Papa" and praised the good parts. Todd similarly responded to a storytelling type song of mine called "Rainy Rainy Clouds." He has retold the hook—"it's a blue song in Tucson / When the rain stays for too long"—in a few of his recordings. Todd acknowledging my songwriting inspired me to keep doing what I do.

We were around the old wood-burning stove in the back room at Cheatham the night we met. Todd was sitting to my left. I remember that because I joke that Todd is to everyone's left. I was really impressed with his songs and challenged by his presence there. Same thing with the other songwriters there. Aaron Allen [whose song "Truth No. 1" was recorded by Willie Nelson] and [New Braunfels-based songwriter] Al Barlow were there, but I was impressed with Todd because I wanted to have a new song like he did for every Songwriters Night, which was on Tuesdays back then. Todd always had a new song ready for the next week. I had a lot more time to write than most college students because I was waiting on one course to graduate. I spent a lot of time with a pad and pen.

Todd often wove in serious themes amid a humorous lyric. He helped me realize that there was more than one way to reach a listener, but I never wanted to emulate Todd's style. I wanted to be my own person, partly because Todd's strongest suit was being an individual. He was definitely influenced by Kent's presence. Kent encouraged us all to be better writers, but Todd was his own cat. Kent and Todd got together quite often. Kent wouldn't do that if there wasn't something special in their relationship. Todd had songs like "Fat Chicks on Mopeds," but he was writing more serious topics with humor with Kent on songs like "Bubba Jesus." I learned from Todd how to break into an ad-libbed story about the song while playing.

Todd's most popular songs online today are the ones where he's telling the coolest stories. You wind up finding cool things in those stories. People definitely think they know you better when you tell stories in concert. I'm sure there are people out there who think they're best friends with Todd because they know him so well through those stories. I'm not just talking about making an introduction to a song when I talk about Todd's storytelling. Sometimes he will tell a story between the second and third verse. That really connects with an audience. Of course, they have never even had a cup of coffee or an adult beverage with him.[17]

john Arthur martinez made his mainstream mark by finishing in second place on the first season of the television talent show Nashville Star *in 2003. His lives in the Texas Hill Country.*[18]

Terri Hendrix

Todd definitely was an artist, a free spirit who was going to do what he was going to do. He could get away with anything. He's a handsome and charismatic songwriter. Who doesn't want to be around that? People would really listen to him at the shows because he was confident and had a laser focus with what he was doing. I mostly saw Todd play at Songwriters Night in 1987, and then he moved to [Memphis]. I was nineteen. Songwriters Night back then was Al [Barlow], Ike Eichenberg, Kent Finlay, Todd, and me.

I wasn't very confident back when we were all around Cheatham Street. Todd and I didn't really strike up a friendship or talk about songwriting. We were just at the same place at the same time, but I had a lot of respect for his writing. I really valued the fact that he was respected by his peers. Kent would tell people to shut up when he would perform, but we both know that songwriters talk over each other's songs. People listened with Todd. There were some really special nights and camaraderie. We all met up one night and shared drinks and songs, and I remember Todd hearing my songs. I was really happy he did.

Even his funny ones were poignant in some ways. They always had a little "gotcha" moment. I always was bothered when people would view him as writing just gimmicky songs. Todd's compositions have always had a beginning, a middle, and an end. Todd is cloaked in some habits, but underneath it all he's a really disciplined artist. People go see Todd for the songs and stories. Watching him grow as an artist was a really great experience. He is an important artist and voice for this time period.

Jason Isbell might have the Americana throne right now, but he got there on the shoulders of Todd Snider.[19]

Joe Ely

Todd, Jack Ingram, and I played in Tyler, Texas, one time. I hadn't seen a better show than Todd's—he's one of the greats—but the evening was strange. The show was promoted by television and posters for the wrong date. This was a show with a great big PA. Seven people showed up, and we were fifty miles from another town. We decided that since we came from different directions we might as well play our sets. We had old friends and girlfriends who came to the show, and we played for them and ourselves. Things could have gotten really nasty with people being pissed off, but we said, "Hey, this is what we do. We don't need to get all bent out of shape. Let's all play. This is what we like to do."[20]

Joe Ely has worked with punk pioneers the Clash, alt-country progenitors Uncle Tupelo, and several between. He founded the Flatlanders with Butch Hancock and Jimmie Dale Gilmore.

Cody Canada

I was playing Top 40 country when I first saw Todd, but I loved how he really paints a picture that explains everything in his brain as a songwriter. I would love to borrow his brain for a while. I have a thousand ideas but can't make them work poetically. I get lucky every now and again. Writing a song takes me days, but I envision Todd writing a perfect song all in one day. I think songs need a beginning, middle, and end. Merle Haggard said songs should be two verses, a chorus, and out. I love Merle, but I think there should be three verses: a setup, the plot, the end. Todd and I have talked quite a bit about songwriting late night after gigs.

Todd is one of the most real people I have met in this industry. I don't know if he meant to do it, but I know a lot of people who met him in the beginning here in Texas who wanted to have the same demeanor as him and attitude toward other artists. He helps other artists and is just nice. There are so many shitheads in this business. Todd was always nice to the openers for his shows. You should always be nice to your opener. Todd was nice to us even before we got to be pals. You will go a lot farther that way. I don't understand why it's so hard to just be nice. You can still be a rebel and be your own person. You want to see someone as real as Todd. Todd fucks up, but being a fuckup is part of life. That's my favorite part with Todd. Most of the world can't admit when they fuck up. Todd does.[21]

Cody Canada was the lead singer for Texas Red Dirt music pioneers Cross Canadian Ragweed for more than fifteen years. He currently fronts Cody Canada and the Departed.

Jack Ingram

I met Todd when my manager gave me *Songs for the Daily Planet* and said, "You're gonna love this." That was one of those moments when someone is like, "You're gonna love each other." Then they look at each other and are like, "Actually, no, I don't like you." You're so much alike, check each other out, but realize you take up each other's space. You're not sure you're gonna like this dude. I knew. We had the same agent who booked us on about twelve shows in 1996. I was gonna go open for Todd when his record was out and mine was coming out. I liked the *Daily Planet*, but something about those songs threatened me.

I watched him play one Tuesday night in South Carolina. Todd fucking slayed. He laid it out there like no one I had ever seen in a bar. I was hooked. He embodied the stories I had always heard about Jerry Jeff. I watched him exit the stage like he was gonna get attacked by the audience somehow. Todd was everything that I got into this business to be. I was like a puppy dog from then on. "Hey, Jack, you wanna . . . ?" "Yep." "Hey, Jack, you wanna . . . ?" "Yep." I tagged along anywhere they went to soak it up as much as I could. Luckily, that didn't annoy him to no end, and we became really good friends.

I became so enamored with his songwriting. You have to let yourself be vulnerable whether you're writing a heartfelt song or you're turning on a line unlike your peers. People think Todd has some schtick, but that first record was very heartfelt even though it felt very raw and immature. You dislike in other people what you see in yourself. Todd was a reminder to me that I wasn't necessarily there as a songwriter. I wasn't sure if it was because Todd wasn't quite there either or if I just saw holes in the songs. I was threatened until I saw him live and realized he's like a brother from another mother. Actually, he's not like a brother. Todd is my brother.[22]

Jack Ingram was a popular regional singer-songwriter for more than a decade before skyrocketing his single "Wherever You Are" to number one on the Billboard Country charts.

Todd Snider

Jack Ingram would play at Cheatham Street. He is very athletic with a very normal family. Jack and I bonded. Strippers before tippers. Our friendship is really deep. People were chipping at him later for being so successful, but they might as well have been chipping at me. I was taking it really personally. Also, Jack was looking for a way out of the world he was in from when he met me. I like to think that I was someone who helped him do that. I like to think that I'm the place where he comes and becomes very artistic. I'm always like, "I could break your fucking nose for you, and you wouldn't have any of these problems. You gotta ugly up that mug, man." I feel like Jack and me have a similar thing to [Guy Clark and Rodney Crowell].

Jack stuck his toe in the water of success. I said, "You're not the first. You're like Rodney and Rosanne [Cash]. Go get that money. Get the bus. Then go apply it to your passion." He's really been getting into the songwriting more now. I worry about him a little because I feel like he's finally getting back to work on being a Townes type. I have always seen Jack as not Pat Green, who is a frat guy who thought singing looked fun. Pat reminds me of KISS or the Stones. The concerts kept getting bigger and bigger, and Mick Jagger had to do these wild gestures. People like Pat Green come along and say their favorite part of the show is the big, wild gesture. Guy Clark did a similar thing. He went through a weird phase where he was doing coke and whooping up the crowd. Well, that's not the show at all.[23]

Greg Ellis

Sundance Records had a half-page ad in the *Austin Chronicle* through our distributor. Half was four album titles we featured at Sundance. The other half was my column called "See You in San Marcos." Well, there was no real music scene in San Marcos then. The goal was to get good enough to play in Austin. I was trying to get people's names in the *Chronicle*, so I wrote an early column on Todd, which was probably the first thing anyone ever wrote about him. You know, Todd followed Cowboy Jack Clement's rules for being a songwriter. One was you had to spend the night in jail. I wrote an article about that and his song "Hays County Jail."

Todd would come into Sundance at least once a week, but all of a sudden he wasn't coming around anymore. I noticed a couple years later in *Billboard* magazine that he had signed with Jimmy Buffett's label. My friend sent me a demo of songs that ended up being on *Songs for the*

Daily Planet. I was blown away. Todd had made huge strides in the three years since I had heard him in San Marcos. What a great record. I was floored, but it was clear something was happening with Todd from the very beginning. He had an innate understanding of storytelling and song structure. I don't think I've ever seen anyone where it was more obvious more early than Todd. He was a natural and had it instinctively. Wild to see. He was just that good.[24]

Jenni Finlay

Todd wrote "Feeling at Home" after he went to Memphis because he broke Dad's heart. Dad didn't understand why Todd would leave, but everybody has to grow. Todd moved to Memphis, and I moved to Nashville, which broke up our family band. Dad was upset with me, too. Dad really didn't understand why either of us would want to live somewhere else. Dad wanted Todd and me around all the time, but we had to move on. "Feeling at Home" was an answering machine message. Todd called and played this whole song on the phone about our house by the river. It made Dad cry so hard. "So easy feeling, so free and easy, so far away from the world / With good lovin' people that treat me like I was their own / And you know that it's worth more to me than any living like I've ever known / It's the closest that I've ever come to feeling at home." Todd only ever recorded "Feeling at Home" as a demo on the unreleased album *Early Daze*.

Verse: Can't Complain

THE MEMPHIS YEARS

Todd Snider effectively launches his career by moving to Memphis in 1989. Importantly, he rebuilds the burned bridge with Kent Finlay as his star shoots skyward. "Dad and Todd made up eventually and kept in touch until the day my dad died," Jenni Finlay says. "Todd would bring people down just to see the house and river and bask in the glory of music." Singer-songwriter Keith Sykes becomes Snider's new mentor during his Memphis years. Snider forms a band called the Nervous Wrecks while studying under Sykes and playing open mic nights at the sports bar the Daily Planet. Nervous Wrecks guitarist Will Kimbrough remains a lifelong musical collaborator.

Meanwhile, Sykes owns an ace up his sleeve: He plays in Jimmy Buffet's touring band. Sykes introduces Snider's music to the legendary songwriter behind "Margaritaville" and "Cheeseburger in Paradise." Snider signs a major label deal with Buffet's MCA Records imprint Margaritaville Records for his debut, *Songs for the Daily Planet* (1994). His follow-up *Step Right Up* (1996) appears on the label two years later after he has moved to Nashville. Iconic MCA executive and producer Tony Brown, who helped create mainstream country's "Great Credibility Scare" by introducing Steve Earle, Nanci Griffith, and Lyle Lovett less than a decade earlier, oversees both. Snider's first two albums include early fan favorites "My Generation (Part 2)," "Alright Guy," "Easy Money," and the hidden track "Talking Seattle Grunge Rock Blues" as well as "Side Show Blues," "Moondawg's Tavern," "Tension," and "Late Last Night."

Todd Snider

Kent had been teaching me songwriting for about three years by the time I moved to Memphis. My dad was traveling and would always be working construction for the local strip club owners. Now he was working in Memphis and would go to a bar where the bartender's sister was married to Keith Sykes. My dad had heard me talk about Keith. Bobby at Sundance had turned me onto him and gave me his records so I sent [Keith my song] "I Can Drink Any Woman Pretty." Keith called me back a couple months later and said the song had potential. So, I moved to Memphis.

Keith said I was a great lyricist, but we needed to work on my melodies and rhythm. He told me that he would sign me to be a writer for other people. Keith taught me to count off songs, how to know what key I was in, and the difference between a melody and a chord progression. He explained many things like how melody should make you sing along, how twelve-bar talking blues went, and how to use three chords or less and avoid going to a weird chord. He would say, "Just go to the same old chord at a weird time instead." One example is "Trouble" by Keith Richards, which is "Shake, Rattle, and Roll" at different tempos. Keith Sykes taught me tone, pitch, time, and scales.

I went to the Daily Planet's open mike and asked the owner, "Can I play here tomorrow night if you like what I do tonight?" He said OK, because I didn't ask for money. I started singing there for eight or ten people. Then one night I went in, and there were rugby players who had come in after practice. I sang my brand-new song "My Generation (Part 2)." The rugby players came back the next week and brought their friends. I had a following all of a sudden. Keith rethought things. "I think you could be John Prine," he said.[1]

Keith Sykes

My sister was working at the Hyatt Regency hotel. Todd's dad would go down to the restaurant bar at the end of the day, and one day my sister mentioned me. Todd sent me three songs. I said, "Look me up if you're ever in the area." He was at my door before he finished reading the letter. We got together, talked, and then I went to see him play live in a nondescript neighborhood in Bartlett, Tennessee. I had never heard of this place, which was pretty big. Todd had never played there as far as I knew, but people were digging it. Todd would sing and people would sing along. The buddy I was with said, "Good lord, man, that's pretty amazing." He had these cool songs that were easy to [win over] the audience, but he also sang more introspective songs. You have to pay attention to his songs. I thought to myself on the way home, "This guy will have a real good shot if he can do that everywhere."

We started working together for a year. We went one baby step at a time and felt each other out. Two songs on that first tape were well put together with nice lyrics, but they weren't great. Todd sang them into a little cassette player. I still have the tape. One song was called "I Can Drink Any Woman Pretty." I thought that was a pretty good hook for a country song. I saw where he was coming from. I was looking for someone like Bob Dylan who could reach all genres with his own sound and style. I've still got that tape. Teaching Todd was easy. You have to understand that he was nineteen. He hadn't been playing guitar long and liked things but didn't know what to call them. I taught him simple things. I would say, "That's called a talking blues like Bob Dylan and Woody Guthrie would do."

I showed him chord progressions. People like me don't know how to write down notes. We have a different language. Todd didn't have any language, so I taught him ours, which is for people who aren't pop musicians who read charts. You just write. Todd has always had a lot of ambition. He just didn't know his strengths and weaknesses yet. Todd was like Jimmy Buffett and Jerry Jeff Walker. He played and people stopped. People don't just go on drinking at their shows. They listen. Todd had a great effect on people. He always went out with both barrels, wanted attention, and got people on his side. Todd knew how to get the audience on his side, which takes a little humor and a lot of talent and stage presence. You don't find that very often in someone that young. It was startling, wonderful.[2]

Singer-songwriter and producer Keith Sykes has toured as a guitarist in Jimmy Buffett's Coral Reefer Band. His songs have been recorded by Buffett, John Prine, and Jerry Jeff Walker.

Todd Snider

I kept playing at the Daily Planet. Kevn Kinney from Drivin N Cryin came to my show one time, and you could never get into a Thursday show again. Those shows were like a mini version of BR-549. [K. K. Rider] came all the time and would yell for a song. I mean, the place held like seventy people, but still that seemed like a lot. I played there every Thursday. I had other gigs, but that was my main one. Sid Selvidge had been playing at this place Zinny's East for twenty-five years. I thought, I'll be the Sid Selvedge at the Daily Planet.[3]

K. K. Rider

I was living a couple blocks away from the Daily Planet and would go down there and play darts with Todd. I was getting up onstage with him next thing you know.[4]

Todd Snider immortalized the Memphis country cover band K. K. Rider with the nearly ten-minute-long fan favorite "The K. K. Rider Story" he often tells in concert.

Mark Marchetti

I was the older dude around Joe McLeary, Joe Mariencheck, and Keith Sykes. They always thought I was gonna die because my marriage crashed and burned. I came home from the casino one night and the only things left in my house were my recliner and the television set. My ex-wife had moved everything out. I never went out and hadn't played a show for about fifteen years. I just wrote and sent songs to publishers. Someone literally grabbed me and said I had to play. So, I went to the Daily Planet for an open mic. I did my tunes and sat down. Then this kid comes up. He touches me on the shoulder and goes, "Hey, man, that was pretty good." I have a weird sense of humor, so I said, "Don't ever fucking touch me, man." He started laughing. Todd sat down, and we drank beers. Then he got up to play. Todd was amazing. I went, "Oh, great. I choose to come out to play an open mic night when I'm witnessing the new Guy Clark or John Prine." Anyone who saw Todd knew he was something special.

Todd would just sit there and not even open his mouth. People were looking at him. Then he started singing. He has that stage presence and can back it up with the songs. You're sold when he starts telling those stories. Some people have that thing where they walk in a room, and you just stop. They're interesting, kind-looking, or give off an energy. Todd had that Huckleberry Finn-like essence even back then that there was something spiritual coming through the music. He would even end his gigs with "Will the Circle Be Unbroken" and always imparted that we should have a good time and treat each other well.

The Daily Planet was a very welcoming hole-in-the-wall like *Cheers*, [the long-running television show] where everybody knew each other. Todd ended up packing the place every Thursday. His shows became an event. Todd was a young guy about twenty-three, but he was always inspiring. We would wake up and call each other to play our new songs over the phone. His were always great. I would cuss him. "Shit, you asshole." He was an aspiring, supportive guy. I never felt competition because I wasn't in the same league. I'm not much of a performer. You have to have a gun to my head to get me onstage. Todd's way of writing would inspire me. I would digest his writing and try to do it my way.

Cowriting Todd's song "Somebody's Coming" really helped me get established in Nashville. Todd and I aren't the cowriting types, but I had written this other song and really liked the verses I had come up with. I just didn't know where to go. Todd came over one day. "Man," I said. "Check this out. I don't know what to do with this." He said, "Let me see the guitar." He just sings the chorus. "Damnit." It was great. I demoed the song, and everybody's favorite part is that chorus that he wrote right off the top of his head. It was perfect. The song was called "There You Go." That was his chorus. I told him I didn't know where the song was going and he went, bop-bop-bop. "There you go." Brilliant.[5]

Mark Marchetti is a Nashville-based singer, songwriter, poet, and farmer who has written for Stax and Chips Moman in Memphis and Sony Tree/ ATV in Nashville.

Joe McLeary

I met Todd when [Nervous Wrecks bassist] Joe Mariencheck and I were going to the University of Memphis. We were in an ensemble at the University of Memphis while Todd was producing a songwriter in the studio there. Joe already had been playing with Todd for a while. He took me over and introduced us. Todd was real nice and easy to talk to. He seemed to be flattered that I had come to meet him. I got a call a couple weeks later to do a gig. They were in the rotating musician era then. I got to where I would just show up at his apartment and talk about what was going on. I loved his songs.

I used to tell Todd that he reminded me of Whoopi Goldberg, who would pin you back into this real dark, serious place and then do comic relief all of a sudden. Look at Todd's repertoire. I don't even think he views what he's writing as comedy. He's just writing from such a different lens that people think his songs must be funny. His ideas are his actual serious view on life and the world. Some are so abstract and strange that people laugh. Todd just isn't a joke teller. He was never the funny guy on the bus or in the van. There were no jokes. You could tell he had been thinking about it a while if he did say something clever. Those very abstract, non-mainstream ideas roll out of his mind all the time.

The Thursday night gig at the Daily Planet was our only one when the record label people were starting to notice. We talked a lot about what he had heard from the record people, what their next move might be, and how Todd might react to their offer. We drank lots of coffee and smoked cigarettes. I had never been involved with something so industry-centric like that. Exciting. I got involved a little late in the game, and Margaritaville Records was already coming around. Todd had interest and had been to Nashville to do demo work. Todd seemed to be anxious to get something going. The music was different for me. I had studied drums at the Berklee College of Music [in Boston]. Then I went to Memphis, and Todd was the first major thing I got involved in.

Todd was so good. I never knew much about songwriters up until then, but I started listening to his songs and realized that I was listening mainly to the lyrics. Supporting those songs was easy because they were so good. It was very fulfilling to just be entertained by the song and play drums to them. The Memphis music scene then was pretty much like it is now. Sun Studios was there. Beale Street was alive and well then. I found Todd before I got too lost into the Memphis music scene. I fit Todd's needs really well.[6]

Joe McLeary served as drummer in Todd Snider's Nervous Wrecks during the nineties.

Stacie Huckeba

I have known Todd since I was going to college in Austin, and we would go down to San Marcos for Songwriters Night at Cheatham Street Warehouse. Then I saw him again after he moved to Memphis and was like, "There's that guy from Texas." Todd was living upstairs from a guitar player named Eric Lewis from Son of Slam when he got to Memphis. Son of Slam was a super heavy metal band and really good friends of mine. They all had really long hair. Todd had this collegiate look and was a barefoot weirdo. Nobody knew where to put him, but Todd loved Son of Slam. He showed up at all their gigs and stuck out like a sore thumb, but we all loved him for being so quirky.[7]

Stacie Huckeba is a photographer, filmmaker, and homelessness activist based in Nashville. She frequently contributes to The Huffington Post and The East Nashvillian.

Eric Lewis

Son of Slam was playing before Drivin N Cryin at the New Daisy Theater, and they wanted me to take pictures around 1992. Todd Snider was opening that night before Son of Slam went on. The place was packed. I was side stage, and Todd was out there doing what he does. I had never heard him before and was completely mesmerized. The crowd loved it. Todd was funny and had them in the palm of his hand. He was telling stories and playing these great songs. I joined Son of Slam when their guitar player left later. Things really took off for us.[8]

Eric Lewis was a key member of Son of Slam, the Memphis band name-checked in Todd Snider's "Late Last Night." He is a freelance musician today.

Kevn Kinney

I met Todd in the break room at Kiva Studio in Memphis. He had been upstairs making a demo with Keith Sykes. Todd invited me to come see him play at the Daily Planet, so we went there later. He blew me away. We started hanging out at Keith's house and with his friend Mark Marchetti. Drivin N Cryin would travel around with Todd's cassettes in the van around then. We were huge fans. Todd even played with us one time when I was sick. We didn't have a guitar player that night, so we had Dan Baird from the Georgia Satellites sitting in. I got food poisoning and had to stop the show halfway. I knew Todd was there. "Todd, man," I said. "Can you get up and play a few songs? I have to go backstage. I feel really terrible." That might have been the first time Dan and Todd played together.[9]

Longtime Todd Snider friend Kevn Kinney founded the seminal American outfit Drivin N Cryin in Atlanta nearly forty years ago. The band has released more than a dozen albums.

Dan Baird

Todd's brother was booking him and called me up. He said, "Do you want to play guitar with Todd?" "Sure," I said. "I'll get to play with Will." "No," he said, "Will's off on another tour." Instant fun to work for Todd anyway. Todd doesn't like any confrontational stuff that could go sideways, but he enjoys barely controlled onstage chaos. He's not a great musician as such, but he gets his point across and has a blast doing it. I did the same in my band as he did: You make sure you're the least musically adept person on the stage. We want to get pushed.[10]

Dan Baird's Georgia Satellites left an indelible mark on modern pop music with the endlessly catchy single "Keep Your Hands to Yourself" in 1986. The band is based in Atlanta.

Eric Lewis

We used to play Rascals, which was the place for a late-night hang in Memphis. We would go on around one in the morning and play until four so [it makes sense Todd would include Son of Slam in the lyrics of his song "Late Last Night"]. The place would be packed. Bands like Alice in Chains and Soundgarden would hang out there when they were passing through town. Guns N' Roses were playing at the Pyramid one time when we had a late show at Rascals and all ended up siting in with the band. Duff McKagen, Matt Sorum, Slash all came up for Stones covers. Then here comes Axl Rose up the stairs in a mink coat around three-thirty in the morning.

Anyway, we would be doing shows around town, and Todd would be playing down the street. We started palling around here and there. I remember running off to see him play one time when he was outside reading a book and smoking a cigarette. We started talking and found out that we both lived in the Gilmore apartments at Madison Avenue and North McLean Boulevard. Todd tells a story about the Circle K across the street [to introduce "Sideshow Blues"]. You definitely want to look over your shoulder in that neighborhood. Todd got the deal with MCA later on. I heard that MCA wanted him to take out the Son of Slam reference in "Late Last Night," but Todd said, "No, man. That's what I was doing. I would go down to Rascals to hear those guys play. Can't change it."

We started doing some Son of Slam and Todd Snider shows. I would play with my band and then play with Todd. We did a few fun shows down in Oxford, Mississippi. I remember thinking at the time that I wanted to play in Todd's band even though I really liked Son of Slam and the music we were playing. I wanted to play what he was playing more than the harder stuff. Todd and I went to lunch and beers one day at a Mexican place. I told him that I wanted to quit the group be his guitar player. "Well, Eric," he said. "That's really nice. I like you and your playing, but I couldn't steal you away from them. Besides you would hate me if you played in my band." I was crushed. "Aw, man," I said. "Okay, let's just keep it that way and stay friends."

Son of Slam was out one week in Texas when Todd had a gig with the Nervous Wrecks at the New Daisy. He didn't have a guitar at the time, but I had a brand-new Takamine six-string I would use for my Sunday night gigs. He asked if he could borrow it. "Yeah, man," I said, "as long as I have it back in time for Sunday." "No problem," Todd said. "The gig's Friday. I can get it back to you on Saturday." I went down to his apartment when we got back to town and grabbed the guitar. I went about my day. Sunday rolled around, and I decided to warm up.

I was mostly doing heavy, hard gigs at that point, but the Sunday ones were an acoustic duo with the singer and me at Murphy's. I pulled the guitar out of the case and the only two strings left were completely black. Dried blood was all over the top of the guitar. What the hell? I had to get a set of strings somehow to play this gig and called Todd. "Hey, man, what happened at the gig the other night?" "I don't know," he said. "What do you mean?" "I just opened the guitar case, and there's blood all over it." "Oh man," Todd said. "I totally forgot. I did a Pete Townsend windmill at the end of the show and cut my hand." He just put the guitar back in the case. I think that's hilarious now, but I didn't at the time.

Son of Slam had played a show another time when the drummer dropped my girlfriend and me off at the Gilmore really late. I realized I had forgotten my contact lens case in the car. I had to wait until he got home—this was before cell phones—to call and get him to come all the way back. The elevator doors opened when we got to the building. Todd and Mark Marchetti came out. They were leaving super early to go up to Nashville for a few weeks. I finally got my stuff from the drummer but forgot my apartment key. I was banging on the door, and my girlfriend had passed out on me inside. I thought, "Who would leave town for three weeks and not lock their door?" I walked down to Todd's apartment on the sixth floor, and sure enough his apartment door was unlocked. I made myself at home and crashed there that night.[11]

Mike Snider

I started working with Todd but didn't know what I was doing. I was the guy that he would talk to about things. Todd and I are brothers, but I was my own guy. He was his own guy. Todd didn't care to listen to anything I said. I had no credibility. I was working on all gut instinct but had an absolute blast. I learned what to do, and that helped me grow in my own career as far as how to listen to artists and deal with their neuroses and changes in attitude. Working with Todd has helped greatly in me not being judgmental of the creatives and to let them go ahead and be weird and help support their weirdness. I'm an agent and partner at William Morris Endeavor today and have been an agent for twenty-five years now. I focus on contemporary Christian music and entertainment.[12]

Todd Snider

I just wanted to work on songs all day and never had an issue working on them. I compulsively have had to put at least three or four hours into it every day since Kent showed me. I wrote "My Generation" for *Songs for the Daily Planet* and kept working on more. I already had "Easy Money." I was working on songs called "A Lot More" and "Turn It Up." I don't even like those now, but they were the two I wrote after I got a record deal. I had the rest already and most for the second album, too. I was playing those songs every night. Keith started sending my songs to anyone after he decided I could be a singer.

Keith Sykes

Todd was writing all the time back then. I think he wrote 168 songs during the first year, and the second year he wrote about eighty while he was touring. He was still writing with the record company on his back. Then I connected Todd with Capitol Records. They showed him interest, but it turned out to be a jive-ass thing. They just wanted to be rid of me so they could be the producer. All they had to be was up-front with me, but they did all that bullshit Nashville stuff. I think the young people have to prove they will cut their elders' nuts off or something. They wanted country, but Todd was a folk artist who liked country songs. He wasn't gonna be a country singer with voices like Garth Brooks and Keith Whitley out there in the nineties.[13]

Todd Snider

There were a bunch of record deal offers, but I was a fairly troubled guy. We started making demos when I got the first one, but they fired Keith and that knocked me off the deep end. We made country and rock tapes, but both were terrible. I got fired for putting a cigarette out on some kid's leg who made me really mad over music, which was a big mistake. I had been living at Jimmy Collins's house [in Nashville] for the last couple months of my record deal, but I came back to Memphis. They had given my Planet gig to Cory Branan, but I got it back. There was this big article in the paper. The guy did me a favor. I got hired [for the record deal], did the tryout, and got fired. That was the gist, but the paper made it sound like I didn't do it their way and made me look more valiant than I really was.

Word got around Nashville. Three or four record companies would come to the Planet. I started making demands the second time I was offered a record deal. I said I wanted artistic control and was holding out. Margaritaville Records was one of the ones who wanted me. I was in the "too country for rock and too rock for country" category at the time. "Why don't you be grunge?" So, I wrote ["Talking Seattle Grunge Rock Blues"] to be funny for my friends. That was back in the days when you would make up a song and sing it for people that night.

My understanding was that if I did well this would break the door down. I did "Talking Seattle Grunge Rock Blues" one night, and Margaritaville Records President Bob Mercer was the first one backstage after the show. "Are you putting that Seattle song on this record?" he asked. "Yeah." "Okay," he said. "One more question: You just played it with your guitar and harmonica up there. Is that how you plan to record it?" "Yeah." "Man," he said. "You can use your own band. You can produce. You do that one, and I don't give a fuck about the other twelve songs." We shook on the deal.[14]

Will Kimbrough

I was playing with Mike Grimes and Tommy Womack in a band called the Bis-Quits at the Extravaganza music conference in Nashville in 1993. Todd was there playing solo. Margaritaville Records signed him that night. I knew who he was because I had seen him open for Jason Ringenberg [of Jason and the Scorchers] and had been knocked out. You remember Todd Snider the first time you see him. I didn't see him again until I auditioned for his band in November 1994. He was living in Memphis and had made *Songs for the Daily Planet*. Todd was planning the tour and didn't have a guitar player. Tom Lewis from Oh Boy knew I had quit the Bis-Quits and called. He asked if I would be interested in playing with Todd. I went over to the Margaritaville Records office on Music Row and picked up a ninety-minute Maxell cassette that I still have somewhere with *Songs for the Daily Planet*.[15]

Will Kimbrough was lead guitarist in Todd Snider's Nervous Wrecks throughout the nineties. He has continued collaborating with Snider as a player and producer for the past thirty years.

Keith Sykes

Todd wanted to be a rock 'n' roll singer, but I didn't think he had a rock 'n' roll voice either. I said, "You can do whatever you want, but I'm not gonna be involved." I just didn't think it was honest. I didn't think it was his strength. Grunge rock had started, and he didn't sound like that. He would be posing. I wanted him to come out with a major label with his debut and said he could do whatever he wanted after that. He needed the support that only a major can give you. You don't get that anywhere else, and you only get one debut. You have to show people who you are. He thought about it and said, "I want to do what we're doing." I thought, "Right choice."

Buffett had opened an office in Nashville by that time, and he liked Todd. So did Bob Mercer, who was running the company. We had an offer from RCA that I wish we would have taken in hindsight. Mercer wanted me out of the deal like the others. The fact that I had worked three fucking years to get Todd to the table didn't mean a thing to him. He let me know that in a meeting. Weeks went by and he said, "You don't call, you don't write." I said, "You pretty much told me that I'm fucked up. Screw you. We got an offer from RCA." So, he sweetened up the deal and put me in the contract to coproduce with Tony Brown. We had this deal with Margaritaville, and Jimmy had all these fans. I knew they would all love Todd, but they wanted three producers on the record, so I bowed out.[16]

K. K. Rider

Todd had signed a contract with Margaritaville Records but had spent all the advance. He needed work. Todd wasn't allowed to play his own songs because of the contract. He called me up. "Come on," I said, "we're playing at Buffalo Bob's tonight." Todd and his bass player Joe Marienchek came down [to play with us]. Todd might have played with us for about a month. He was a mellow guy who would come over and just hang out at my place when we weren't playing music. He would smoke pot and watch television, but he also was constantly writing—I mean, constantly. He would write ten or fifteen songs in a week, and they would all be good. I would write ten or fifteen songs in a week, and none would be worth a shit.[17]

Tony Brown

They moved Jimmy Buffett from ABC Records to MCA Records in Los Angeles. He became a platinum-selling artist when Irving [Azoff] managed him. [MCA President] Jimmy Bowen told Buffett, "You know, your first two records were cut here in Nashville with Don Gandt. Nashville's opening up to acknowledging that people like Kenny Rogers could be country and pop. Your music fits right in." Bowen moved Jimmy to our division for the albums *Riddles in the Sand* and *Last Mango in Paris*. "I've got a guy in Memphis working with Keith Sykes," Buffett said. "You need to cut a record on him."

Buffett brought over Todd Snider. I loved that first album *Songs for the Daily Planet* and the hidden track "Talking Seattle Grunge Rock Blues." I still play that song for everybody, but the young people missed that era and don't think it's funny. I still think "Talking Seattle Grunge Rock Blues" is funny as hell. Todd had a Mark Chesnutt hit on that album called "Trouble." I was always pitching Todd's songs to Ronnie Dunn to do with Brooks and Dunn because he loved bands like the Georgia Satellites and edgy Southern rock bands.[18]

Tony Brown toured as guitarist in Elvis Presley's TCB Band and Emmylou Harris's Hot Band before becoming a hugely influential and successful producer with MCA Records in Nashville.

Joe McLeary

We already rehearsed so much at the Daily Planet and through touring that we were all warmed up when we went in to record the first album. We had already experimented with the songs and picked them apart. Todd would make abstract suggestions on how to play. He never wrote out music or anything. We just went for the best take we could get. There was no, "Hey, let's go back and add a couple extra measures after the chorus." There wasn't any need. Same on the second album. We had toured so much by then that we walked into the studio, they hit "record," and we started playing. We did songs two or three times and finished in a week.

I had recorded in studios before, but I had never been involved with such high caliber people as the ones behind the glass for those albums. Todd wasn't allowed to bring his own musicians the first time he went to Nashville before my time, but he was allowed on those first two albums. He was pretty comfortable by then. Both records were great, but the first was more nerve-racking. I didn't have the right gear. I wasn't a session player. I didn't have a click track set up. I showed up with my drums and a metronome that had a little ear bud that I stuck up through my headphones. That was the most pathetic thing ever, but I figured I better have something. It was all very exciting and nerve-racking.[19]

Mike Grimes

I met Todd when I was in the Bis-Quits with Will Kimbrough. We were on Oh Boy Records for two and a half years from 1992 to 1994. I became aware of Todd when our band broke up and Todd snagged Will to play guitar for him. Also, my girlfriend and I had broken up. He started dating my ex-girlfriend. I was like, "My band broke up. My girlfriend and I broke up. Todd's got my girlfriend and guitar player next thing you know." I was introduced to him around 1995 and was so glad that Will got such a cool gig when I heard *Songs for the Daily Planet* for the first time. I was taken with his artistry and performance style from the beginning.

There was no denying that Todd was badass. I would be around him any time Will was playing with him. Joe quit the band and Will called me. "We're in a spot," he said. "We're playing this festival on the river [in Nashville], and Joe isn't gonna be able to play bass. Could you woodshed the set?" No rehearsal. So, I played bass with Todd for one gig around 1997. That was nerve-racking but really fun. I had quit playing music for a little while around then. I've always straddled the line between being an artist and working industry jobs. We were friends from then on. Todd obviously was such a good songwriter.[20]

Mike "Grimey" Grimes performed with Will Kimbrough in the Bis-Quits in the early nineties. He has boosted East Nashville with endeavors including Grimey's New and Preloved Music.

Tommy Womack

Todd had heard my song "Betty Was Black and Willie Was White" from our Bis-Quits album. I wrote that song cleaning the house one day before even moving to Nashville. Every time I would see Todd he would say, "Betty was black and Willie was white." Todd was a man-about-town back then. He would go to shows around Nashville. I ended up opening for him and learned a lot from watching him.

I was playing bass for the Nervous Wrecks a few years later. People would always ask me, "Is he as fucked up onstage as he appears, or is it a Dean Martin thing where he's pretending?" "No," I would say. "He is absolutely, genuinely that fucked up." But I have never seen him walk onstage without a set list. I've never seen him open his mouth without knowing exactly what he was going to do, and no matter how polluted he got and how late he was up, he was always up the next morning at six o'clock working on a song. I'm sure he's already been up this morning working on a song. He had a work ethic about songwriting. He's one of the most naturally talented dudes I have ever met.

Same with Will Kimbrough. Being onstage with Will is daunting. I'll never be able to play lead guitar like him, but we trade licks back and forth like Keith Richards and Ronnie Wood. Say you're Will and play a lead part. I immediately start playing quieter so people can hear him. Nine out of ten guys will keep playing rhythm guitar at the same volume. I think he was happy to find musical things like that in someone. We've had hundreds of great gigs together. We communicate on guitar great. Listening to Will play is like hearing a record that's already been mixed, mastered, and produced. He's one of the best guitar players in Nashville, which makes him one of the best in the world.[21]

Singer-songwriter Tommy Womack was in the Bis-Quits with Will Kimbrough and Mike Grimes in the early nineties. His songs have been cut by Jimmy Buffett, Todd Snider, and more.

Will Kimbrough

The *Daily Planet* record came out, and the label pushed it hard. We toured for ten months and capped it off with the *Austin City Limits* episode. That was the only *Austin City Limits* where the band was really on its game. We had finished a tour and were not intimidated to be on *Austin City Limits*. We tore it up. We were working all the time from 1995 until early

1998. We would go in and make a record as soon as the tour was over. The band was all younger Memphis guys and me. Todd was closer to my age but still two years younger. He had never been on tour, but I was a road dog for over twelve years before that. I was the grumpy old guy in his early thirties.

We went out in the van and trailer to play shows and got opening spots for Jimmy Buffett. Did some television and made a video. Went through a bunch of tour managers. Todd really came into his own as a bandleader. He had been a folk singer on his own like he has been for the past twenty years now. He was really learning how to front a rock 'n' roll band and fell into it immediately. You play in Columbia, South Carolina, then you have to be in Tampa at 6:00 a.m. to be on the radio, which is extremely important to do. So, you literally drive from eleven at night until six in the morning, and there's some radio guy sitting at a fake fifties diner in a strip mall. He's surprised to see you. "Oh, we just need Todd for five minutes." That happens a lot when the label is working your record. You go home pretty quickly if the label doesn't give a shit.

Joe Ely

Todd and I were on MCA Records together in the mid-nineties. We ended up playing the *David Letterman Show* at the Ed Sullivan Theater [to promote "Oh Boy" from 1996's *Not Fade Away: Remembering Buddy Holly*]. Someone told us that night about being there when Buddy Holly and the Crickets played Ed Sullivan around 1958. The three bandmates got into a shoving match backstage. Buddy's front tooth was broken, and he was going on in fifteen minutes. Someone ran down to the drugstore on Forty-Second Street. He brought back white gum that they fashioned into a tooth. They went out and sang "That'll Be the Day." Struck me as being really hard to sing on national television with gum replacing a missing half tooth.

Cody Canada

I saw Todd Snider on *Late Night with Conan O'Brien* in 1995. I thought, holy shit. His hippie-like free spirit and not-give-a-shit attitude appealed to me. This was my music and attitude. If you don't like my songs, fine. If you do, come on, let's go. Todd was writing these songs for himself, and bonus if other people dug them. I probably saw him play shows ten, twelve times a year for the next three or four years. I would see where he was playing and drove or flew in. I very fortunately got to be friends with the guy over the years. Watching Todd and Will Kimbrough together really helped shape what we've done over the last twenty years.

We still could play the first two records—*Songs for the Daily Planet* and *Step Right Up*—front to back. I brought out Todd's "I Believe You" during a sound check once. There were a few fans, and they asked what song that was and who wrote the song. They wanted to know if we were going to record it. We said, "Yeah, we're gonna record it." We had been playing that song for years. "Late Last Night" really felt like the perfect song for where Cross Canadian Ragweed was. I'm all over anything with a Chuck Berry riff. I played "Alright Guy" every Tuesday night at the Wormy Dog in Stillwater for like six years. Everybody loved that song, so I learned it and never forgot. Todd was 75 percent of the influence that got me going as a songwriter.

Will Kimbrough

I had been on a label that had a brief smidgen of the label backing the record, but I had never had backing like Todd did. I kept reminding everyone, "Hey, they're into it. You might as well do the most you can no matter how exhausting it is." Hardly anyone ever gets that much attention from a label. I don't know if Todd understood that or if anyone can. They even sent us to Europe and wanted Todd to do a press tour. Todd's record was doing great in Europe. He was on the cover of glossy magazines and had songs on the charts. He wanted to bring the band, but they said, "No, you have to do a press tour first."

You go to the capitals of Europe every morning on a press tour, sit in the hotel, drink coffee, and do interview after interview. Then you do showcases and come back in a couple months and tour when the press was hitting the stands. Nobody could make Todd understand that. We were happy to go, went, and had a blast. We would go and have three days off in Munich or Vienna while he did interviews. Then we would go to the next. Todd had to work his tail off getting up at six in the morning to do interviews and then do his showcase. Then we would travel. He didn't go back to Europe for a long time. My impression is that he thought touring Europe was brutal, which it can be. I was going, "Man, my band never got this."

We were working up the songs that would be on the next record on that tour. Todd was writing a lot. The set would always change, so it was a very dynamic time. Todd was really into the dynamics of the show with a band. We would have it all planned out from night to night. "You guys are gonna walk out in the middle of this song. Then I'll play a song, and you guys run back onstage when I say 'avocado.'" There was no phoning it in. We had a really good time. The audience showed up and were excited. Well, not every night. Sometimes Todd was unhappy about the turnout or how the crowd was acting, but that's normal. Todd hadn't figured out that he could walk offstage and still have a career at that time.

I thought Todd was a great songwriter. He wrote really personal, poignant stuff that worked. He wasn't corny when he wrote about something dramatic and sad. I don't know how you define being a great songwriter except for the use of language and its effectiveness in moving you one way or the other as well as using musical styles to propel the story forward. There's a mood throughout *the Daily Planet* that sounds like 1995, but he could play those songs with just his guitar and the songs would have carried. The songs and stories have carried him through his career. I think it was incidental that for a few years he could front a band and make rock 'n' roll records. That would go on for about ten years through *The Devil You Know*. Then Todd figured out that you need to learn to play by these days or the economics will be really hard to sustain. You have to learn to play solo and make it mean something. He had that from the beginning. People loved it. I think they loved it more than Todd with a band.[22]

Paul Griffith

I was friends with Will Kimbrough and met Todd in Reno when he and Will came over to see our set when I was drumming for Amy Rigby. Todd was at [John Ascuaga's] Nugget [Casino]. He was charismatic like a golden god and said, "I want to record with you." I hear that five times a day, but he ended up calling me later to play on *New Connection*. I love singer-songwriters and immediately noticed his empathetic songwriting, which not many writers can do. I liked his wonky feel as a drummer, which I understood because I had played with John Prine. You stay out of the way when you're playing with those two.

Some drummers are like a frozen rope and play the same every night, but I much prefer following the Bob Dylan model where you hang on for dear life. Prine was less frenetic about it than Todd and would play close to the same every night. Todd leans heavily toward the Dylan model. I wouldn't know how a song was gonna go until he started singing every night. There were times when I wasn't even sure what song we were doing until he started singing. Playing with Todd is like a high-wire act every night. Playing those shows is still a lot of fun even when it doesn't work.[23]

Paul Griffith frequently plays drums for Todd Snider in concert and in the studio.

Jason Rigenberg

My first exposure to Todd Snider was when I was doing a record release show for my new album on Capitol Nashville in 1992. He was an unknown opener who was still living in Nashville. He opened for Jason and the Scorchers during the nineties. Sometimes he would do full tours throughout the Midwest. He had Will Kimbrough on guitar and Mike Grimes on bass in those days. Todd had already had the big record with *Daily Planet* and was facing the sophomore slump [with *Step Right Up*]. He was just out opening for us, and we weren't much to talk about during those days. I didn't get to know Todd very well in those days.[24]

Jason Rigenberg formed the iconic cowpunk band Jason and the Scorchers more than four decades ago. He has released four kids' albums under the name Farmer Jason.

Will Kimbrough

Step Right Up was a typical sophomore record with good songs, but the album didn't do what the first record did. Todd had been on Margaritaville and then was signed on MCA. We were assigned an A&R guy. Every other word out of his mouth was, "Joe Satriani." We would say it back to him. "Yeah," we would say while fingerpicking some folk song, "I like Joe Satriani. This is just like Joe Satriani." We thought that was funny. Then we did the Monsters of Tube Socks tour with the Bottle Rockets and Jack Ingram and his Beat Up Ford Band, which was our further mocking of the shredder guitar Joe Satriani A&R guy. Todd and the label weren't jibing at all. Todd didn't have a powerful manager to throw his weight around and was fending for himself. I know that from when my band had a label guy who would show up in a stretch limo and a *Miami Vice* shirt in the late eighties and announce, "I don't hear a single."[25]

Todd Snider

Kimbrough has always been like a marriage. I get jealous. I think he does too. We're slightly competitive, but I would go get my shovel if he told me he killed a guy. It doesn't always feel great when he plays a song I love. I'm like, "Ohhh. I'm not very good." Play me a Jeff Tweedy song that's amazing, and I'm like, "That dude's good." Play me a Will Kimbrough song that's amazing, and I'm like, "Man, I need to work on my melodies." I'm always wanting to keep up with him lyrically and musically. He became like Keith Sykes in the years that the Wrecks started. I was learning about music from him. He taught me arranging. He was our Nashville ringer. We really got a good one. Kimbrough taught us to be a band and how to tour and live on the road before I moved to Nashville in 1996.[26]

Dan Baird

You're all musically in the kids' trampoline room at McDonald's playing with Todd. Nobody's gonna get hurt, but anything can happen. That's why you play music, man. Putting on a show wasn't as important to Todd as making an exploding piece of music. I live for exploding music. The idea is to realize the possibility that hasn't been realized before. Crazy tightrope walk. Todd loves being the tightrope walker. The band is on the ends holding the rope tight. Most people are terrified of doing that. They want to hear that they did a good job and nobody in the crowd wants their money back, but we're not symphony players. We're rock 'n' rollers. You're supposed to come out of the show with some skinned-up knees and elbows. Hopefully, you don't knock your teeth out, but if you do that's why they have dentists. Todd knocked a tooth out on his thirtieth birthday.

We were playing behind the Exit/In in Nashville. Todd was nervous as hell. He decided to hit the tequila early and not quit. We went onstage, and the place was packed out. Todd slipped and fell on the first song. His head came down, caught on the monitor, and busted out his tooth. He finished the show. My wife and a piano player who is a very good friend came over after. The piano player said, "That's the worst show I've ever seen in my life." My wife said, "That was the best show I've ever seen in my life." I go, "We did our job, then." We just turned into the razor blade. There was no fence to ride. You're going one way or the other. The show was messy and rocking.

The highlight that night was when Todd was stumbling about the stage. He had laid the acoustic guitar about three feet behind him and went staggering backward. I reached my left foot out and kicked it out of the way as his foot came down right where it would have been. "Oh my god," Todd said later. "I completely blew it." Then [keyboardist] Ross Rice comes backstage. "Oh my god," he goes. "I've been waiting my whole life to do that show." Absolute chaos. Wonderful. Todd does the shaman thing onstage correctly. In fact, I may have learned some of the last finishing pieces about how to open yourself to the possibility of being a shaman while playing guitar with Todd. That's an exalted state. You're not only not thinking. You're in the act of doing and bringing other people into the doing way past knowing.

You've gone to the point where you don't know [the answer] anymore. You don't have to have an instrument in your hand, but you have to stay the leader on top of the horse. You can't lose your saddle. The whole shaman magic would erode if he would walk away to take a piss during a solo. The idea is you get run over if you get run over. You grow tall if you grow tall. People write books on how to be a success or be artistic. So fucking simple: You either have it or you don't. You can't even nurture it. It's in you, or it ain't in you. Period.

You have to practice your craft enough to the point that you can do your art. You want to feel that electricity again and again. Pure dope. You want it and don't want to settle down. One time isn't enough. Ten times aren't enough. A hundred times. You keep going for it because there's a physical and spiritual release. Look, it's bad when you rehearse the rock 'n' roll out of a song. There's no stank on it. You don't wanna know that the flash pops will go off onstage at exactly one hour and twenty-three minutes in. There's no excitement in that. Shit, I want to be excited every time I take the stage. Why wouldn't I? That excitement doesn't come from playing the song correctly. That's like having sex correctly. You don't rehearse for music, sex, or cooking. You get in there and cook.

You get past the craft and then you're all about explosiveness and whether I can as a player make Todd remember why he wrote this song right now. He will open up if I can. That's a sideman's job: Learn the song, get the singer to open. Todd feels like I'm on his team, committed, going over that barbed wire with him onstage. He wants to feel like he's with a bunch of badasses who have his back and reacts to that well. "I have your back. You won't get too far out there. I'll take it one step farther. Come on, third verse, what do you got?" Todd loves that challenge.

I understand the spiritual elements of playing music. You know when the big thing that no one can see is coming up onstage. You're like, "Oh, man. Let's rock it."[27]

Peter Cooper

I first heard Todd like most people with *Songs for the Daily Planet*. I thought the songs were fresh and funny. Such a cool record. Todd was on my radar from that moment. The first time I saw him play was at a concert at the riverfront in Nashville. I had never seen a performer like that. I was writing for *The Tennessean* newspaper by then and was charged with writing a review. I said something like he was like the guy who your wife begs you not to invite to the dinner party, but you know you're gonna invite him to the party anyway. Todd will be the life of the night. He's so captivating, funny, and smart.[28]

Late Tennessean music writer and singer-songwriter Peter Cooper has written songs with Todd Snider and assisted in his memoir, I Never Met a Story I Didn't Like.

Jason D. Williams

Todd Snider has a great mind. I lived down the street from him in Memphis. He was nervous to come down to talk to me because I had been signed to RCA Records, and he idolized me. Then I heard about him playing at the Daily Planet. He was a great songwriter with really cool hair and a wonderful stage presence. Todd is one of the neatest guys in the world. His songs are a lot like Michael Hurley. Michael Hurley is to songwriting what Chuck Berry is to rock 'n' roll. Every songwriter from Bob Dylan on down has revered him. I thought Todd's songs were clever, innovative, and very [complex]. I think the toxins make him remember them. Todd told me once that pot is the breakfast of champions, which is the absolute truth in his case. His mind's too big and his soul's too creative.

Wild man Jason D. Williams mirrors Jerry Lee Lewis's stage presence in his outrageous live shows. In fact, Williams played all the hand shots in the Lewis biopic, Great Balls of Fire.

Kevn Kinney

Todd has always been really honest. So many performers are so entrenched in being somebody else and let their influences guide them. Todd always told the truth. His songs were always believable. I heard his piano version of KISS's "Rock and Roll All Nite," and it was so believable. I don't do many cover songs. I have to be in the moment. My main thing in teaching songwriters to write—even if you grew up in the suburbs with shag carpeting, a bright yellow kitchen, a yellow stove, and posters with naked people on the wall—is tell your story. You have a great one. Todd does that.

Listen to Todd sing "Lonely Girl." Fuck, man. That shit is fucking real. I was drawn to Todd the first time I saw him because I knew that guy was fucking real. I'm looking for that when I come see you sing, and Todd still does that for me. His songs "Thoughts and Prayers" and "Is This Thing Working?" are Todd just telling his truth. That carries you through the next seventy years. Kids will buy his stuff in fifty years, and the songs will stand up because they're real stories about his life. He has lived an incredible life. He's always been that guy who's open to sitting there and listening from the corner of the room.[29]

Marshall Chapman

Todd was the first artist signed to Jimmy Buffett's Margaritaville Records. I was next. We met at Bob Mercer's house one night. Bob was married to one of Jimmy's former wives and was running Buffett's label. They had an ulterior motive for inviting us. My friend Chris is a physician, and they thought Todd was smoking too much dope and doing too many drugs. They wanted Chris to give him a physical and tell him, "You've gotta quit taking this and that." Instead, Chris said he was as healthy as could be. He gave Todd a completely clean bill of health. That was not what they wanted to hear.

Bob Mercer was really important to Todd. He became a father figure and always wanted to take care of him like that. They got real close. Bob was an interesting guy. He was involved with all the heavies like Pink Floyd. He would always have us over for dinner and call me every day to play golf. I used to be a junior golfer growing up in South Carolina, but then I decided it was a just a sport for Republicans with ugly clothes. I quit. Bob helped me get back into it. He was a member of this really nice golf club. We played barefoot.

Marshall Chapman has released more than a dozen albums from Me, I'm Feeling Free *(1977) to* Songs I Can't Live Without *(2020). She was on Margaritaville Records with Todd Snider.*

Kim Richey

I remember when Todd came out with his first record. My publisher and I drove around in his car and listened to it. We loved his lyrics and take on things. I like his outlook and how he sees things in songs like "Alright Guy." He's always funny but hits you emotionally. Todd doesn't sound contrived and songwriter-y. I remember liking his honestly. You can write in character, but it still needs to be honest. A friend told me years later that Ray Kennedy was making a record with Todd. They needed somebody to tap dance [on "The Ballad of the Devil's Backbone Tavern" from *Happy to Be Here*]. "I can tap dance," I said. "I took tap dance for a million years when I was a kid." My friend called Ray. Everybody was like, "You can tap dance?" "Yeah. I told you." Ray gave me some money, and I went to Green Hills. There was a shop that sold stuff like dance class shoes and outfits.

I went in and tried to buy a size ten tap shoe. The lady was skeptical. "Can I go somewhere that has a surface I can tap on?" She led me back through this storage room where I could tap. "You can tap dance?" she said. "I know," I said. "I keep telling everyone." I went back to Ray's, and he had gone to Home Depot. He bought all these different surfaces for me to try tapping on. He had me tap along on one kind of wood, then some plywood. Finally, I ended up just tapping on the floor of the studio. I was really good at tap as a kid, and it was something that I never forgot. Who knew it would come in handy?[30]

Kim Richey has released nearly a dozen albums from her self-titled debut (1995) through her seamless Thorn in My Heart *(2013) and* Edgeland *(2018).*

Marshall Chapman

I had just recorded my second record for Margaritaville called *Love Slave*, and Todd came into the office one day. He wanted to hear the whole album and wanted to really listen—and with me sitting right there. I couldn't believe it. He would look at the titles and say, "I can't wait to hear this." One he liked was called "Just to Torture Myself." Fitting. He later sang on one of my albums. We were at a studio in a house out beyond the airport and beyond East Nashville in far East Nashville. We only did one take. We let it rip and it was fabulous. Todd showed up and then disappeared. He's that way for shows too.

We got to hang out backstage doing some shows in Charlotte and Wilmington. We did one at the Poor House in Raleigh. They feed you this incredible meal before the show there, but Todd had [his former road manager] drive him to the closest door to the stage about two minutes before he was supposed to be onstage. I would stand around and talk and sign merch after my shows. Todd would be gone. I had this bass player who used to say, "Let's hit it and quit it." I love that expression. That's Todd. Mr. Hit It and Quit It. He's like an apparition. He just shows up onstage then disappears. I mean, I was on the road with him and would never see him except the two minutes before he went onstage. His self-preservation instincts are admirable.[31]

Jimmy Collins

I was there the morning MCA dropped him. He had fingered a bunch of people. I was like, "Todd, don't do that. You're on MCA." He would throw the finger at the whole crowd and walk off. There was a time when we thought Todd was gonna be a big rock star. He needed the MCA machine to be supporting him, but it all came out in the wash. I mean, Todd would drive a red Galaxy back in San Marcos, and it would break down. He would go over to Kent's instead of getting it fixed. Kent probably would try to talk him out of it but then Todd would leave the car and get another one.[32]

Keith Sykes

The label sent Todd around the world. He probably moved to East Nashville because the possibilities were more limited in Memphis. We don't keep in touch so much anymore. Todd has never screwed me over on the publishing, but we were supposed to do a tour together one time when he fired me. He booted me at the very last minute for whatever reason. That left a sour taste in my mouth and was a last straw. I'm proud of Todd and everything he has done, but I'm not sure a friend would do that to someone. I thought, "Well, maybe we're not so much friends as business associates."[33]

Pamela Des Barres

I've known Todd forever. Everything started when my good friend Kim Britton was a publicist at MCA and was handling this character Todd Snider. She wanted me to write his bio. Of course, I went to see him and loved him so much. He's right up my alley. I'm a big Gram Parsons fan.

Gram turned me on to alternative country when he was in the Byrds back in 1968. Also, I'm a big Dylan fan. Todd fit both those bills. He also was incredibly cute. This must be twenty-four years ago. He came over with his whole band, and we hit it off so well. We played Elvis records forever.

I also was there the night he walked off the stage at the Whisky a Go Go. Same time frame, same band. Everyone from MCA was there. The whole team felt pressure. We could all tell, but you can't tell Todd what to do. You cannot coerce him in any way. He's like a cat. "Here, kitty, kitty." No way. You can't make him. MCA wanted to re-create him into a rock star. He wasn't having it. He got up onstage, looked at the audience, and walked off. He went out the back door, onto Sunset Boulevard in his bare feet, and back to his hotel. That was one of the best things I've ever seen. Who would do that? No one.

Iconic groupie Pamela Des Barres's adventures with rock stars from Mick Jagger and Jimmy Page to Waylon Jennings and Jim Morrison fill pages throughout her memoir, I'm with the Band.

Todd Snider

That Los Angeles show was so weird. People really loved it. Madonna's brother and sister were there [with] the MCA Records people, and they had tons of press. I've met four hundred of the two hundred people who were there over the years. Prine also had the video and loved it. The show was entertaining. I had on three coats. Someone should have known then. I think I said, "I'm just gonna play one more and go, 'Fuck y'all. Y'all bore me.'" They all just turned white. I put all my coats back on, jumped off the front of the stage, and went out the front door. I remember as packed as it was you could hear that door click because everyone was silent. I went down the street and got drinks.

Pamela Des Barres

Of course, MCA dropped him, but that was a good thing. Everyone at MCA was horrified, embarrassed. They had invited all kinds of press to the event and let him know it. I believe that he could feel their coercion and desire to train him in a certain way. That didn't feel right to him. He's turned other things down because he had to go his own way. What made Dylan the way he is? There are a thousand books on it. It's an inside job. Todd is overly sensitive to the point where things hurt him. That's why he's very isolated for the most part. He has good friends, but he spends lots of time alone. He has been able to do exactly what he wants since then.[34]

Joe McLeary

I was with the band about five years from 1992 to 1997. I stopped because I had watched the whole thing build up and go to Nashville. We were touring all the time. There was a lot of, "When are we gonna do this and that?" I didn't leave because Todd didn't make it big. Things were happening in my life. I was married before I met Todd, and we had a daughter during that time. I needed more flexibility. I was devoting everything to the Todd gig. It all culminated on a long trip when we were up in New York visiting my wife's parents' house. I was supposed to do a gig with Todd in Key West on New Year's Eve at the end of that holiday. I woke up in New York and went nonstop from there to Memphis to Nashville to Miami renting cars, trains, and planes.

We did our typical band gig at Jimmy Buffett's Margaritaville on Duval Street in Key West. Todd had sentimental reasons to have the band with him on New Year's, but I think it's better to take a break when the holidays come. You can go back to work after. Todd was new to everything and was excited. Buffett showed up the first times we played there but not that night. They had a slimy, greasy apartment for bands above the venue. Somehow they decided it would be appropriate to have a big bowl of fruit there for us. We started throwing everything out the window one by one: a grape, an apple, pineapple. Pretty soon Duval Street was covered with fruit. Cars were driving by squishing it.

Then later Buffett said, "Come open for our arena shows." We opened these thirty thousand seat arenas, and Todd had gotten radio play with "Talking Seattle Grunge Rock Blues." People wanted to hear that, which was the only song they would have heard on the radio at that point. That was a fun, Buffett-esque tune with humor and a songwriter who knew what he was doing. Buffett wanted us to go out and do that song, but Todd wouldn't at the arenas. Maybe he did it one time near the end of the tour. Todd said he didn't want to get pegged as the comedy guy, but that begs the question, "Why did you even allow it on the record?"

I'll never forget one night on tour. We were playing "Late Last Night" at the Vogue Theater in Indianapolis. We were toward the end of our set. Maybe our encore. Will starts it off, and it's a pretty fast and physically demanding song the way I used to play. We're playing it, got through the solo, and were vamping and waiting on Todd's cues on how we're gonna end. Todd turns around, and says, "I gotta take a piss." We're playing this fast song with everything we have. Will does another solo. I look over and three minutes has gone by. We're cramping up and hurting. Joe Mariencheck's almost crying. His arms are burning. I look out and see Todd sitting at the bar. He's hamming it up with the audience. I laughed. Todd never flinched.[35]

L-R: Todd Snider and Kent Finlay outside of Snider's first tour bus, which, he told Jenni Finlay, was formerly owned by the Judds, Luckenbach, Texas, 1994. Photo by Diana Finlay Hendricks.

Early Daze / Todd Snider

1.	can't keep a good man down	1:52
2.	this ol' world ain't gonna get the best of me	1:42
3.	we don't talk much anymore	2:38
4.	this ain't no way to get to heaven	2:42
5.	i've gotta quit this shit again	2:35
6.	bless her broken heart	2:15
7.	foster brown	2:59
8.	that woman proved me wrong	2:26
9.	lisa marie	3:10
10.	hold me down	2:27
11.	feeling at home	3:05
12.	who says it's lonely	4:19
13.	look back kindly on me	3:28
14.	is it live or is it memorex	3:05
15.	keep off the grass - first demo	1:52
16.	my and my guitar	2:54
17.	looking out for #1	3:38
18.	songwriter's prayer	2:33
19.	minor in possession	2:26
20.	i'll get over her if you'll get under me	2:24
21.	there's got to be a better way	2:18
22.	now that i've fallen for you	2:36
23.	happy hour hero	2:54
24.	guitar	4:59
25.	back in the company of friends	4:24

Todd Snider San Marcos-era demo tape. Courtesy Jenni Finlay.

L–R: Jenni Finlay (fiddle) and Todd Snider at Jerry Jeff Walker's inaugural Laborfest, Luckenbach, Texas, 1996. Photo by Diana Finlay Hendricks.

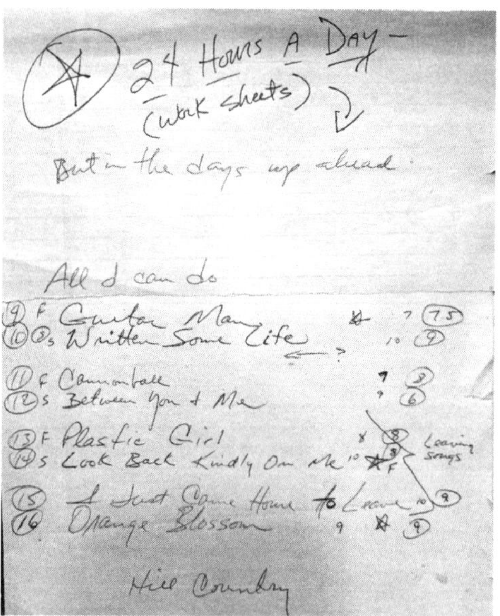

24 Hours A Day —
(work sheets)

But in the days up ahead

All I can do

9 F Guitar Man 7 7.5
10 S Written Some Life 10 9
11 F Cannonball 7 8
12 S Between You + Me 9 6
13 F Plastic Girl 8 8 Leaving songs
14 S Look Back Kindly On Me 10 8 F
15 I Just Came Home to Leave 10 9
16 Orange Blossom 9 9

Hill Country

Kent Finlay's handwritten lyrics to "24 Hours a Day," cowritten with Todd Snider on August 1, 1995. Photo by Brian T. Atkinson. Courtesy Jenni Finlay.

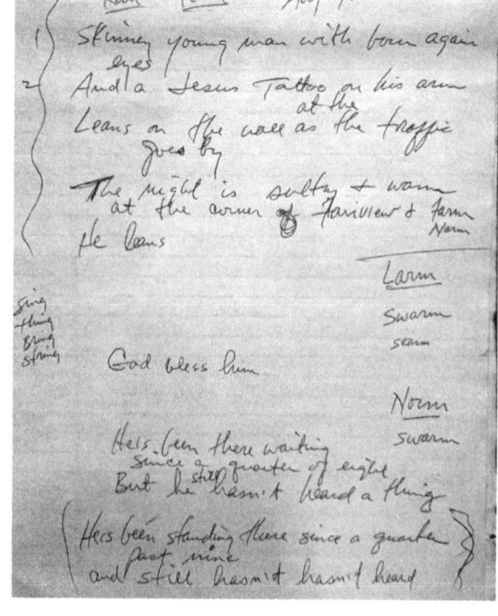

Kent + Todd Aug 1, 1995

Skinny young man with born again eyes
And a Jesus Tattoo on his arm
Leans on the wall as the traffic goes by
The night is sultry + warm
at the corner of Fairview + Farm
He leans

Larm
Swarm
storm

Sing
thing
Bring
string

God bless him

Norm
swarm

He's been there waiting since a quarter of eight
But he still hasn't heard a thing

He's been standing there since a quarter past nine
and still hasn't hasn't heard

Kent Finlay's handwritten lyrics to "24 Hours a Day," cowritten with Todd Snider on August 1, 1995. Photo by Brian T. Atkinson. Courtesy Jenni Finlay.

Todd Snider Memphis-era demo tape. Courtesy Eric Lewis.

Todd Snider, signing the MCA Records contract for his debut album, Songs for the Daily Planet, *at Newby's, near the University of Memphis, in the mid-1990s. Photo by Anita Webb.*

L–R: Michael "Moondawg" Webb and Todd Snider in the Memphis area, mid-1990s. Photo by Anita Webb.

Center, L–R: Todd Snider and Joe Ely in Memphis, mid-1990s. Photo by Anita Webb.

Todd Snider, performing in Memphis, mid-1990s. Photo by Anita Webb.

Center, L–R: Todd Snider and Kent Finlay in Memphis, mid-1990s. Photo by Anita Webb.

Todd Snider, performing in Memphis, mid-1990s. Photo by Anita Webb.

Todd Snider, opening for Drivin N Cryin at the New Daisy Theater in Memphis, mid-1990s. Photo by Eric Lewis.

L–R: Sheila Lewis, Teenie Hodges, who wrote the Al Green hits "Take Me to the River," "Love and Happiness," "L-O-V-E (Love)," and "Here I Am (Come and Take Me)," and Todd Snider. Photo by Eric Lewis.

Todd Snider at the What the Folk Fest in Memphis, March 9, 1996. L–R: Eric Lewis, Will Kimbrough, unidentified, Todd Snider, Robert Jordan, and Kevn Kinney. Photo by Sheila Lewis.

Todd Snider promotional photo for Margaritaville Records.

Todd Snider, Step Right Up *release party in Nashville, mid-1900s. Photo by Anita Webb.*

Todd Snider opening for Jerry Jeff Walker at the Denver Pavilions, outside of the Pepsi Center, in Denver, Colorado, July 28, 2003. Photo by Brian T. Atkinson. Snider's set list was bookended by "Can't Complain" and "Alright Guy" with "Beer Run" as the anchor.

Todd Snider performs at the Nevada Museum of Art in Reno, Nevada, July 23, 2004. Photo by Stacie Huckeba.

Contact sheet with photos of Todd Snider performing at the Rocky Mountain Folks Fest in Lyons, Colorado, August 21, 2005. Photos by Brian T. Atkinson.

Todd Snider at the Rocky Mountain Folks Fest in Lyons, Colorado, August 21, 2005. Photo by Brian T. Atkinson.

L–R: Will Kimbrough and Todd Snider at John Ascuaga's Nugget Casino in Sparks, Nevada, February 1, 2006. Photo by Stacie Huckeba.

Todd Snider at South by Southwest in Austin, Texas, 2007. Photo by Brian T. Atkinson.

Todd Snider at Eric McConnell's studio in Nashville, 2007. Photo by Stacie Huckeba.

Todd Snider at his home in Nashville, 2007. Photo by Stacie Huckeba.

Todd Snider at the Eastside Sluggers Baseball League, June 2007. Photo by Stacie Huckeba.

Todd Snider at Eric McConnell's studio, September 22, 2008. Photo by Stacie Huckeba.

L–R: Keith Sykes and Todd Snider at Sykes's house in Memphis, October 6, 2008. Photo by Stacie Huckeba.

L–R: Unknown, Burt Stein, and Todd Snider at the Ryman Auditorium in Nashville, November 20, 2008. Photo by Stacie Huckeba.

L–R: Todd Snider, Tim Carroll, and Peter Cooper at Elmo Buzz rehearsals, December 3, 2008. Photo by Stacie Huckeba.

Todd Snider at the Troubadour in Los Angeles, California, February 2009. Photo by Stacie Huckeba.

Todd Snider, at home, Nashville, May 7, 2009. Photo by Stacie Huckeba.

East Nashville Bulldogs rehearsal. Photo by Stacie Huckeba.

Todd Snider at Bonnaroo Music Festival, Manchester, Tennessee, June 14, 2009. Photo by Stacie Huckeba.

L–R: Don Was and Todd Snider at Bonnaroo Music Festival, Manchester, Tennessee, June 14, 2009. Photo by Stacie Huckeba.

L–R: Todd Snider and Don Was rehearsing backstage at Bonnaroo Music Festival, Manchester, Tennessee, June 14, 2009. Photo by Stacie Huckeba.

L–R: Don Was at Todd Snider at Bonnaroo Music Festival, Manchester, Tennessee, June 14, 2009. Photo by Stacie Huckeba.

Todd Snider reading a newspaper article about himself at Bonnaroo Music Festival, Manchester, Tennessee, June 14, 2009. Photo by Stacie Huckeba.

Todd Snider at the original Family Wash location in Nashville. Photo by Stacie Huckeba.

Todd Snider with the reunited Nervous Wrecks at Levitt Shell Auditorium in Memphis, Tennessee, June 19, 2009. L–R: Will Kimbrough, Todd Snider, Joe Mariencheck, and Joe McCleary (not visible). Photo by Stacie Huckeba.

Todd Snider with Cowboy Jim at home in Nashville, July 6, 2009. Photo by Stacie Huckeba.

Todd Snider at Shelby Park in Nashville, September 2, 2009. Photo by Stacie Huckeba.

Todd Snider on the Volcano Radio Hour in Nashville, October 19, 2009. Photo by Stacie Huckeba.

Chorus: East Nashville Skyline

THE NASHVILLE YEARS

Todd Snider crashes creatively with *Viva Satellite* in 1998, but his final album for MCA Records yields two masterworks: "Can't Complain" and the closing "Doublewide Blues." He signs with John Prine's Oh Boy Records as a Nashville resident. "My John Prine connection started in Memphis," Snider says. "Prine was making two-song demos to shop around for *The Missing Years*, and Keith Sykes was on the short list for producers. Prine came to Memphis and did four songs: 'All the Best,' 'You Got Gold,' 'Everything is Cool,' and 'The Missing Years.' Then they did a Tim Carroll song ["If I Could"] just for shits. Keith knew that I knew all John's songs, so he hired me to be the runner on those sessions. I drove John around. We got friendly. He came to the Daily Planet and went on about a song of mine called 'Lisa Marie.'"

Snider immediately builds momentum with the label on *Happy to Be Here* (2000) and *New Connection* (2002). The former features standout tracks such as "Long Year," "D. B. Cooper," "Lonely Girl," and "The Ballad of the Devil's Backbone Tavern," while the latter offers his signature "Beer Run," as well as "Rose City," the Kent Finlay cowrite "Statistician's Blues," and "Waco Moon." Snider showcases most on the seamless live album *Near Truths and Hotel Rooms* (2003). Then he officially lays claim as East Nashville's favorite son with his high-water mark, *East Nashville Skyline* (2004). "*East Nashville Skyline* was the only record I nailed the whole way through," Snider says. "I told a couple friends that there's a point where your training meets the peak, and I knew I really had to figure out songwriting. I learned that the grift doesn't work unless you're really vulnerable. You have to open your heart and show people what's in there. I don't think I started really singing from my heart until *East Nashville Skyline*."

East Nashville Skyline sparks a consecutive creative crest. The following five albums—*The Devil You Know* (2006), the outtakes collection *Peace, Love and Anarchy* (2007), *Peace Queer* (2008), *The Excitement Plan* (2009), and *Agnostic Hymns & Stoner Fables* (2012)—showcase the songwriter in finest form. The albums include Snider classics "The Devil You Know," "Looking for a Job," "Just Like Old Times," "Happy New Year," "Is This Thing Working?" "Is This Thing On?" "East Nashville Skyline," "Nashville," "Cheatham Street Warehouse," "Greencastle Blues," "In the Beginning," "Brenda," and "In Between Jobs." He starts his own independent label, Aimless Records, releases the superlative full-band live record *The Storyteller* (2011) with Great American Taxi, and puts out a rowdy garage rock album *East Side Bulldog* (2016) by his alter ego Elmo Buzz along the way.

Jenni Finlay

The Houston Oilers picked Nashville when they decided to move to Tennessee, but they had to camp out in Memphis while the stadium was being built. Memphis was rubbed pretty raw. The city had always considered itself the "red-headed stepchild" next to Nashville, so you can imagine how upset they were that the Oilers used them as their "practice" town. This all was going down right when Todd was moving from Memphis to that funky little Fairview house outside Nashville. Memphis had been good to him more than not—even though it's the only place he's ever been mugged at gunpoint. So, Todd moved to Nashville and said, "They're probably going to hate me in Memphis now, too."

I'm pretty sure they still take his calls.[1]

Todd Snider

I would go backstage at John Prine's shows and was getting to know [his road manager] Mitchell [Drosin] and Al [Bunetta] and got a record contract when Keith got a call from John that he liked my record, which meant a lot. I went on the road with John for the *Lost Dogs* tour. I was always intimidated but got friendly with him. Then we made the third record. Al listened to it and said, "It's a great record, but something stinks." "What?" "The script." "You're right." I had thirteen songs and was trusting him as a song person. I was still managed by Mercer and was still on MCA, but he said, "Can you play these songs for John?" I went in the next day and said, "Did you like those?" "John says you have one song here." I was hurt but was thinking he was right even though I didn't know what was wrong.

He broke down what was wrong with the songs. I essentially was trying to win arguments and wasn't showing my heart and being vulnerable. I was using the craft as a weapon. I knew I was doing something wrong but couldn't figure it out. I threw those songs out when he told me that and started working hard on *Happy to Be Here*. Then I hired Al [as my manager]. I didn't fire Bob Mercer. I would call and tell Bob anytime Al would call and tell me something. I would do what Bob said. One guy came up with an idea, and I would do it if the other liked it. I thought I was really into songwriting during the first two records, but then I was really into melodies, clothes, and drugs with the third. I was getting into the idea that girls liked me. I found morphine around that time. I got myself together after that record, but the morphine was starting to win. I didn't try that hard on *New Connection*, and I knew I was disappointing John.[2]

Dan Baird

Todd camped out early in East Nashville. He writes these really fucking good songs that are usually simple in musical structure, but the simpler the skeleton the more weight you can hang on them. Many guys over there who had a foot in folk music and saw him get up there and go crazy. It's like, "Wow. He's free." Todd's grinning like a cat eating shit when everything is clicking. I mean, he's on-fire happy. That goes out to the crowd, and they get happy too. They come back not because it was a good show but because they felt something. Young songwriters see that and go, "That's what I wanna do." Todd is as close as those younger songwriters will get to having their own personal Bob Dylan.[3]

Will Kimbrough

We made *East Nashville Skyline* and *The Devil You Know* years later. Wonderful records. Chalk up *East Nashville Skyline* to Todd. He had the songs and knew what he wanted it to sound like. He just trusted me to hear what he said. I mean, Todd's favorite records influencing him definitely aren't recording engineers' favorite records. Todd's not name-dropping Steely Dan's *Aja*. He doesn't want to spend two hours getting the Ringo Starr cymbal sound. He just wants to set it up for a performance with a concept that either works or doesn't. Might take a couple days or weeks or might be an immediate, "Yes, that's it. We're done." Todd was in a pretty delicate state at that time. [Snider's friend] Skip [Kenneth Francis "play a fucking train song" Litz] had died. Todd had found him when he passed away. I think Todd had been partying with him. Todd was fresh out of treatment and raw but totally 100 percent on top of his artistic game.[4]

Todd Snider

I went over to Eric McConnell's house to smoke weed when we did the *East Nashville Skyline* record, and we were complaining about some demos that I had done in Memphis that week. He had a studio, so we started like, "Show me the beat the guy was playing." We put down the original guitar and drums of "Play a Train Song." Kimbrough brought me into the cult rock 'n' roll underground of Nashville. They were the non-mainstream crowd here. Will is part of that social group. I was set back by him in a few ways. He's driven more melodically than lyrically. I tried to do that for a while, but it wasn't satisfying. It didn't work like therapy anymore. I had to stop writing like him.

I called Will that night and was like, "I think we did it. I just need someone to clean it up." He came over was like, "Dude, you did it. This is the song." We found the train beat that did it. My guitar part was wobbly and all over the place, so he replaced it. I was like, "Hear my guitar part? Can you play that but good?" He did it. Then we just kept working, which is how he came to produce that record. We didn't even talk about it. Will held my hand and showed me how to do things myself. That's his production style. Same with Don Was [who produced 2009's *The Excitement Plan*]. Most producers come at you like, "I always heard you in this way . . ." Will and Don are like, "Yeah, I'll produce you. What do you want to do?" They just wait and wait and wait until you say you're stuck. "Oh, okay. I have a thousand ideas . . ."[5]

Will Kimbrough

I was able to be the conduit on *East Nashville Skyline* and not throw too much paint at the wall. [Bassist] Dave Roe would walk down the street and poke his head in. We would say, "Hey, hey. Come play bass." We only had Eric McConnell's one-inch eight-track tape machine and would do background vocals and tambourine on one track like you read in the Beatles books. Some songs like "Tillamook County" were just Todd by himself, or we had Todd's acoustic and my electric. We had great players who were perfect for the way we recorded. I mixed the record because I had eight faders. What a joy. I just had to make sure the vocals and instruments were in the right place. Todd would sit at my ear like a first-base coach.

He would murmur a direction in my ear so no one could hear, and I would say things to the guys like, "So, Todd wants to do it in F sharp, but keep your eyes closed the whole time. Don't look at your instrument." Todd would give me some way to interpret what he wanted for the musicians by referencing a record only Dylan freaks really love like *Self Portrait*. Todd was obsessed with that stuff. I'm lucky he asked me to do it, and I guess he's lucky because I don't have rules about which records are good. I just know what I like. We had a real good understanding between us during that particular miserable, rainy, dead-of-winter, cold Nashville winter. What a thrilling thing to do.

The bedrock of our friendship is mutual respect for each other as songwriters. There will be ups and downs working with anybody for twenty-five years off and on, but playing with Todd was a wonderful relief and learning experience for me. I got to just play guitar and sing harmonies for the first time. I could sing all the harmonies and not stomp all over somebody's song with too much playing. I respected the song, but I could take a solo if someone wanted. We were and still are a great partnership. We don't see each other that much anymore but still email at six in the morning. Our affection for each other's music always has been powerful and has never felt anything but good.[6]

Todd Snider

You usually give the label the songs. They give you the money to make the album. You record the songs. I felt like that part had become a stumbling block. I wanted to take ownership of everything and take control. I didn't tell Oh Boy when I made *East Nashville Skyline*. I went over to Eric's house because we got grass from the same guy. I had heard this Loretta Lynn record [the Jack White-produced *Van Lear Rose*] that had been made there. I liked the guy a lot. I figured if Loretta Lynn didn't say this place was too rinky-dink it was good for me. The only song I had was "Play a Train Song." I recorded it with Sykes but didn't like it. I was over at Eric's smoking pot one day, and I told him about the song and how I wanted it to go. "Wait," he said. "That's just not possible."

He started to explain arranging music and theory, and we recorded "Play a Train Song" together that night. Then we called Will and got going.

I told Eric and the musicians that I didn't have any money and might not ever. I felt like if I made a record without any label help it might be better. "I'll take what we do, and give it to Oh Boy," I said. "They'll pay us if they like it. We'll just have to figure it out if they don't." I supplied all the weed, and we dove in. We hadn't planned it, so we were at the mercy of whoever was home that day. I didn't realize that *East Nashville Skyline* was a breakthrough when we recorded it, but my friend Peter Cooper did. People were kinder after that record came out.

I don't have an issue with having an album that's better than others. I'm just glad to have a good album, but I do still try to re-create that record to this day. I don't consider a record to be going now until I have caught that wave. Every time I go to an engineer I tell them I want to record a demo for an unfinished song. I don't say, "We're recording an album." I say, "I'm just gonna come in and noodle around." Then you tell everybody about halfway through, "Fuck it. I'll put this out." That seems to keep the red-light fever off everybody. People don't change their strings. Nobody gives a shit. They don't want to do anything over because they think we're gonna do the whole thing over later.

East Nashville Skyline was stories about people I knew. No more gospel. No religion. I liked John Lennon and Bob Marley when I was younger. They knew, didn't they? I realized the more I looked into it that they had so much to lose by saying the things they did. Everything goes back to, "Write what's in the room, man." That's what was in the room for Bob Marley. He got to reap the benefits of what he had to see and say about it. Go stand somewhere and say that, but don't try to be a Bob Marley. You don't live in a war-torn country. I think "Bobby McGee" and "The Gambler" are as good as songs get.[7]

Chad Staehly

East Nashville Skyline is a masterpiece. The record has all these amazingly deep and heartfelt lyrics while making social commentary. That balance and rawness became a calling card and stamp for the whole East Nashville scene. The songs and melodies and everything really spoke to us in that moment. The chemistry with us was there right with Great American Taxi and Todd from the start. Todd had started doing tours with Yonder Mountain String Band around then and was developing an interest in the jam scene. He improvises in his own way, plays to the room, and understands it. His show is just a little different than ours in that people pay attention to his words in the song and between songs.[8]

Keyboardist Chad Staehly has backed Todd Snider with Great American Taxi and as a member of Hard Working Americans. He belongs to Snider's management team today.

Mike Grimes

I played on three tracks during the *East Nashville Skyline* sessions. None made the record, but one was the song "East Nashville Skyline" that came out later. Todd did a *Live at Grimey's* CD not long after that. I remember that day well. The feeling is palpable when Todd Snider is singing two feet away from you. The way he could completely touch a crowd brought me to tears. He's one of the best performers I've ever seen. The Eastside Bulldogs played the Basement East three years ago around Christmastime. We're both busy doing other things, but we have a mutual admiration society. Todd's brain is wired differently.

"Incarcerated" [from *East Nashville Skyline*] motors and is one of my favorite fucking Todd songs from *East Nashville Skyline*. The lyrics are hysterical. Of course, that whole record is incredible. "Conservative Christian" speaks for itself. "The Ballad of the Kingsmen" and his Skip tribute "Play a Train Song" were great. I was running the Slow Bar then, and my partner Dave Brown was running the Radio Cafe down the street. Skip would hang out there. Dave has a "Play a Train Song" tattoo. Skip was this boisterous vet, crazy fucking biker-type dude who lived by his own set of rules. He would come in and scream, "Play a train song" no matter who was playing.

Skip would shake things up. He was a sweet guy who probably partied himself into the ground. Skip told funny stories, but he was pretty obnoxious. I was pretty accepting of eccentricities at the time, nonetheless. We had other people who were eccentric pains in the ass in other ways, but we still liked them. We were glad to host the bohemian culture going on at the time. They were gravitating toward East Nashville. I didn't have a girlfriend and wasn't married. I was like, "Fuck, let's rock." Skip was somebody to stay up later and drink with. Somebody had to drive him home half the time because he mostly was lit.

You're rooting for that guy. You're crossing your fingers when it's third and seven. You want him to hit that ten-yard crossing route. I really got to know Todd the day that Skip Litz died. Skip was the unofficial mayor of East Nashville and was famous to all his friends. He once led the police on a chase on his motorcycle going five miles an hour past every East Nashville bar. There were several police cars behind him. He wanted to wave to everybody. Skip had been Todd's tour manager and was a friend to everyone in the neighborhood. Skip was found asleep on his couch with a smile on his face after he died just like Todd says in "Play a Train Song."[9]

Peter Cooper

I was writing for *The Tennessean* newspaper and wanted to do an appreciation of Skip, which meant going over to his house and talking with everyone who was there writing down Skip stories. We talked about Skip's absolutely critical insanity and completely different way of looking at the world. For example, Skip was hungry one night after the show and had a hundred- dollar bill from merch sales. They went to Taco Bell because they knew it would be open and got in the drive through lane. "Can you change a hundred?" he asked. "Um," they said. "No, sir." "All right then, give me a hundred dollars' worth of tacos."

Skip kept all these cassettes and discs from nights when he would run sound at the Radio Cafe in East Nashville from shows by Victor Mecyssne, Gillian Welch, and Todd. Skip cared so much about the music and kept it all around him. There was a note one time that had been sent from Davidson County that he was being fined because he hadn't mowed his lawn and his neighbors were complaining. Skip had written to them himself but never got to send the letter. He had written "deceased" on the envelope that he was gonna send back to the county. He wasn't gonna pay that fine.

Todd had met Skip walking around this circle in his neighborhood. He was walking one morning, and Skip was on his porch smoking cigarettes and doing whoever knows what else. Todd heard his next album coming from Skip's jam box, but he hadn't been giving out copies of that album yet. He stopped for a second and was like, "Hey, man." "Hey, man," Skip said. "You can walk all you want, but you're still gonna die." Todd took to him from that point forward. One main duty [Skip had] as Todd's tour manager was to handle Todd's dog Lulu. Lulu was a very small, white, puffy dog. They got to their hotel one time, and Todd checked into his room. Skip went back to the bus and got Lulu. They were walking in, and a clerk saw Skip walking in with Lulu. Dogs weren't allowed in this hotel. This nineteen-year-old clerk guy says, "Excuse me, sir, is that a dog?" Skip turns and looks the guy right in the face while he's holding Lulu to his chest. "No." He takes Lulu to the room.

Todd did a lot for Skip. Skip did a lot for Todd as well. Skip was someone who was more than the mayor of East Nashville. He was a whiskey-swilling Dali Lama. He had his own perspective and Todd could buy into the theology of Skip. I wasn't around when he was writing "Play a Train Song," but I did get an advance copy of *East Nashville Skyline*. *East Nashville Skyline* is where Todd really became Todd Snider. Todd had heroes like Guy Clark, Kris Kristofferson, and John Prine whose first efforts stand with anything and everything they did. Todd took a little longer to grow into himself. That's not to say that he didn't have moments of brilliance in his early albums, but *East Nashville Skyline* was him working on his side of town with his friends and was totally him.

East Nashville Skyline was one of the best things that I have ever borne witness to. I related to the song about Skip on so many levels, but I immediately knew it wasn't because I knew Skip or knew Todd's affinity for him. Specificity immediately leads to universality, and the express route to universality was through details. "Smoking long black Cadillac winding down / Parked it up on the sidewalk like he owned the whole damn town." Well, Skip did. He owned the whole damn town. He did park up on the sidewalk. There was something that struck me that that's how Todd operates like the way Woody Guthrie did in "This Land Is Your Land." "I saw a sign that said no trespassing / But on the other side the sign said nothing / That side was made for you and me."

I was absolutely blown away by *East Nashville Skyline* and found a kindred spirit in Todd. I really felt like he fully revealed his heart through an entire album on that—even on the cover songs like Fred Eaglesmith's "Alcohol and Pills" and [Herbert Magidson and Carl Sigman's] "Enjoy Yourself." I went on a tour chronicling Todd then and saw how true those songs are to him. We went to Northern Virginia and up into Maryland. I really got to understand him as a person on that trip. We went to see a Kris Kristofferson and John Prine concert on that trip. I saw how they related to Todd not as an aspiring young buck but as a peer. You're doing pretty good when those guys see you as a peer.

Kevn Kinney

Todd's garbage can is the only thing I have ever thought about stealing. He will have his garbage can full of half-written songs and lyrics. Todd wakes up early around five in the morning and writes, types, and thinks. He knows his shit. My friend was there once and asked Todd about Bobby Bare, and Todd gave him a two-hour speech. "This is where this shit comes from: Bobby Bare followed Kris Kristofferson, then this guy wouldn't exist if this one wasn't here." Todd has had some really great mentors. His breadth of knowledge with Americana music, where it came from, and why what you're listening to is original is [breathtaking].

Todd is the real deal walking around in his bare feet and playing guitar all the time. He's found people in his audience who like the truth and can be patient enough to watch him up there for an hour and a half. He has his "Beer Run" songs, but he doesn't have a weird moment where he went techno for a while or went to England to have his records produced by Dave Stewart from the Eurythmics. He's been very consistent with his vision. People gravitate toward that. Todd pushes his own envelope for us. I love it when he's so vulnerable in his songs. He influenced me a lot as a songwriter. I think we've influenced each other. I'll go see him any time I can when he's playing in town. I know he won't be there if he doesn't want to be.

Peter Cooper

Many people stop listening to music after they make it their living. They don't turn on music at home because that's what they do for a job, but Todd really does have a dusty pile of vinyl records on his floor. He will put on Keith Sykes and Jerry Jeff Walker, whose soft, contemplative songs he loves. Todd really gravitated to song like Jerry Jeff's "Mountains of Mexico" and "Too Old to Change." It wasn't like Todd listened to those folks and thought, "I'm done with that textbook. Now I'll go somewhere else." He has kept those people close to him. He listens to Dylan incessantly. *New Morning* is his favorite. He said, "You can't steal Dylan. I tried, but you can't. You walk into the song and try to lift something, but it's too heavy." Todd knows the Prine stuff so well he almost doesn't have to listen to him, but he does.[10]

I learned on that East Coast trip that Todd is all about intention. He goes onstage, and people often think that he's just flying off the cuff. "Here's the tipsy gypsy giving you whatever's on his mind at the moment." He's in his mind for hours and hours before he steps onstage. He spends so much time on set lists and sometimes discards them entirely. He thinks through everything he does. We were talking one time about Kenny Chesney, who may not share many fans with Todd. Chesney's a stadium-filling country performer. Todd was talking about Chesney and said he could see what went into his shows.

Chesney knew months before the show that he would come out in the dark. Then this light will hit just his face and hat at the twenty-two-second mark. Then he's gonna lift his hat up and be revealed to the crowd. Then he'll do this and that. Todd was so impressed by Chesney's intent on putting on a show. I'm not saying that's the way Todd puts on a show, but he sure thinks about that before he walks onstage. He knows how to tell a story, but he edits his own stories before he hits the stage almost like an athlete's visualization process. You think what to do when the pitcher throws you a slider on a two-two count. You're gonna hit to right field. That's part of his songwriting process too.

Todd has talked to me about how he wants a Rocky punch in his songs. Many people reveal their whole story in the opening verse and chorus to a song, but there's a point in the *Rocky* movies where he gets the opening and clocks you. You'll notice that so many of Todd's great songs open you up with laughter and empathy in the third verse and give you a Rocky punch that you did not see coming and from which you will never recover. "Just Like Old Times" [from 2006's *The Devil You Know*] is one. The narrator's in a hotel room with a hooker and drugs, and a cop bangs at the door. He knows a cop with a hooker and drugs is not a positive development. He says, "No, sir, officer, you don't understand. We're just two old friends drinking wine. I know she is but that's not all she is. She's also an old friend of mine."

I'm cracking up just saying that. "I've got her high school picture in my wallet from 1982." Then he ends up saying, "You have a good night too." The officer is leaving. You just don't see that leaving. It's funny and a grift to the officer. He's saying, "Hey, we know each other." She's still a hooker in a hotel room doing drugs. Then he tries to play it off to her. "Hey, we've got the cop taken care of. This picture is no big deal." It clearly is a big deal, though. There's an emotional heft to that song that's pretty incredible. Todd has so many like that where he reveals himself in writing about other people. He can write a song about the truth without writing a song that's journalism.

Justin Corsbie

I wrote my movie *Hard Luck Love Song* based on Todd's song "Just Like Old Times." Todd was pretty excited about the film. His attitude was like, "Go for it. Sounds good to me." We went over some [ideas] as I was writing the script, and I sent the script to him when we finished, but his was a very hands-off approach in general. I think that's just because film is a medium he's not used to working in. Another part is that I know his catalog so well, so I didn't need a ton of guidance. I had a good handle on what to infuse into the film from his music.

The film's main character, Jesse, was inspired in part by Todd. For example, Michael Dorman, who was the actor who played Jesse, and I went to see Todd in Asheville, North Carolina, before we started shooting the film. Michael had never seen him. We were visiting with Todd on the bus before the show, and he said this line, "I don't not gamble." I thought the double negative was hilarious so Jesse says that in the movie. I infused things like that and references from his songs and stories throughout the film. I think Todd even lost count when we screened the film for him and his crew. Another example is when I have the character Skip, named after a character from "Play a Train Song," say, "Come over here, you little shit," which is a line from "The Ballad of the Devil's Backbone Tavern." The film is full of Easter eggs like that.[11]

Writer and director Justin Corsbie's debut feature film, Hard Luck Love Song *(2021), was based on Todd Snider's song "Just Like Old Times."*

Peter Cooper

Todd and I wrote a song about Phil Ochs called "Thin Wild Mercury" [from *The Devil You Know*] about a confrontation he and Bob Dylan had. Ochs was angry at his lack of superstardom and was jealous of Dylan while he was riding high but perhaps was a little on edge around his old friend. Ochs criticized a Bob Dylan song while they were in a limousine that Dylan had paid for. Dylan stopped the car. He said, "Phil, you're not a writer, you're a journalist." He made Ochs get out of the car. Sometimes great truths are in fiction. Todd's heart appears in songs that aren't on the surface about him.

The songs I've written with Todd have sprung from conversations. He used to live just a few blocks from me, and we would be talking about the stuff we always talked about, which was music and sports. We would sit on his upstairs porch. He was very proud of that porch. He built it from songwriting royalties. He also bought the Major League Baseball television package from those royalties, so we would sit up there and drink wine, talk, and watch baseball. Sometimes those talks resulted in songs like "Thin Wild Mercury." I don't remember ever sitting down with Todd and saying, "Okay, it's ten in the morning. Let's write a song."

Stacie Huckeba

Todd convinced me to move to Nashville in 2006. Todd and [his ex-wife] Melita [Oshoewitz] found me a house that was directly behind theirs. Our back yards kissed. We would go over there every day. We all got really drunk one night over at Todd and Melita's house and made it snow. I think it was Martin Luther King Day. Peter Cooper's wife, Charlotte, was a schoolteacher and didn't want to go home to get up early for work. Todd was like, "Let's make it snow." It was fifty degrees in September, but Todd started calling his friends and news stations. He told them snow was pounding down. We all wanted to stay up and party and made enough calls that the news reported there was snow in East Nashville. I filmed it on this little point-and-shoot camera and put it together just for us to have. Todd loved it. He was like, "Shit, you can make movies." *Come to East Nashville* was the first movie I ever made.

Then he started calling me to film everything. I did the "Unbreakable" and "Highland Street Incident" videos [from *The Devil You Know*] and other promotional ones. I think I'm the only person who shot promotional photos for him for ages. Todd's fantastic to work with, but he's nuts. I think one reason they call me in all the time is that I never tried to put constraints on him. I never said, "This is our vibe and our look." He doesn't respond well to directions. His instinct is to do the exact opposite if you tell him to do something. He would get an idea, and we would run with it. For example, we shot a cover photo for the *East Nashvillian* one time and Melita put all these looks together for him. We went to the 3 Crow Bar to shoot. The photos were great. Then he called me two days later and was like, "Meet me at the Family Wash and bring your camera."

I go over and he has his old white car and a T-shirt he had written "Titans #1" on. "I forgot," he said. "I don't give a shit." It was the most give-a-shit moment to prove that he doesn't give a shit that I have ever witnessed. They made me pull all the rest of the photos. That's what he submitted for the cover. I think they had hired someone else for the last photo shoot I did for him about a year ago. It apparently was a bigwig. The story was that Todd chased him out of the house with a frying pan. They had to call me in to do the shoot. They had me bring lighting and all this stuff. I didn't go, "Hey, do this." I think Todd is a rebel at heart. I really do. I think he really buys into the philosophies he lives by.

I don't think people necessarily believe it when they find out he doesn't have a driver's license or insurance or a set of keys. That shit is true. Todd has zero responsibilities. None. He lives by his own life codes. That's just the genuine nature of who he is. His gig isn't a gimmick. He doesn't lock the doors at the house. He doesn't care about possessions. Anything at the house is something other people have brought in. He would be fine if there wasn't a bit of furniture in the house. I think he forges friendships through that and how he's honest, but you constantly break up with Todd. You're like, "Can't you just be fucking normal?" You have to remember this is normal for him. He's gonna frustrate the piss out of you. He's gonna do crazy shit sometimes, but that's truly who he is.

Melita had a very calming presence. You would never really see them fight until the divorce. Nobody was more surprised about the divorce than I was. Melita called and asked if she could come stay at the house. "What?" I thought for sure she would be there a couple days, and they would get back together. They were this force and saw themselves as like a Guy and Susanna Clark couple. They really were. They canoodled, held hands, played kissy face even after seventeen years being married. She could bring him down from a level twelve down to an eight. Todd took a while to find his footing after the divorce. That's simply my opinion, but nobody was that anchor for him. He could be tricky to be around.

Todd has no responsibilities. He does not pay the light bill, the insurance, the rent. All the money goes through [his manager] Burt Stein. Burt and Brian Kincaid are probably the only people who actually know how much money he has. He consistently comes up with these big plans and expects everyone to be on board. Todd's like, "Sure, we're gonna pay everybody," but the reality for Brian and Burt is that there's never a budget. You never know what's gonna happen. Here I sit all these years later with what is probably a really great movie, but there's no budget to make it. He has made records that no one will ever hear. He makes a record, and it lands on Burt's desk. "What? He made a record? We don't have a marketing budget."

The city of Nashville should pay Todd a tax dividend for what he's done to promote East Nashville, but Todd would defer to Mike Grimes and Skip Litz because they were there before him. There were only about five or six of us who were a part of that scene when I moved over there. Everything else was run-down. There were no coffee shops. We had Bennie's gas station, which has been a BP and a Marathon, and was the only place to get a coffee. We called it that because the guy's name was Bennie. Mike had the Slow Bar. They really only moved in there because Melita was more comfortable in a neighborhood with brown people. She came from New York. She was used to diversity, and it made her comfortable. Todd loved that about her. She exposed him to so many other people, and everyone was so creative.[12]

Kevin Gordon

I was working at an art gallery when I moved to Nashville. We were carrying Todd's former wife Melita Oshewicz's art. She knew that I was a musician. I was with her in the car when they were dropping off some new art. She introduced me to Todd in the middle of Fifth Avenue. I got to know him gradually. My friend Paul Griffith plays drums on most all my records and was playing with Todd at the time. He helped facilitate what would become me doing gigs with Todd's band gigs in the East Nashville Bulldogs. We had great fun. I don't remember all of it, but it was really fun for me to just play guitar. Todd preferred that I not know the songs going in. That worked perfectly from my own perspective. He had a punk aesthetic that I was familiar with, even though we weren't playing punk rock.

There are some still photos at the end of the *East Nashville Tonight* movie that he put out from those gigs. There was a crazy show in New York. I'm really glad they didn't use any audio from that show. I only really remember little snapshots from then. I remember almost nothing from playing the gig. We got to New York and the venue had a balcony with some backstage area. Todd had the balcony closed off so we could have a party. All I remember is bottles of bourbon and joints as big as my fist being passed around. I don't partake very much. I'm a lightweight, but we were almost done with the run and it felt like the thing to do.

Todd opened solo, then I played, and Chuck and Elizabeth played. Then we went back and played with Todd. I was in that environment swilling bourbon and smoking reefer during the time between my solo set and our band set. I don't know what the results were like, but the response was great. Todd is extremely functional. He used to tell me when I opened shows, "Well, I know it's time for me to start smoking when you go on." He hangs back there and smokes to get in the right place for the gig. I appreciate his level of functioning.

I really love the apparent spontaneity in his shows. You can be on the road with him and see six shows in a row with the same stories. He has a delivery that presents those same stories multiple times and nobody is too worried about it. Doesn't hurt that the stories are funny as hell no matter how many times you've heard them. He always changes the stories a little. He's very giving as far as responding to song requests. His perspective is like, "Sure, if someone remembers something I've written I'm happy to play it no matter how many times I've done it." Todd has a very non-jaded attitude and an odd combination of youth, experience, and maturity as a writer. I thought his saying about peace, love, and anarchy summed him up perfectly. He believes in benevolent anarchy, but it's definitely anarchy.[13]

East Nashville-based songwriter Kevin Gordon's songs have been recorded by Levon Helm, Keith Richards, and Hard Working Americans. He graduated from the Iowa Writers' Workshop.

Peter Cooper

East Nashville has been changing. There are plenty of people who want to talk about distribution now. That frustrates people like Jon Latham who are all about the music and creativity. I think a big anthem for East Nashville was "East Nashville Skyline," which wasn't even on that album. "From a Rooftop" is a beautiful piece about our part of town. "East Nashville Skyline" is about how things change. I think Todd, Mike Grimes, and Skip created East Nashville. People think East Nashville is a proper city, but it's actually in Nashville. I think that has a lot to do with *East Nashville Skyline*.

Todd and the guys he talks about in "From a Rooftop" really made up East Nashville. He just decided that East Nashville would be this magical place in the same way Hondo Crouch did about Luckenbach, Texas. People believed Todd because he was so beautifully poetic. "East Nashville Skyline" is a neighborhood portrait. I played guitar on "From a Rooftop." I wanted to do something that we didn't have to copyright and thought it would be cool if that song was connected to "East Nashville Skyline." The guitar was intended as background to make that connection in people's minds. We were heavy into hanging on the east side around then. We even kept my dachshund barking in the mix.[14]

Mike Grimes

I had about eight thousand records and decided to open Grimey's record store. My business partner David and I left a session and went across to Shirley's to have a beer. We said, "This is cool as shit. Could be the place."

We arranged to come back a few days later and hook up with the owner, Shirley. We said, "How long have you been here, Shirley?" "Seventeen years, and I'm ready to get out. They're gonna turn this into a Tennessee Titans bar." "Hold on," I said. My naivete was ridiculous. "Could I purchase the business from you now if I talk to the landlord?" "Fuck yeah," she said. I used all the money I had from the first year with Grimey's.

I wrote her a check for $10,000. She had a big going away party three days later. Had all her buddies come over and drink the rest of the beer. We added a few menu items. It was beer only, and we were off to the races with no background in opening a bar. We had no plans to do music, but we started doing a handful of shows over time. Our friend asked to do a gig. Cool. Ryan Adams was recording *Heartbreaker* across the street while we were doing that. They said, "Ryan wants to play tomorrow." Okay. We weren't gonna do music, but then we had one band, and Ryan Adams wants to play. We started booking more.

You eventually realize that no one's coming if you don't book music because they expect it. I learned by default. I had to book music every night to keep it open. We've had everyone on their way up somewhat due to the fact that Exit/In closed for six to eight months. We had the Black Keys for a hundred bucks. Everybody played for the door charge. We had the Shins, My Morning Jacket, Kings of Leon's first two shows, Postal Service, Big Star. Nobody took pictures. I have some grainy Black Keys photos. I've seen no photos archived of the Kings of Leon's first performance. Maybe that all adds to the mystery of it.[15]

Patty Griffin

I met Todd in Nashville because he was friends with [instrumentalist and producer] Doug Lancio, who I worked with for years. We had never hung out for any length of time before the day I sang on the *Peace Queer* album. Todd was really, really funny and kind in the studio. I had seen him open for John Prine at the Paramount in Austin, so I knew he was hilarious. He was enthusiastic in a way that was like being a little kid in the studio. He fell down on the ground with his feet up in the air because he liked what we did. He was literally jumping up and down and fell back into a beanbag chair like a bug. Really sweet.

We did the session at Eric McConnell's postwar ranch style house that probably was built in the sixties. You step down into the studio in his basement, which looked like a very dated and carpeted seventies living room. Doug ended up setting up an isolation booth [for me to sing harmony on "The Ballad of Cape Henry" and the Credence Clearwater Revival cover "Fortunate Son"]. Doug is so low-key with a dry sense of humor. We nicknamed him "Eeyore." He always seems glum, but he's not really. He comes across as very laid-back, intense, and funny with a very droll sense of humor. They definitely had a camaraderie in the studio that comes from being neighbors in Nashville.

I later played a show with Todd at the Paramount Theatre in Denver. Our gig was on the Saturday of the week when weed officially became legal. Todd made the most of that. He's so much fun. I'm always amazed at his brain. I've known some extremely funny people, but the way his brain fires amazes me. His timing seems very natural, but I'm sure it's not. I'm sure there's a level of discomfort at all times being that funny. I imagine something is always going on in your brain like hearing music all the time in your head. You can't shut that off. Your brain's constantly telling you things to say.[16]

Patty Griffin entered public consciousness with her album Flaming Red *in 1998.* Downtown Church *(2011) and her self-titled album in 2019 both won Grammy Awards.*

Don Was

I though Todd was brilliant. We started talking about making a record, which turned out to be *The Excitement Plan*. We were at a hotel in Milwaukee and shot video with a camera on us. The most exciting thing about the three days in Milwaukee was going to a Brewers game. I have no problems going anywhere with strangers, but Todd's different. We were minding our own business, but two completely unrelated people tried to pick a fight with Todd. It made me think of those lines from "Greencastle Blues": "Some of this trouble just finds me / Most of this trouble I earned." That Brewers game summed it up. Sometimes he does the shit that messes him up, but sometimes trouble just finds him.

I produced *The Excitement Plan* like a documentary on Todd and wanted to capture the essence of who he is instead of trying to make singles. What he was doing wasn't fashionable. I wanted to show a sense of what it's like to spend an hour with Todd. I think the record is hugely successful in that regard. It touches on all the bases of who he is not only as an artist but as a human being as you go through song by song. *The*

Excitement Plan touches on his life and temperament and his outlook on life. His voice is right up front and dry, and it's a very personal record if you listen. We were in agreement that this would be a folk album about him and his guitar. We wanted to capture truth about doing honest songs showing what he was doing in that moment. It wasn't about putting down groovy musical textures, although those were fun sessions with a fun band to play with. We knew it would be a document of a moment. We weren't trying to make the Beatles' *Sgt. Pepper*.[17]

*Legendary producer Don Was has captained albums by the Rolling Stones as well as Bonnie Raitt, Ziggy Marley, and Todd Snider (*The Excitement Plan *and* Time as We Know It*).*

Otis Gibbs

I agree [politically] with Steve Earle, but goddamn he's boring to listen to when he preaches about this shit. Todd has a gift, and it's the part people don't think about when they're trying to express themselves. He has that in spades. Billy Bragg has that. He's just a beautiful guy. You just like him. I was touring with Billy about twelve years ago, and we ended up in San Francisco because he was playing the Hardly Strictly Bluegrass Festival. He was gonna do a songwriter round with Guy Clark and Steve Earle. Todd played right before that. Billy had never heard of Todd. We were standing on the side of the stage, and there were between ten and twenty thousand people out there. Todd was just being Todd. People loved it.

Billy was like, "Who is this guy?" Then Todd played "You Got Away with It (A Tale of Two Fraternity Brothers)" [from *The Devil You Know*]. Billy was floored. He fucking loved it. He went up to Todd and introduced himself right after the show, which is the worst time to meet anybody. I toured with Billy a few times after that and he would always say, "Hey, man, ever hear anything about Todd Snider?" You could tell Billy was really rooting for him. Billy had been looking for other people who talk about important things, but he had never found one who would deal with it with humor. Billy witnessed Todd preaching important shit to people. He thought it was a rare thing that needed to be celebrated more.

I think songwriters should write whatever they want to write however the hell they want. You have to realize that people are there to be entertained when you're standing onstage. You want to reach people. You should head toward it if there's an avenue you find that reaches people. Todd uses humor as his way. You see it with comedians. They're great at that. They're able to say things that songwriters can rarely ever get away with because they make you laugh. You get away with it through that. You hide truths in there. Listen to Steve Earle's albums. I don't find any preachiness in there at all. Listen to his stage rant, and you're like, "Oh boy." Todd has the gift. He's able to turn the pills into something digestible. Hard to do.

Most people don't even know how to try that. Very few who do try can pull it off. I don't wanna pretend that I know what Todd's day-to-day life is like. Maybe he just learned along the way that his life was easier if he made people laugh. There was a moment in time when Howard Stern was what everyone on the construction site was listening to. He had an anti-establishment voice. He took the XM deal and wasn't on the terrestrial radio anymore. That voice was replaced by Rush Limbaugh. Then when the Bush years happened there was nobody there who could speak out against all that. I believe that Howard Stern would have been that, but there's this chasm. Then in walk comedians like Bob and Tom.

They would have Todd Snider on. Those folks listening would buy records, attend shows, and end up learning more about who this person really was and about the people who probably meant a lot to him. I wonder what the years would have been like if there would have been that voice on the construction site saying, "Bush shouldn't invade Iraq." I think you're either that person who's a storytelling songwriter or not. You can't decide, "Okay, I'm gonna be a great songwriter." Either you have that in you, or you don't. You can't decide that you're gonna be funny onstage. Todd has natural gifts. Todd has all that in him and has a little volume nob that he can turn up. People react to that. Doesn't feel like it's somebody's jacket he put on.

There's all that talk about drugs with Todd. People are afraid to talk about that, embrace it, and make fun of themselves. Todd does. It doesn't seem like there's much ego about what he does. Todd has a huge amount of charisma. Richard Lewis has a lot of charisma. He was saying things that were always making the punch line on him. His neurosis was the butt of the joke. I think there's some of that with Todd. I can't give a recipe to make that all work. It's just there. Todd just happened to have a big record deal and could do it. He was doing it in front of a lot of people. I will say that I didn't give a shit about the music business and all that corporate crap when I moved to Nashville.

I cared about the history. I first heard about East Nashville counterculture because Todd was waving the flag so damn hard. I remember seeing the video of him driving around that Stacie Huckeba filmed. Todd went by this lesbian bar in Five Points. "Oh, there are some beautiful girls in there." That was an inside joke that he had for you. He would be able to hide little things in there. It's like, "Man, I'd like to live there. That sounds fun." I'm not worried about some suit working at a label. Todd seemed real and counterculture. A bunch of people saw that video and thought, "That would be a cool place to live." The truth is that Todd, Chuck Mead, Sergio Webb, Kevin Gordon were just having fun and living life.

Todd planted a flag, but there was a creative community in Nashville before Todd. His neighborhood was Old Hollywood. The Everly Brothers lived right there. Everything they recorded as demos was in those houses. Marty Robbins started writing "El Paso" there. Grady Martin, one of the most recorded guitar players ever, had Skip Spence for a neighbor. We're talking about a very small neighborhood on two streets, a couple blocks. There's history right there. Guy Clark lived a little ways away. That famous picture of Guy with Townes playing fiddle on the porch was just a few streets from my house and Todd's. Saying it began with Todd isn't right, but there was a swing when the gentrification started going nuts.

Everyone here points to Grimey as being an engine toward that. Mike Grimes never gets credit, but when you're in a room with these people they'll tell you he was there really early with the Slow Bar. Some of my earliest memories there are going to the Slow Bar and Radio Cafe. The "Road Mangler" Phil Kaufman would be bartending. Gillian Welch and David Rawlings would be sitting at the bar. Ryan Adams would be over in the corner. I remember going in and seeing Todd's wife, Melita. I didn't know her but thought that was cool. I was just a guy from Nowheresville, Indiana. That was cool, man. I'm a history nut, and there were all these things happening. Todd was the first one I remember really talking about it. He would say, "Come to East Nashville."

Todd emailed me one time. "Hey, man, we're gonna have a party tonight. Here's the address." I go over to this house in East Nashville that's bigger than most. People call it the mansion. I have no idea who owns it. I pull in the back, and there's a big privacy fence. Todd had befriended a young rock band called the Turbo Fruits, who were throwing a party. Chuck Mead and Phil Kaufman were there. They're playing Sly and the Family Stone all night. There was a two-foot brick wall that faces the pool where everybody is. There's a projector showing the lowest, D-grade sixties porn you've ever seen on the wall. Strange, fun evening. There was positive energy.

Todd called me one time on a Tuesday night. "Hey, man," he said. "I really love your podcast. I listened to Tommy Womack. I wanna be on it." "That would be great, Todd." I made a little wish list when I started the podcast and Todd was on it. He's entertaining as hell. Nobody's promoting anything when they come on to talk to me. It's mainly history like the time they were with such and such. "Man, I would love to have you on," I said. "How about next Thursday?" "No," he says. "I want to do it right now." I think he came over a little past midnight. Todd and Brian Kinkaid came over. Brian grew up in the neighborhood in Indianapolis where I live now. [My partner] Amy went upstairs and we talked in the living room. Todd had a list of things he wanted to promote.

I don't do that, but Todd is an anarchist. He did it in the most entertaining way possible. Todd had been doing ecstasy and mushrooms for two days and hadn't slept. He was feeling no pain. I joke that Todd Snider tripping balls on your couch is about as East Nashville as it gets. Most people in those situations might try to hide it, but he's like, "I'm Todd Snider. I'm high as a kite." Pretty damn funny. That's so far out of most of our realities. I really enjoyed talking with him. I started asking about him being around Guy Clark. Guy could be so grumpy, and I could see Todd and him not completely meshing because Todd has flowers in his hat. "What the hell is that about?" Guy asked. Todd said, "I like flowers in my hat."

Todd got serious when I asked him about John Prine. He fucking loved John Prine. We all love John through his music, but Todd actually got to spend a lot of time with the person. It's a beautiful thing when the person's exactly how you wanted them to be, and you could tell that's how he felt about Prine. We had a really nice, fun, strange evening. Brian drove him home after. That's important to say. Todd isn't a guy jumping behind the wheel while he does these things as far as I know. Somebody's taking care of him.

I really love Jerry Jeff Walker and found out that Todd really loves Jerry Jeff. He can talk about him for a while. Todd's version of "Backslider's Wine" is as good as it gets. He started singing that in my living room. Those are moments where you realize you're communicating with someone and understanding each other. I feel that way when Todd talks about Jerry Jeff or Prine. Todd was in lots of rooms we would love to be in. He earned his way into those rooms. He cares enough about those people. There's never really any malice in the stories he tells. The joke's always on him. He's the outcast if there is one. That draws people in like with [Snider's East Nashville live streaming studio] the Purple Building.

You don't run into people at the Purple Building who moved there because there was a good investment opportunity. These people care about being a part of something. Todd was always a part of something. He was always loose at those gigs he did there to warm up for tours. He would stumble through to get them right. These were free gigs, and he wanted to get it right for the paying audience on tour. I remember going to five or seven of those shows over the years. Really good time. There was never any announcement about it. You would find out about the shows if you were supposed to find out. The musicians from the neighborhood would be there. You would drive by and see eight East Nashville weirdos smoking cigarettes by the door at this building that's always closed. You walk in and wouldn't even know the time for the show. The Purple Building felt like the neighborhood.[18]

Indianapolis native and longtime East Nashville resident Otis Gibbs has released nine studio albums from his debut, 49th and Melancholy, *in 2002 through* Hoosier National *in 2020. He hosts the popular podcast* Thanks for Giving a Damn.

Stacie Huckeba

I'm not sure if Todd owns or rents the Purple Building. Todd probably doesn't either. Todd truly doesn't know what's in his bank account. That's not bullshit. For example, I needed to get into the iTunes on his computer for some project we were working on right when I came to town around 2007. So, I set up iTunes on his computer. Of course, he didn't have a credit card. Melita was off somewhere doing something, so I used my bank card to set up his iTunes. I was hoping he would never open it again, but then a week or two later I went to the store and my card was declined. I was like, "What the fuck?" I got home and found an email from Todd: "Did you know that you can get every Bob Dylan record, every Stones record on that thing you did?" He had literally maxed out my credit card buying all this music. Never even dawned on him that somebody was paying for it.

Todd Snider

I haven't had one bill sent to my house so far. I never know how much money I have in the bank. Ever. Not in thirty years. I had to go to the bank once with Burt. The president of the bank came out and called everyone around. "This guy gave me $10,000 in 1994," he said. "He never called again." True. I've never called once. I go on long tours and never ask what we made. I just don't have expensive taste. Sometimes I'll find a cool jacket and say, "Hey, I want to get this for $400." They'll be like, "All right." I just bought a car because I've been renting one for two years. I saw one I liked, and everyone said, "Okay." No one said how much it was. I just got a boat that cost $6,000. I certainly have $6,000, right? I don't know, but Brian Kinkaid knows. He checks. I've never cared. All I have to do is be in one place for ninety minutes.

Stacie Huckeba

I had to call Melita. "I need a check now. Your husband has just bankrupted me on iTunes." He opened it up and was just scrolling around and checking out songs that were on his mind. Money never dawns on him. I can guarantee he doesn't know who his insurance is with. He has no keys. He in charge of absolutely fucking nothing except coming up with these ideas and roping people in. I have always been able to hang because I've never been disappointed by the adventure. I have gotten frustrated, things have gone badly, but the adventure has always been worth it.

Todd loves being around people who are down and struggling and different from him. He pulls from that for his stories. Their stories get bigger as time goes on just like Todd's get bigger. I think that's why he loved Skip Litz so much. They bonded heavily, but Todd was the one who decided East Nashville was cool. Then *East Nashville Skyline* came out and changed the face of the neighborhood. Songwriters just started coming. Todd still believes in East Nashville even though he lives in Hendersonville now. Also, he always wanted that Purple Building. Doing everything he does there now shows how much he still believes in East Nashville and that concept of creating your own hippie commune dreamworld in your neighborhood. That still very much exists here.[19]

Peter Cooper

We wrote the East Nashville Bulldog song "Ways and Means." "When I was down on my luck / You and me driving your pickup truck / I ran into Warren Pash / He owed me fifty bucks in cash / Pulled it out of his jeans / He had the ways and means." We even referred to the fact that Warren had cowritten the Hall and Oates song "Private Eyes." There was another that we wrote on separate computers that went, "There are only two kinds of people as far as I can tell / The terminally ill and the worried well / Did you ever wonder, of course you did." It's called "The Last Laugh" on *The Excitement Plan*. We wrote that on an email riff.

You'll be sitting for three minutes and have two minutes of a song just ping-ponging with Todd, but as fast as he is in the initial creation, he's slow and deliberate in editing. It comes down to intention again. Something that seems tossed off is not at all. His brilliant mind can make something very quickly. Then that brilliant mind will hit something from every angle to make it right. There's absolutely nothing that he's saying that he doesn't mean to say. Todd is incapable of going, "Well, that's good enough. I think that will do."

The Bulldogs were just a fun band at first. I played bass for a while. We would just show up at a club in East Nashville and play at the Five Spot. Todd just wanted to rock. He was becoming more and more known as a solo performer, which he's fantastic at doing. He also likes to just rock. He was so happy to write a song about Bocephus. Todd is never really screwing off. Those songs are good. They were a way for him to do something else and become Elmo Buzz for a while. We talked a lot about music criticism. He was frustrated. He said you open your heart and then somebody who doesn't know you has a job to tell you that you didn't open it far or well enough. It's hard to get onstage every night to reveal your truths and what you care about. It can be tough when you're alone. I think East Side Bulldogs was a way [to avoid that for a while]. "Nobody wants to talk about distribution. Go back to Franklin, pretty boy."[20]

Robbie Crowell

I met Todd when I played sax on the *Eastside Bulldog* record. Todd is a smart songwriter with a good sense of humor. Not taking yourself too seriously like Todd is a rare thing in this genre. My favorites don't have this attitude, but Americana and folk music can be pretty precious, self-absorbed, and serious. I spent eight years playing with a band called Deer Tick that was on the fringes of that but also very irreverent and loud live. Those things don't go over well with the Americana people. The Americana Music Association is a pretty self-contained unit. The same people present and win the awards every year. The Americana and major label country worlds are very insular. They don't realize exactly how inconsequential they are in the grand scheme. That's why I like Todd. He clearly does not give a fuck or do that self-referential thing. "Now, this is serious music. You should sit down and listen in a very serious way." Todd has a big sense of humor.[21]

Multi-instrumentalist Robbie Crowell has performed with Todd Snider's East Nashville Bulldogs and has worked with Snider on his solo projects.

Todd Snider

I went on really late at the Americana awards in 2014. They said Elizabeth Cook and I had robbed the Belcourt Theatre, smashed out all the bottles, and had thrown up all over the place. That word got around town really fast. Then I showed up late to my show. What really happened is that I got into a fight with the stage manager. I didn't like him and told him so. I said I don't like the trophy shows. It's almost all backstage and no show with those. That was a chaotic night. I had been awake almost a week straight and shouldn't have been there. We were supposed to play the after-party, but there were a bunch of openers [and the show went late].

The stage manager kept trying to shove me onstage during Jason Isbell's speech. Then he got on the walkie-talkie and told them I wouldn't go on. "You think I'm not gonna figure out how to sing in front of the microphone by the time it's my turn, young fella?" This kid is telling me I needed to make my mark before the zippity do. I don't have to make shit for anything. I don't have to do any of that. "I'm gonna sing the first line of the song when they start. I didn't promise you fuck all. And I'm not being paid. I'll walk out when I want."

I didn't understand what he meant by "make a mark." Who gives a shit? I've been taking stages since I was twenty. I'm not gonna lose two seconds of sleep if I decide not to sing right now. Same thing as when I walked off the Don Imus show. Those things can get a little foolish. My side is that I come sing at your thing for free, but you don't get to teach me about making my mark and when to sing. I say, "I'll leave and never think about it again." "But it's on TV," they say. "You heard me. I'll leave and never think about it again." They could be cooler about things. I was downstairs the whole time waiting my turn to play. I almost took off after the awards, but Burt talked me out of it. Anyway, I got banned.

I was supposed to give the next award away.[22]

Robbie Crowell

Todd exists on the strengths of his personality and work. All the great songwriters from John Prine and Kris Kristofferson to Willie Nelson and whoever didn't take themselves too seriously. Humor is a weapon like anything else. Prine's "Your Flag Decal Won't Get You Into Heaven Anymore" isn't a light, fluffy song. He's talking about some serious shit, but the song is pretty funny too. Todd has carved out a unique space. He's so good he's undeniable. Someone like that will eventually carve their spot no matter what help they get or don't from the industry. Todd's also an undeniable character in addition to being a really good songwriter. Those two don't go hand in hand all the time. I know some really good writers who are incredibly boring live and mediocre writers who are incredible live.

Todd recently asked me to play sax on some more tracks. Aaron Lee Tasjan, Paul Griffin, and all the Bulldogs went in, and Todd started writing on the spot, which was fun. That's a rock 'n' roll approach and attitude that most people don't have these days. His songwriting is good with the Bulldogs. Also, rock 'n' roll should just be fun sometimes. I think people miss that these days. There are a bunch of really great Stones songs that aren't all that deep. You'll stop listening to Led Zeppelin if you try to analyze their lyrics. I love Zeppelin, but you just gotta accept they're not really great songs as songs.

I wasn't on the whole first Bulldogs record. The sax chair for them was like the drum chair for Spinal Tap. The players kept dying. Todd warned me that was the case when I came in. They originally had [legendary Rolling Stones and Joe Ely saxophonist] Bobby Keys, but then he passed away. Todd was like, "You've seen Spinal Tap, right? You know what happens with their drummers. Well, that's been going on with our saxophone players." That record was pretty much 100 percent improvised. Todd would get the lyrics and melodies and structures down, and we would just go for it.

Todd can self-critique in an accurate way that's very rare. The new album [*The First Agnostic Church of Hope and Wonder*] is just Todd and me playing. I was playing drums and percussion. He played everything else. He learned to play bass for the record. This record is more conceptualized than the Bulldogs. Todd had all the songs written when he came in. I don't trust many artists who self-produce and have seen many things go awry like that. I understand that it's difficult to step outside yourself and see yourself objectively. You have an idea of how a song is gonna go. You have it put together in your head. Todd would come in and say how the parts worked.

We tracked one day and listened back. "You know," he said. "That ain't it." He scrapped the whole time except the lyrics and melody. We went back in and tried it five or six different ways until something became apparent that's how it should be. I've seen artists come in with an idea or how a song should be. They're shooting pool with a rope, but they're unwilling to concede that it's not working. They just go further and further into it, and the song will never be good. It was interesting with Todd. He had the ability to see when the initial vision didn't work and had the willingness to totally scrap the works. That makes for a much more creative and satisfying recording and end result.[23]

Jason D. Williams

Fast-forward to several years later when I paid Todd fairly well to produce a record on me. Then fast-forward a little more. He wanted me to do three shows with him in the Northeast and gave me a piano onstage. I got three standing ovations in fifteen minutes. I apologized to him for some reason, and then he never talked to me again.

Todd Snider

I've done lots of producing, which is a harder job than making up songs. I pretty much was the producer on *East Nashville Skyline* and the *Bulldog* record. I edited it all. I like to do that arranging and tone-finding. I hardly produced the Great American Taxi record. I mostly did what Tony Brown did for me, which is guard the door and let them do their thing. I was really proud of producing the Jason D. Williams record. That was one of the great experiences of my life. He asked for songs, so I sent him thirty. He said they were the best songs anyone had ever sent him. He showed up to the studio to cut them.

"He was like, 'What are you talking about? What thirty songs? You sent me thirty songs?'" Okay, now I see what we're here with. He had all his clothes off thirty minutes later. Dan Baird and I had to think fast. The best we could get him to do was make up songs on the spot. Dan and I would say he could dictate the lyrics. Then we would change them and give him back what we wrote. Fucking craziest thing I had ever been around. We got it done, and the weirdest-ass record came out. I have never met a guy like Jason. He shot golf balls through his neighbor's house one time. His neighbor came out. "What are you doing?" "What?"

"You're shooting golf balls through my window." "No, I'm not." He was standing there holding the balls and golf clubs. "I see you standing there with the balls and club, Jason." "No, no, some kids did it." "Why are you such a jerk, Jason?" He says, "I'm the devil." Goes inside his house. He would do shit like that everywhere we went. The sessions were insane. Insane. He was naked for Christ's sake. Then we went to make the second record, and I could tell he was mad at me. I had seen him turn on people. I could see he was gonna turn on me. He was saying he needed more atmosphere. There was a little party atmosphere.

He sang a song about Nashville, but I wasn't sure if it was supposed to be aimed at us. Then he told me he needed some garbage. Well, first he needed wine. Then he wanted there to be homeless people around. I thought, "Okay." I went downtown, offered these guys some liquor, and came back with four homeless guys. He's like, "We need garbage, too." I know I'm being jerked around. Now there are four homeless guys drinking on the floor with garbage all over the place. He has his shirt off. Now he wants there to be girls. I knew this roller derby team and called them. Now I have four drunk homeless guys with garbage all over and roller derby girls. Jason might be ready to get into a fight.

I went into the bathroom, locked the door, and smoked half a joint. Then I opened the door and police lights were ripping through the lobby window to the studio. They were everywhere. I shut the door again, locked it, smoked the rest of the joint, and waited in the bathroom for about half an hour. I opened the door, and there wasn't anyone there. Not one person. I walked out to my car and drove home. Haven't heard from Jason since. I never did find out what happened. There's something going on with him, but it's not alcohol or drugs. I was knocking on his head one time going, "Is there anybody in there?"

Peter Cooper

Todd got a book deal later [for Da Capo Press's 2014 memoir, *I Never Met a Story I Didn't Like: Mostly True Tall Tales*]. He called and said, "Hey, man. I have a deadline. Can you help me?" I may not be much of a writer, but I can type like a motherfucker. We had an extremely tight deadline. I think we wrote the thing in two months. I would go over to his house around eight o'clock in the morning, and we would sit at a table. Todd would tell stories, and I would type them. I took that home and worked on it whenever I could. The book is basically straight from Todd's mouth. It's so Todd. I would send what I had to Todd at night, and he would say, "All right. We got six thousand words today." He loved the word count. He liked doing the math. What's incredible to me is that all the stories come full circle. People think of Todd as an elliptical thinker, but he's not at all. You read the Jerry Jeff's balls chapter and think, "Where is he going with this?" Then he brings it back around.

Todd was never going to let himself be the hero in the book. It starts with him having dangerous hard fruit thrown at him by Jimmy Buffett. Buffett was like, "You might want to play your new single tonight." Todd says, "Nah." The stories in the book are Todd realizing what a petulant dude he was back then and what he must have seemed like to these people. He never gets into the ironic cynicism that's in a lot of rock music books. There's also a chapter on Garth Brooks. You think, "Oh boy, he's gonna roast Garth Brooks." No, he tells you the sweetest Garth Brooks stories ever and how Garth helped him in so many ways. You learn that Todd is always taking things in, and he's reflecting on all that in the book. I always wonder if Garth has read his chapter in Todd's book. I bet he has.[24]

Don Was

Garth recorded "Alright Guy" live in the studio for his *Chris Gaines* record that I produced in Nashville, and he had Todd come in and sing the guide vocal while he learned the song's nuances. I can't remember why we didn't put it on the record. It would have been a hit song. [The fact that Garth paid Todd] for the song even though it didn't make the record is pretty righteous. It's a very Todd story to come that close to having something on a Garth Brooks record. Garth was the biggest recording artist in the world. Having a song on his record would be game changer, so I'm sure it was hugely disappointing to Todd.

Garth didn't have to give him any bread for that, but he threw everything into that vocal. I remember thinking, "Garth's gonna have to step up to top this." I was impressed that he did. The song was fucking great. I really liked Todd from the get-go. He's a very lovable cat who's fun to hang out with. He has a good heart and wears it on his sleeve. We did a Was (Not Was) tour about eight years later and got Todd to open the shows solo acoustic. That's when we really started hanging out. We had fun on that tour, and I loved what he was doing. I hadn't seen him live. I sat in the audience and watched the whole set every night. I went on to produce the Jerry Jeff Walker tribute Todd did with his band Great American Taxi [2012's *Time as We Know It: The Songs of Jerry Jeff Walker*].[25]

Vince Herman

Todd wouldn't tell us what songs were going on the Jerry Jeff tribute, *Time as We Know It*, when Great American Taxi recorded with him. He taught us the first song on the first day in the studio. Then we learned the second song as Don Was did the final mix on the first. Todd wanted to do it that way so we wouldn't know the songs or have time to plan solos. He didn't want us to know the arrangements. He wanted everybody to be heads-up and focusing on the song and not so much on the calisthenics we could be doing while performing. Worked great. Most were first takes. Todd consistently delivered. What a great process of learning but not learning too much. You honor the song. That's why they call it playing—not executing—music.

Todd was all about making the song better and having the story come across more clearly. Todd definitely was not about any pyrotechnics on the guitar. He wants everyone to come into the present moment, which is what you're really after with songs and storytelling. You want a completely absorbing moment that takes the audience away from whatever they left before coming to the show. You're fully engaged in that moment. Todd is good at pulling that out of the musicians. Then he produced our Taxi album *Paradise Lost*. We knew it wouldn't be overproduced with Todd, and we appreciated his spiritual approach to songs. Todd made everything comfortable in the studio. We had a spiritual endeavor because he set the right tone.[26]

Former Leftover Salmon lead singer Vince Herman has recorded and toured with Todd Snider. His band Great American Taxi served as backing band on Snider's live album The Storyteller *(2011).*

Don Was

We really flew through *The Excitement Plan* and *Time as We Know It*. Todd didn't have the bread to mess around in the studio. I worked them for free. We just cut a whole bunch of songs every day. I don't think either record took more than five days. I don't remember any tension at any point in my dealings with Todd. We always had fun. He did *The Excitement Plan* last Sunday on that weekly broadcast he does and told the stories behind the songs. I love that song "Money, Compliments, Publicity (Song Number 10)" and the notion that you're successful when you don't care about that shit anymore. That doesn't mean you don't have all those three things as much as you need.

You just don't care. That's how Todd defines success, which tells you a lot about him. He certainly has the talent, focus, and clarity to go after all that if he craved those things. I've always admired that he doesn't seem to have an interest in that as much as some others that I have worked with in the past. He can go out to dinner without having worry about how he's gonna be or whether he'll be photographed by paparazzi. Many people would trade their arm to have that. I never viewed Todd as a fuckup. I think he's one of our greatest writers. Shame that more people don't know about him, but that doesn't alter his body of work. His work is stellar.[27]

Ramblin' Jack Elliott

I met Todd Snider at Jerry Jeff Walker's birthday celebration many years ago. I thought Todd was unique and fresh. We met up again about a year later when he was playing out in California not far from where I live. He was very hospitable and invited me to sing a song with him onstage. Then we visited with his friends on his marvelous bus. We mostly talked about buses and traveling that night. Musicians are like museums. We collect a lot of stuff while we're out on the road. Musicians who are good enough to make their bread have to keep traveling all over. You may wear out your welcome somewhere after a couple days. You have to keep going to the next town and the next.

Buses and trucks are my favorite topics of conversation because of the ever-present need to travel. So, conversations with Todd and other musicians usually aren't about music. We talk about travel and transportation. Cars, trucks, buses, motor homes. Fun. Todd and I traveled on a very nice bus when we did a tour. We played about a dozen shows in two weeks in Colorado, Oregon, California, and Washington. Very enjoyable. Todd was recording me the whole time when we were together. The best part of traveling with him was that we could visit any time of day or night. We had a party any time we felt like visiting. I've been telling stories for eighty-nine years now. Todd uses language that young folks do that's beyond my understanding, but I'm very amused by it.

Todd has invited me to come visit him in Nashville, but I don't particularly like that city. I was a guest of John and June Carter the first time I went to Nashville. I thought it was a pretty friendly place naturally. Everybody was very friendly around John and June. I was mistaken. I went back there later to do some recording and got in a taxicab. I asked the driver to take me to Seventeenth Avenue South. He turned around and stared right into my face with his gimlet eyes and said, "Who do you know on Seventeenth Avenue South?" He wanted to know who I was going to see. "Will you kindly drive this cab?" I said. Everybody wants to know where you got your guitar and from whom if you're in Nashville because they have one too. Everyone came here to be the next Johnny Cash. There's competition and jealousy. I was rather put asunder the way people were treating each other in Nashville.[28]

Legendary folk singer Ramblin' Jack Elliott's close apprenticeship with Woody Guthrie secured his place in history. Elliott largely made his name interpreting songs by Bob Dylan and others.

Todd Snider

Ramblin' Jack Elliott is a hero. I talked with him on the phone recently. Jack invented the healthy way to be a troubadour. I just toured with him and felt like I learned a lot about touring and being happy. I used to think I would stop doing this when I got to the point that you realize that the alphabet is a hoax. You don't use it anymore. I feel like I'm gonna use it even more now that I know it doesn't work. These new songs are circular logic word salad like "Ain't That Some Bullshit." I'm saying, "Look, you can use the words I put in a row without really saying anything." My dad died at fifty-four. I could go around and see America again. I smoke pot a lot, but I don't really take drugs anymore.

I'm semiretired as a Mark Twain wannabe. Ramblin' Jack and I were different together because we didn't look for trouble. We only looked for horses, trucks, and boats. I could see myself getting into that. The gypsy thing is real. I took an oath and joined the cult in the eighties. He started seeking daytime stuff. I thought, "Oh, that could be a thing." He smokes pot but doesn't look for trouble. Gypsies are free to travel, steal, and lie. Do what you have to do to get to the next town. He invented that and has found a way to make that a noble pursuit. Sometimes the lie makes everybody feel better about themselves. Then you fucking get out of there before they figure it out. I wonder if I could be like Jack, but I doubt I will go on much longer. I don't know how he's healthy.

Jack was way worse than me with the drinking, taking drugs, and not eating. Not eating is just as bad as taking drugs. People take drugs and don't eat or sleep. That's my problem. A drug is affecting you poorly, but maybe it wouldn't if you slept and had a sandwich. I have a hard time getting around on my bones these days, so I don't know where it's gonna go. I made a TV show and a podcast during the pandemic, but I didn't like them. I got back to work on songs. We built our own studio while we've been at home. I went last week and recorded a song called "Never Let a Day Go By." I could see traveling, but I also could see just vanishing if I worked toward it. I don't have a plan and never did. I prided myself in being rudderless and goalless and always trying to find another song, but that's starting to wane too.[29]

Pamela Des Barres

Todd helped me plant an apple tree in the front yard one time. I don't live there anymore, but I drove by recently and saw it flourishing. Todd and I hit it off in so many ways. I've always been attracted to rebels—edgy, dangerous people. Todd might not seem dangerous, but he certainly is. He doesn't follow any rules. He still doesn't use a cell phone or text. I admire anyone who goes against the grain like that. He always has. We've been really close friends since we met. I have driven so many miles to see him play. I'll drive to whatever city if it's within driving distance. I've even flown places to see him.

I stay in the hotel, and we talk for hours. Todd's a kindred spirit. Did you read the groupie chapter in his book? Crazy how much importance he gave me. He compared me to Jimi Hendrix. I really liked that. We hang out on his porch in Nashville when I'm there and look at the lake. We commune in very deep ways. There was a point when he was having a very deep religious crisis. He was brought up in a very religious family. You concern yourself with how far to take Christianity when you're a rebel like Todd. I turned him onto this book called *The Gospel According to Jesus* by Stephen Mitchell.

I turned many people onto that life-changing book. Biblical professors got together and wrote that about what they thought Jesus actually said, which was very few words. There are only thirty-three pages of what he said. That book seemed to help Todd. He mentioned it the other day during his Sunday concert. I mean, I gave that to him twenty years ago. That was very nice and feels good. I was born-again as a kid. It can be a really difficult breakthrough to come to terms with who Jesus really was and what he means to you without the guilt. That book really helps.

Todd is a genius old-school musical journeyman who's on the road all the time. However, he's also touchy, which comes with sensitivity. I've seen him walk offstage more than once if he gets people heckling him or demanding a certain song. He won't play a song if he's not in the mood. The person can keep at it, but he'll curse them out and walk offstage—or not say anything. He might just put down his guitar and leave. That's part of his charm. Nobody does that. He's true to himself. I knew the minute I laid eyes on him that he was one of my favorite people in this world. I'm drawn to his looks, rebellion, and words because of my nature. I have a groupie heart. I'm a lyric whore because of Dylan, so I long to see Todd.

I have seen him fifty or more times, but his fiftieth birthday show at the Ryman stands out. He was on fire that night. Everybody was there to celebrate him. I went to Nashville just to be there for that show. He also put on a great two-night show in Portland one time. I also saw him at the Ryman where he stormed off the stage, but that's okay. There really isn't anyone better than Todd in his genre. No great artist knows where the great shit comes from. It just flows out of him like magic dust, and it floats onto everybody. Getting into Todd is a lifelong thing.

His fans all know the words to these cryptic, celebratory songs. There are lots of words, but they feel so united through them. We get Todd Snider. We feel connected to him immediately. Probably because Todd is unbelievably generous. He doesn't care one shit about a physical object. I went to visit him one time. He was going to change his shirt in the room he calls his closet. There were piles of clothes on the floor. Pants, shirts, jackets. He just pulled something out of the pile to wear. He collects really cool things for his house, but he doesn't really care about those objects. He'll literally give you the shirt off his back.

Todd can fill decent-sized theaters, but he doesn't let that go to his head. In fact, he sometimes doesn't feel like he deserves anything. He has incredible humility. Todd is a regular guy, but he's very special on top. Todd is just a dreamboat in every way. We've never had one harsh word. No thorns. We're always so pleased to see each other. He emails me sometimes just to say he misses me. We talk about everything. Todd loves my history. He loves the Rolling Stones, and I was one of Mick Jagger's girls way back when. We talk about the Stones and Dylan. We quote lyrics and play records for each other. We turn each other onto new music. You know how two connected people talk. Everything is very comfortable and relaxed. Todd wants to hear all about being on the road with Led Zeppelin or being onstage with the Doors. He's a huge music lover who's not afraid to gush. What a rare thing in the position he's in.[30]

Peter Cooper

I believe in charisma. I witnessed it in Johnny Cash and Kris Kristofferson before Todd. You can't take your eyes off these people. You would realize something had changed even if someone like that walked in the room when you were looking the other direction. You would turn around to see what's going on. Todd has a natural way of drawing your attention and admiration. He's also one of the funniest people on the planet. That doesn't hurt. Hard to dislike someone who's making you laugh that hard. He also walks through the world being himself in a way that most of us are incapable or unwilling to do. He's wide open. You don't have to wonder where you stand with him.

Todd is himself all the time. Kristofferson called it the truth in beauty, which is evident in Todd at all times—even when he's screwing up. Most aren't willing to screw up in public. Todd's okay with that. Hard making connections with people who are guarded, like having property with a big old wall around it. You can wonder what's on the other side, but you may not get to know. Todd has no wall around his property. He can sit for hours with an aspiring artist or sit in thrall with a teacher like Kent Finlay. He can sit for hours with Rahm Emanuel. He's at ease in all the situations and understand his role in each one. He's encouraging and inspiring.

Todd doesn't need you to meet him on his terms. He doesn't need to meet you on yours. There just are no terms. I would argue—and I believe Todd would as well—that Nashville gets a bad rap. Nashville is a creative free-for-all. The city is not defined by corporate, major label, contemporary country music any more than New York City is defined by Donald Trump or Austin is defined by the guy who shot people from the tower at

UT. People have spent years in Nashville being atypical artists like Guy Clark, Emmylou Harris, and John Prine. This town is a lot bigger than a radio slot. People like Guy, Emmylou, Rodney Crowell, and John Prine recognized Todd's brilliance. Even people who have ruled the radio like Garth Brooks can instantly identify what's great about Todd.

Tony Brown has produced albums that have sold in the millions, and he understands Todd. Todd has never tried to be on a radio playlist by Rascal Flatts. He doesn't do that. There are lots of different music games. Thinking Todd wouldn't be successful because of who he is like thinking that poor Hank Aaron wasn't accepted in basketball. These are different games. I think Nashville is a place where creative people come to do what they want to. Now, are there people who want to fit into a corporate system that exists here? Sure. There are, but they're a minority of working musicians in Nashville.

I don't buy the notion that Nashville is a cold, gray corporate place. I don't think there's a better place for Todd as long as he wants to make music and be around creative people. John Byrd and I wrote a song called "If Texas Is So Great What Are You Doing Here?" The song goes, "Guy Clark was your favorite son / He moved to Nashville in 1971." I love Texas—particularly Austin—but there's a reason why Todd can tell stories about his early days gambling with Guy Clark, John Prine, and Townes Van Zandt in Nashville. That was just a wild, regular Tuesday night here. Nashville is a magnet. Webb Wilder had a great album called *It Came from Nashville*. Very few people came from Nashville. They came to Nashville to assert their own creative visions. Todd has given lots of hope and assurance to people who are individualists.[31]

Bruce Robison

Todd, Robert Earl Keen, and I toured for a month together all on the same bus. I really got to know Todd then. It was interesting because Robert and I are more from this planet. It was fun to have Todd in there and see his relationship with the fans. I really got to see the enormity of that thing Todd has developed over the years—his combination of songwriter stand-up storyteller. I honestly don't know anyone you wanna trade songs less with than Todd because he's so funny and poignant. My songs are not like that. Todd gives an amazing, funny experience for seven minutes. Then I would play a two-and-a-half-minute country-pop song that hopefully is crafted well.

Ours are such different things, but he's so inspiring and a rare thing. It was wonderful to spend time seeing [behind the curtain] in ways I don't get to do much. So, we get to the end of the first gig. [Someone] came back and said, "Are y'all gonna go out and sign [autographs]? We all looked at each other. We hadn't thought about that. Robert and I said, "Well, yeah, sure." Todd said, "No. I'm not gonna do that." We were both like, "Yeah? You don't want to?" "Nope," Todd said. "People will be mean to me." We both looked at each other. "What?" Todd did end up going out with us. Thirty seconds into the thing somebody came up and said, "You know, this other person is really my favorite songwriter, but you guys are really okay." Todd just looked at both of us like, "I told you." Todd had his antenna up in a different way.

He was picking up on something that Robert and I were just letting wash off our backs as part of things. There are many things it seems like Todd isn't willing to put up with, which is interesting and cool. I'm falling all over myself to get along in this world, so it's really something when you see someone who is doing that. Sometimes they do it anyway. It really was a special experience to spend time with those guys. They're at the different ends of the spectrum but are both are a couple of the best storytellers that I know of on the planet these days. Those two go way back, so I was a bit of the odd man out, but it felt like Robert and I were looking at each other and relating sometimes when Todd was really out there. I think Robert and [his wife] Kathleen and Todd go back further than I did. You could feel the respect about his songs. I feel like there really is something that resonates with Robert about Todd's songs.

I probably played the same songs every night. Those two might not have played the same song twice ever. "Play a Train Song" was the one song Todd probably played every night on that tour. That song is a master class on imagery and phrasing. I hope people can see how rare it is to do that. Some people can do that and make it seem effortless. Doing that character study and going from point A to point B in such a short amount of time is so rare. I'm the kind of guy who just doesn't care at all how you dress or how funny you are or if you smoke weed or not. I care about listening to a song like that. "Play a Train Song" is up there with anybody's songwriting. "Play a Train Song" has all the melody pieces in line like Dylan and Paul Simon do when they choose to. Todd has a fair amount of those tunes.

Todd has an amazing connection with the fans, which looks like it's masterful and honed over many years. I hope and wish Todd has had an impact on Texas music. My close friends like Jack Ingram and Robert are close with Todd in a way that I'm not. I definitely have friends who love Todd. I feel like Todd and Chris Knight are north stars for people who really want to dig into songwriting. [My brother] Charlie and me are in-between. I feel like I've been better friends with Rodney Crowell, Jerry Jeff Walker, and Guy Clark than I am with the guys who came after me in the Texas music explosion. Jack has talked about Todd so much. I know seeing Todd freed Jack to approach his music in a way he hadn't been. Todd really opened him up in a great way.[32]

Bruce Robison has written hits for several artists such as the Chicks' "Travelin' Soldier" and Tim McGraw and Faith Hill's "Angry All the Time." The longtime fixture on the Texas music scene pleases crowds throughout the state when he sings his song "What Would Willie Do?"

Kevin Russell

The Gourds played this festival years ago. Todd was onstage when we got there, and people were going crazy. I was like, "You're telling me that one guy can play by himself with no rhythm section and get people to go crazy? How does he do that? What the fuck am I doing?" Todd did it with songs. He takes songwriting seriously. I don't know Todd very well, but we have a mutual admiration. The last time I saw him was at the Turnpike Troubadours festival up in Oklahoma. His bus was there, and I was expecting him to come out, but his tour manager came out and said, "Todd wants you to know that he would come out, but he can't move because of his back."

He seems reclusive, but [having an aversion to socializing] is common with entertainers. They become artists because they're introverts. Then that art takes them into the public forum, and they're like, "What the fuck am I doing here?" It's a portal to fame that maybe they weren't looking for. We've seen it happen over and over. I understand. Of course, I don't take it personally. There are plenty of people to talk to. You get to a certain level where you want to avoid certain types of people. Todd gets to share his art, but he doesn't want to be in the crowd. I would guess that he never really liked crowds much. I know other artists who have gone through what he has on the way to fame and who got stage fright. They didn't plan for it psychologically. Todd is just a normal guy who became famous and was like, "Oh shit. Now what do I do?" There are expectations. People project shit onto you. Your fans will read into your songs.

People think they know Todd, which is where it gets weird. A fan thinks they really know you. They talk to you like they have some intimate knowledge when they don't know you at all. I always immediately dispel that. "No, it's not about that. This song isn't about me. It's about somebody I knew or it's totally fiction that I made up." People don't want to hear that, but I make sure to say it. I'm not gonna play along with some myth that someone creates. I'm gonna create it myself if there's gonna be a myth. They aren't gonna put it on me.

I call Todd the Fonzie of Americana. You're at the family gathering, and no one knows you. Suddenly, you're somebody. I've experienced this with my wife's family. They treat you differently. You can see that in different ways. I made sure to let them know that nothing has changed. I'm no better than you. It's a sensitivity, a naivete, an idealism. I see Todd as a romantic and a bit naive. Many of us artists are. That feeling of detachment can be traumatic.

He's self-conscious and doesn't want anyone to know that he's fucking brilliant. "Dude," I would say, "you're fucking brilliant. Accept it. Own it. Be it." There's no shame in it, but some people become ashamed by what makes them great, which might be a way to try to stay grounded and humble. I feel like talented people often fall into that trap. They're not prepared when they fall into it and can't get out. Then they feel the best way to deal is to tunnel under. They make a space within the trap, stay in there, and come out at night when no one's around.[33]

Kevin Russell entered consciousness as a front man and songwriter for the popular Austin-based band the Gourds in the nineties. He fronts the soul band Shinyribs today.

Verse: Play a Train Song

THE SONGS

Todd Snider's finest songs stand tall against modern music's most celebrated compositions. A simple mantra guides his journey: "Live the song. Be the song. Make songs real. Don't use big words." Snider always credits his teachers along the way. "Todd reveres his mentors," close friend and songwriter Elizabeth Cook says. "Kent Finlay took me for tacos once. He was very much like a mentor talking with me. Todd speaks about Kent in a father and son way like how it was between him and Jerry Jeff Walker."

"I really mean it," Snider says. "Live the song. Be the song. Make songs real. Don't use big words. For example, I made up a song one time called 'Once You Find This.' We played it back in Portland for this family I grew up with. I say some ninety-dollar word like 'crucifixion' or 'resurrection' in the chorus. Someone said, 'Good show. What was that one verse in that one song?' I could tell that my friend was really saying, 'Why did you say that big word? What did that word add to the song?' I was probably being pompous or speaking with an authority that I don't have. It took years for me to get over talking like that."

Todd Snider

I feel young songwriters groping for those words. I think, "What does going for those words really do?" More syllables don't mean more [depth]. Young songwriters want to say words like "consecration." I like Pat Green's song "Wave on Wave," but it has a college word in there. He says, "We're all looking for redemption." I guess that's okay. Who the fuck am I to judge? I just try to avoid those. I learned that from Prine. I only work with about ten people in the trench, but I listen to every single one. Someone will say, "Are you sure you want to say that?" "Well, yeah," I say. "I get what's itching you, but I want to say it." Most times they're like, "Okay. Yeah."

"My Generation (Part 2)"

"My Generation" was the first song I came up with after moving to Memphis. I was staying upstairs at my dad's house and had gone to an open mic at the Daily Planet. That was when I told the owner that I would play for free if I could get the Thursday night gig. No one came to the first shows, but slowly we built up. I was upstairs at my dad's and feeling like the thing I wanted to do was gonna be something I couldn't do. I wanted to be a folk singer, which wasn't happening on any level in 1989. Especially in Memphis. That song was my angry response to people not coming to see my shows at the Daily Planet. The eighties didn't feel very troubadour-y.

Rugby kids decided to have their big party at the Daily Planet the third time I played Thursday night. There were four people there to see me and this big table with like twenty rugby players. I started with "My Generation," and they all went batshit. They asked me to play it three more times. That was it. Memphis was on. I had an "I would rather lose at rugby than win at softball" sticker on my guitar case. They saw that and were rooting for me out of the gate. Then I sang my own song, and I was theirs. They came every time. They had a little contingent, and they just kept coming to the shows.

"Moondawg's Tavern"

[Michael] "Moondawg" [Webb] lived in the Memphis area. His speakeasy was in Frayser, Tennessee, which is the white part of Memphis. His story was so sad. Moondawg's sister Anita invited Joe [Mariencheck] and I out to Moondawg's Tavern. We didn't think it was real, but Moondawg said we could come out whenever. We started hanging out there all the time. Moondawg was this anchor to many people in a really hard part of town, which was as close to wholesome as that could have been. Then he got his penis cut off from cancer and carved the word "fucked" in his arm. Those were six dark months. He got into coke and heroin then, and he was dead pretty soon. "Can't Complain" was "dedicated to Michael 'Moondawg' Webb, Wreck of Honor" when I recorded it. I still talk to his sister Anita all the time. She and her family still live down in Frayser, which is a lot of guns, poverty, and violence.[1]

Anita Webb

I met Todd before his record deal at his first What the Folk Fest in Memphis in 1991. Todd got local musicians together to help feed the homeless. A *Memphis Flyer* article about the festival described the Todd I met: "No one had ever heard of him when Todd started doing What the Folk Fest. He raised sixty dollars and gave it all to the food bank when he did not have sixty dollars [himself]." I fell in love with Todd's songwriting and began to follow him. I volunteered to be the "street team" leader and posted posters all over the Memphis area for What the Folk Fest. We had volunteers in four counties. The proceeds were up to over $5,000 to help feed the homeless by 1996. Todd made it grow that much.

Todd's songs grab you by the heart. He reminds me of my favorite songwriter, John Prine. I kept showing up at his packed Thursday night Daily Planet gigs and shared my pot. Todd was and is a rebel. I think Margaritaville Records was trying to change and mold him. We were at a showcase in Nashville one time when Margaritaville bought Todd this expensive jacket, shirt, and tie. He goes, "Anita, man, I do not want to wear this. You want to wear this jacket and tie tonight?" So here is Todd, who is six-some feet, and I am five-four. I go in wearing his jacket and tie. Moondawg literally howled.

Moondawg had lived in a duplex in Clearwater, Florida. He cut a door in the wall to the other side of the duplex to make it a full bar with a pool table, bar, stereo, posters, lights. He would put the kids to bed at night and go through the door to the bar. Building his own bar was his solution to getting kicked out of many bars with my older brother. Moondawg had a rare heart disease and moved back to Tennessee, where he was on the transplant list at Vanderbilt. Experimental drugs kept him alive for eight years. He turned his garage into Moondawg's Tavern, but you had to be invited to the tavern because Moondawg sold newspapers filled with the best pot in Memphis. He was careful about who he sold those newspapers to in the nineties.

Selling reefer was his supplemental income. He did not get out much. So I had met Todd and kept telling Moondawg about him. I told Todd about the tavern because I knew they would be buddies. I finally got Moondawg out to meet Todd. Moondawg was so taken with Todd. He noticed Todd did not have shoes. Moondawg offered to burn a big one with Todd and gave him his shoes. Well, Moon wore a nine-and-a-half and Todd was a thirteen, but Todd accepted those shoes. I saw them in

Todd's closet at the Gilmore later. Moondawg started going with me to see Todd, and we finally got Todd out to the tavern. Most of the time Joe or I drove Todd to the tavern. Moondawg would say, "That kid is gonna be big if the right person hears him."

Todd liked Moon's biker story. So they are talking about it one day, and Moon says, "You know, I used to go in this biker bar, and one day the bartender asked me what I rode. I told him a Schwinn." Their senses of humor clicked. Moon really loved Todd songs like "My Generation": "We'll buy anything from Diet Sprite to one thousand points of light / Well, I admit we're not that bright, but I'm proud anyway." Moondog was glowing the day Joe and Todd showed up to play his song "Moondawg's Tavern" for him. I could see how happy that made him, but all he said was, "Great song. Did you make it up on the way out here?"

Todd made so many of Moondawg's bucket list wishes come true. He invited us to a castle in Franklin, Tennessee, for his *Daily Planet* album release party with Jimmy Buffett and some of the band. Buffett was Moondawg's absolute favorite, and he got to meet him. Todd treated us as family. Then Todd told Moondawg he could go on the road. They had this huge bus. Moondawg packed and waited, but it turned out he couldn't go. Moon was pretty upset. I thought this might be a huge issue between Moon and Todd, but Todd showed up at the tavern after the tour. He said, "Well, I couldn't make it happen, but I stole Jimmy Buffett's socks for you, man." Moon hung them up in the tavern. Then we partied.

Moondawg played "Moondawg's Tavern" for every person who walked in that bar. Then Moon got penile cancer, and they removed the diseased part. My brother was never the same, but Todd tried to cheer him up as best as he could. Todd knew the depression was overwhelming. Moon turned to a drug for pain relief, but I always thought he sought relief from mental anguish. Anyway, this is from the last letter from Todd to Moon: "People like you are heroes in heaven. I love you, Dawg, and I will not judge you. I will be your friend as long as you live, even longer." Not too long after that Moon took that rocket to heaven like what Todd sang about in "Can't Complain": "I got a one-way ticket to cruise in the passing lane / I can't complain."[2]

Anita Webb is Michael "Moondawg" Webb's sister. Todd Snider wrote the songs "Moondawg's Tavern" and "Doublewide Blues" for Michael Webb. Anita Webb lives outside of Memphis.

"Doublewide Blues"

TODD SNIDER

There was a pig-in-the-ground cookout one time where this guy had a mustard stain on his V-neck T-shirt, and I kept that picture in my mind. I had been hanging around in Frayser for about a year and was drawing on stuff I had seen for "Doublewide Blues." I wrote that for Moondawg after he didn't like "Moondawg's Tavern." The story is all little slices of sagas that I saw go on, but Wild Bill the manager is made up. I was trying to tie a song up by the time I got to him. Most of the words were inside jokes. I had another verse—I wrote lots of them like [Shel Silverstein's] "Rosalie's Good Eats Cafe"—about a satanic ritual with kids gutting a cat. I look back and think, "Man, something in me as a songwriter was just dying to stay alive with 'Doublewide' and 'Can't Complain' from *Viva Satellite*."

[*Viva Satellite*] producer [John Hampton] is dead now, but I sent him all my songs back then. He graded them. He gave "Can't Complain" and "Doublewide" A-plusses. The rest were B-minuses. I would write eight more if I had it to do all over again. Moondawg died during the making of *Viva Satellite*. I had done his song on the last record and did "Doublewide" on that. Moondawg heard it because he had been hanging around the studio, but he died from an overdose. I remember when we recorded "Can't Complain" I had a tie on because we had just gone to his funeral. His whole funeral came over to the studio and had a big party.

"Can't Complain"

JACK INGRAM

Todd wrote "Can't Complain" after we played the Rockbar in Scottsdale one night. The crowd did not give a shit. Two hundred people were there to be seen. I remember thinking, "Oh, this fucking sucks." I did my thing before Todd, but you don't stress as much as the opener. Todd played a couple songs, and the crowd wasn't listening. It's one thing if they don't dig what you do, but it's another when they're not even paying attention. That's when you want to punch people in the throat. "You're not even giving me a chance to wow you." Todd told them, "You know, my mom told me never to play at Applebee's." Then he said it again and again and again. "My mom told me never to play at Applebee's."

That night reminds me of how Todd, Jerry Jeff, and I have based our careers. The only way for it to truly be brilliant is to accept that everything might fall apart. That's what's so rock 'n' roll about Willie Nelson,

Waylon Jennings, and the Rolling Stones. They seem reckless, but the songs come in with a bullet. They're powerful when they come together in the end. People celebrate them in ways they don't at a Celine Dion or Rascal Flatts show. Those guys have all the right ingredients but don't have that thing where everything explodes. Something has to land perfectly when everything could have fallen apart. Todd isn't scared about everything falling apart because sometimes he lands it. Totally worth it.[3]

"Tension"

TODD SNIDER

I was living with my old girlfriend in Atlanta when I wrote "Tension." I had a record deal but didn't have a record yet. I remember I did an interview the day I wrote "Tension." Then I watched this movie [1992's *Unlawful Entry*] with Ray Liotta after the interview. I remember there were seventy-five minutes of the bad guy just being genius. Then Kurt Russell picks up a gun at the end and just shoots him. I made up that verse about how the good guy just shot him in the head, and everyone was like, "Oh. That did it." The whole rest of the song came out. I thought it was just a poem.

"James Dean's Car" (cowrite with Jason Rigenberg)

JASON RIGENBERG

I had Todd guest on [Rigenberg's 2002 solo album] *All Over Creation*. We cowrote the song "James Dean's Car," and Todd came in and sang on the song for the *All Over Creation* sessions. I was living out here in Dixon, and he was close by in Fairview. I had just found out that Todd was my neighbor. There weren't too many civil people out here for either of us, so we started getting together. We started becoming friends and collaborators then, but our friendship really cemented when I started the Farmer Jason character. Todd began to guest on those records. That's when we developed a real bond.

He was so generous with his time. Kids related to him. It's really interesting watching kids who don't know him from Adam out there relating to Todd Snider. People think they know Todd. They want to think that Todd is their friend. All is right with the world if you are friends with Todd Snider. He has that everyman thing. He's very approachable despite his unique talents. You can see the guy has the chops. Todd Snider is one of the premiere songwriters of this generation. No question. He's unique. Todd is a half-generation behind me with the crowd that spawned Uncle Tupelo and folks like that, but Todd stands out in that crowd.[4]

"Long Year"

TODD SNIDER

John Prine listened to the eighteen songs I had written for *Happy to Be Here* and liked "Missing You." He picked "Long Year" as the worst. I had originally titled the song "It Gets Harder to Listen All the Time." Instead of singing, "It's been a long year," I was singing, "It gets harder to listen all the time." I asked John what was wrong with my songs. "Listen to yourself singing about this thing like you're above it." The song was about a girl who went to AA.

"Listen, you're even making it about a girl," he said. "It's not even about you and you're still winning the argument. This is steroids. This isn't songwriting. You went to AA and got your feelings hurt. Now you want to use AA to zing them with a great song about going to AA and getting your feelings hurt? You've wasted that on the song where you went to AA and made some jokes about how dumb they are. Good for you." I went home and changed the song to my point of view. I changed "It gets hard to listen to other people," which is a pretty shitty thing to say, to "It's been a really long year." I took the song out of A minor and put it into D major, which is more wistful and less angry. I sang it for him. He said, "You're getting it. You should record that now."

"Lonely Girl"

I wrote "Lonely Girl" around the same time as "Long Year." They wouldn't let you have music or radios in rehab, but the kitchen guys got to have one. I would sit as close as I could to hear that play music. I could hear music through the door. I would sit there and do what I was supposed to do, and Melita was over there smoking cigs at a table. I was sitting on the floor in a hallway. I saw her in the cafeteria. That's why I say, "The music plays, but it doesn't help." I'm taking about being over here listening to the radio. I just wrote that song for Melita. She was in there for throwing up. I was in there for opiates.

"D. B. Cooper"

"D. B. Cooper" began a big part of my life. I can put my foot on the rock when I sing that song because my dad wanted them to catch [Cooper]. Now I sing about not agreeing with my dad every night of my life when it sounds like I'm telling a story about a guy who hijacked a plane. I can drift off and go into a trance when I sing it. I started to do that with all my songs. "Easy Money" is that way accidentally. I think Kent knew how to do that, but it's a hard thing to put on a kid. You learn it as you learn it. Someone can tell you to go through a certain intersection, but you really know after you've gone through it and paid the price.

I had about an eighteen-month period where I was writing songs for concerts. I wasn't writing them for specific girls but girls in general around *Viva Satellite*. Like not for the girl the song was about but for the girls who were gonna hear it. That was as close as I came to not caring what the words meant to me or where they came from. I learned later that the girl and heartache have to be real if I wanted to go on a bus to California or St. Louis again. Songs are just a waste of time if they're not a genuine form of therapy.[5]

"Beer Run"

BOB KEVOIAN

We played "Alright Guy" on *The Bob and Tom Show*, which made Todd a favorite. We had never met him but were blown away from that first time we heard his music. Todd eventually made his way into the studio and debuted "Beer Run" with us. "Beer Run" became the most requested song we ever had. Todd is a great musician, poet, and storyteller. My wife found out about Robert Earl Keen from "Beer Run" and became a huge fan because of Todd. He introduced us to a number of artists like Robert and Guy Clark.

I know Todd has gone up and down through the years, but we always were able to get him on the happy days. He was on the show countless times because we all had so much fun after his first visit and kept him coming back. In fact, one time he was with us on his birthday. We found out about a week before and arranged for a birthday cake and a topless lady to present it to him. I think that was the first time I had seen him smile from ear to ear. Todd was definitely one of our favorite songwriters to have on the show and always had something new when he came in. He would play a new song, and we would go, "Where did he get that idea?"

Todd writes funny, quirky songs that fit our format perfectly. We only played a little music on *The Bob and Tom Show*, but when we did it was someone like Todd who had a humorous song with a great melody. I think Todd liked us too. He would be scheduled to show up, play a couple songs, and take off, but he always would end up staying the whole morning. We had such good conversation. He would even try out new songs out for us. We would listen like we were hanging around in a living room. Sadly, he would be on tour when he came in, so we didn't get much of a chance to hang out off-mic.

"Beer Run" instantly was a great feel-good story song. Our audience was beer-drinking males aged eighteen to thirty-four. I'm sure that had to do with the success "Beer Run" had on the show. Unfortunately, I never got to see Todd play an actual concert. We had to get up so darned early for the radio show and could never go out late to enjoy the artists we had in the studio. He's a good man and hang as long as you're not bullshitting him. Also, you have to admire a guy who has an alter ego called Blind Lemon Pledge. His mind never stops.[6]

Bob Kevoian cohosted The Bob and Tom Show *with Tom Griswold. It debuted on WFBQ in Indianapolis in spring 1983 and has been syndicated nationally since 1995.*

"Sleepy" John Sandidge

Todd Snider mentions me in "Beer Run." He references the Robert Earl Keen song that also mentions me ["I'm Coming Home"]. I'm famous now. I have been recognized everywhere down to the heart of Mexico because of those songs. People will come up and say, "Are you that Sleepy John?" Greg Brown and Fred Eaglesmith also refer to me in songs. I guess they just thought it would be cool to put me in a song because I've brought a lot of those guys' music to the West Coast, have been promoting concerts in Santa Cruz for forty years, and have been a DJ on KPIG for forty-five years. They never discussed it with me but what a great honor. Todd paints a great picture of Santa Cruz in "Beer Run."

Todd is a big hit on KPIG. People demand his songs. They particularly like older ones like "Doublewide Blues," "Moondawg's Tavern," "Vinyl Records," "D. B. Cooper," and "Ballad of the Devil's Backbone Tavern" as well as "Tillamook County Jail," "Play a Train Song," "The Ballad of the Kingsmen," and "Conservative Christian, Right-Wing Republican, Straight, White, American Males." We played "Can't Complain," "Statistician's Blues," and "Talking Seattle Grunge Rock Blues" from the live album. "Beer Run" was a local hit because Todd mentions KPIG and me. People like hearing their names in songs.[7]

"Sleepy" John Sandidge is a longtime disc jockey on Santa Cruz's landmark Americana radio station KPIG 107.5 FM. He is mentioned in songs by Robert Earl Keen, Todd Snider, and others.

Kent Blazy

Kim Williams's daughter Amanda cowrote "Beer Run" with two or three other country artists. Garth Brooks heard that and asked if he could use that title. I don't know if he had ever heard the Todd Snider song. "Amanda has this song," Garth told me. "I don't want to use anything in it, but I want to use the title." We wrote it with Kim. We divided the song between us, Amanda, and her other writers. I don't even know if Garth took credit for it. Then I heard a story about how there was another song called "Beer Run," which Todd takes to a whole other level.

I knew Todd from our Americana channel in Nashville [89.9 FM]. They played those songs when Americana was pretty early. Todd was an out-of-the-box guy, which I liked. He has a different take on things and is eclectic and funny. He reminded me of a young John Prine. I followed Todd in the *Nashville Scene* weekly newspaper. Todd is quite a character, so they wrote about him a lot. I like that he can pull off a great show with just an acoustic guitar or a full band. You have a good lyrical sense and can tell good stories that engage people if you can pull off a show with just a guitar. I look for that in any songwriter: Can the song stand up on its own?

I have a plan for when I finally meet Todd. I'm gonna tease him and say, "You are a lying son of a bitch, but I love you as an artist." I've heard him tell his "Beer Run" story onstage and on the radio. He talks about meeting me even though we never have. Good schtick. There's nothing wrong with [embellishing a story]. Todd is funny. I understand. People wanna hear the stories behind the song when I go out on the road as a singer-songwriter. Todd has a great comedy sense and knows how to work a crowd. You embellish them sometimes to make them more interesting.[8]

"If Tomorrow Never Comes"

KENT BLAZY

I had a demo studio in 1988. You get demo singers to do your songs if you're a singer-songwriter like me who isn't a really good singer like me. They make them sound way better. I was using people like Martina

McBride, Faith Hill, Billy Dean, and Trisha Yearwood. They all went on to be famous, but the way they made a living back then was singing other people's songs for demos. Garth was cleaning churches and selling boots when I met him. He knew he could make more money making demos. He met me and said, "Here's a cassette of six songs. I would be glad to sing for you if you could use me on some demos." I loved his voice and the songs I heard.

"You know," Garth said. "I write a little, too." I told him we could get together to write. You and your cowriter hopefully both bring in ideas. He came in the first day, and I was sitting on the couch with my guitar. He was wearing this big, long, leather duster and a cowboy hat and looked eight feet tall. He stood above me and said, "I have this song idea that I've run by about twenty-five writers, but nobody likes it." Gee, thanks. "Don't you want to hear it?" "Sure," I said. "Go ahead and play it for me." He had the skeleton for this song and said, "What's wrong with that?" "Well," I said. "Mainly, you're killing off the star of the song in the first two lines. That's like killing the star of a movie in the first three minutes. Not much of a movie after."

I thought we had a really good song at the end of the day. He went up to my studio and did a little guitar and vocal demo. We pitched it around town for about a year. Everyone passed. "Nobody's gonna sign a guy named Garth. What would they say to radio? Garth?" Then he got to play a song at the Bluebird one night because an artist didn't show up. He sang "If Tomorrow Never Comes." Someone from Columbia Records was in the audience. They had just passed on him for the third time that week. The Columbia guy came up after. "Maybe we missed something," he said. "Why don't you come back in?" "If Tomorrow Never Comes" ended up being his second single and first number one.

"If Tomorrow Never Comes" was a miracle. I had always asked the universe to be able to write a song that would really change people's lives. I felt like we did that with "If Tomorrow Never Comes." The song became exactly what I had been asking to write for all those years. This was the first song that I had written that really touched people. We got cards and letters and people who would come up after the shows and talk about it. That showed the power of a song and to not give up on something that you believe in. "If Tomorrow Never Comes" could have been just another song, but one twist of fate changed that.

I'm flattered by Todd writing his song "If Tomorrow Never Comes."

We're all singer-songwriters just trying to make a living. I'm happy for him if it works for him. I would love to meet Todd and say, "Hey, I'm the guy you've been talking about but have never met. I love your stories. God bless Todd for having that sense of humor and take on how things could be. I think Todd is a phenomenal talent. He cracks me up. God bless him for making music his own way. He's being a troubadour. He's not trying to be the next star or voice. He just does what he does and does it well. He's his own thing. Todd's like Townes Van Zandt in his own way.[9]

Kent Blazy has written singles for Garth Brooks including his first number one hit "If Tomorrow Never Comes." He cowrote the George Jones duet "B Double E Double Are You In?"

"Conservative Christian, Right-Wing Republican, Straight, White, American Males"

TODD SNIDER

We had just made the live record [*Near Truths and Hotel Rooms*], and I decided that I would do more social shit. I tried to back out a few years later, but I remember making up "Conservative Christian [Right-Wing, Republican, Straight, White, American Males]." There was this thought, "Hey, you're cutting off half the people. Why would you do that if you're mainstream? Cutting people off was never part of it in my mind." I just never gave a fuck about that. That's not where I come from. Every song is supposed to lose them in a way. I remember at the time really thinking that that was good, but a couple records later I thought I went too far. I don't think that now.

"Conservative Christian" opened it up. They said a certain person wouldn't care for the song. "Yeah," I said. "That's a person I don't like. Who cares if they come to the gig? Who wants that?" They said, "Lots of the 'Beer Run' guys who come to the gig don't want to hear that." "Well, I don't know what to tell them. That's just not the way I grew up." My main thing is I'm a folk singer who doesn't care if I change the world. I need as many songs as I can get now. They don't come very often. I need the song for work if one happens to be about politics. Get into the melody if you don't like the lyrics. I don't have time to concern myself with being liked. I have deadlines. Also, I'll make up thirty songs, but I'll only like the ten that have a connection. I knew "Conservative Christian" had legs.

I have lots of songs that are way less offensive, but they don't [work]. You're down there fishing for that one main line and get stuff out of it.

There are frequencies, and you're trying to tap into that main one that's genuine. It's easier to tap into the ones that aren't, and they're sitting right there next to the one that is. You reach down and grab the cable. Half the time it's bullshit, but there are songs that came from the "Train Song" place. I like "Train Song," "Too Soon to Tell," "In Between Jobs," "D. B. Cooper," "Can't Complain." Some feel foundational. I feel like I could sing "D. B. Cooper" on the electric chair. You could set me on fire, and I could play "Can't Complain." Sometimes when you're on acid you see a faucet that's coming out like a fire hose. "Can't Complain" came out like seventeen gallons of water.

"The Ballad of the Devil's Backbone Tavern"

I type out and edit my stories for songs like "The Ballad of the Devil's Backbone Tavern" [and "If Tomorrow Never Comes"]. I started approaching them like a song and kept my antenna open for more stories. There were two in particular that I realized I had something. One was the time Kelly Keller [K. K. Rider] got hit by the rope string. That story hit me like a ton of bricks. I knew I could tell that onstage. I wouldn't have thought twenty years earlier that I could make up a story about Kelly Keller. Now, I was like, "No. No. I'm gonna tell that story and really hone it." I wrote it all out and put secrets and twists in there.[10]

"The K. K. Rider Story"

K. K. RIDER

I'll just say this: The K. K. Rider story is Todd's story. I don't believe I was ever knocked out, but I definitely was knocked down that night at Buffalo Bob's. His story is about the same [as mine] other than me not getting knocked out. Well, he got the song wrong. I wasn't singing [the Rusty Weir song] "Don't It Make You Wanna Dance." I never knew that song. We played the country hits of the day. I think that he just wanted that song in the set and used his K. K. Rider story to get there. I do have people [who know me from that story]. In fact, I have a song called "Famous in Nashville." I'm always signing autographs and taking pictures with people when I'm in Nashville. Not so much around here.

Todd did sing backup for our band K. K. Rider, but we weren't allowed to call him by his name or advertise that he was playing in the band. I would call him "Todd" not "Todd Snider" when it was time to introduce the band. Todd already had a very good following around Memphis. He packed them in every Thursday at the Daily Planet. We had a PA system go out on us one time, and Todd loaned us his. It was the first time K. K. Rider played under that name. I had forgotten that Todd loaned us his until I saw a VCR tape recently. I thank him at the end. I had to get it to him after the gig because he was playing somewhere on the strip. That was even before he played with me.

I moved away from Memphis a while back. I didn't hear from Todd again until he played a bar in Carbondale, Illinois, and his manager got in touch to let me know he was playing at a bar about seven miles from my house. The night took a weird turn. I was the disc jockey at a strip club at the time. I got drunk and took the night off to see Todd. I had T-shirts from the strip club and squeezy boobs for him and went down to the club to see him. Somebody wrestled me to the floor thinking I was attacking Todd. He didn't even realize it was me until the next day. Todd and his manager came to the bar to see me when he figured it out, but I wasn't there.

"Looking for a Job"

TODD SNIDER

[My former tour manager] and I used to joke that we were arch nemeses. One of his riffs was, "I was looking for a job when I got this one, boss." That was his way of saying, "No, I don't wanna do it." I was like, "Man, you know that thing you say all the time? That's pretty good." "Hey, man, go get us more weed. Fuck you. I was looking for a job when I got this one." He always says, "Write a word, get a third." I said, "Okay." So, he gave me that riff for "Looking for a Job." My dad was a construction foreman like the one in the song. He didn't do labor just like the guy in the song. He drove around in a truck checking on the labor. We went around from boomtown to boomtown.

There would be only five paint crews in town for those jobs. You recruit them to win favor. My dad's job was half being boss and half keeping those guys around. I remember riding around in his truck with him, and he would get in these arguments like I did with Buffett. There was a seriousness, but you were laughing. Buffett was laughing the time he threw fruit at me, but he was also mad. "Who's gonna drive if you piss me off?" It would be like saying to the manager of a restaurant, "Who's gonna wait tables when I quit?" "Any other kid."

"The Devil You Know"

I'm usually studying some kind of music that [influences my new songs]. I was taking a deep dive and studying the history of rap when I wrote "The Devil You Know." I guess all that came from that was I used the f-word like fifty times in the song. It was like, "Who cares?" They say that in rap all the time. "The Devil You Know" was just a simple Chuck Berry song. The story was real. Helicopters over our house were common. You could tell they were low that night. They ended up getting the guy on a golf course a couple blocks away. I sat down and wrote that song in one sitting. No edit. Really rare for me. I recorded it the next day. I knew how the chorus went, but I just started singing and was like, "I don't know where the chord changes are but I'll feel them. It's gonna be "Johnny B. Good." Every time I felt like going to the four [chord], I was like, "No, not yet."

I had so many chords that I thought I better wait. Then I never changed the chord. I remember thinking, "Okay, we got that version. We'll get the groove. We'll get the chorus. I'll find chords as the day progresses." Then we went in and listened to it. "You know, that's it." The verses just sit on the one [chord]. You can't really count it like twenty-four bars in E. It's like twenty-three bars the first time and twenty-eight the second. You just have to stay with the story. The only way you can show that to a band is say, "Okay, you guys have to listen and hear the story. You can't count and go to the four. Wait for a Chuck Berry cue. I'll stomp my foot and say, 'Helicopters over the house again' and go up to the four." I did that before on a song called "Forty Five Miles," which is one verse in like eleven bars.

"Happy New Year"

"Happy New Year" fell out in this real stream-of-consciousness way. I didn't have to work very hard for it, which is why I didn't trust it. I knew it was Country Joe's birthday, and I always liked him. I recorded the song like Chuck Berry's "Johnny B. Goode." Mercer was at the studio looking at me funny and said, "What is this?" I said, "I don't know." "Sounds like you don't want anyone to hear about the revolution you're trying to start." I didn't even know what that meant, so I [threw it out]. [My former tour manager] was like, "No." So, I whipped it through the old "Can't Complain" box and presto-chango. I had a song.[11]

"Greencastle Blues"

People like "Greencastle Blues." I made that up on the piano. [My former tour manager] and I were in the Cadillac. We were gonna do Bloomington, Indiana, then come home. We went through Greencastle, and the cop was behind the billboard like in the movies. We weren't speeding, but the guy got behind us because we slowed down so much. We got surrounded by lots of police. We had been taking turns driving. It was my turn. I went into the jail and was the oldest person in there. I was just sitting in there mapping out my phone call—even though I never made one. Weird day.

I heard my own record playing down the hallway. I was like, "Motherfucker. Do I tell them?" Doing that can really go south like in Tillamook, so I kept my mouth shut in Greencastle. We got a call from Sheriff Mark Frisbie later. He wanted to know if Todd Snider from the jail was Todd Snider the singer. He said, "Man, I was just listening to *The Devil You Know* in my office this morning." Then he showed up at the gig. He said that a woman claiming to be Loretta Lynn called and told them to let me out. Mark Marchetti said that Loretta actually did call. Mark had talked to [my old tour manager]. I wrote that song to get out of trouble. I could tell my wife was getting sick of that stuff. I was talking my way back in the house.[12]

Mark Marchetti

My friend was going through a divorce when I was still living in Memphis and said, "Come up to Nashville and stay with me. You can clear your head and get back on your feet." I was terrified and depressed when I moved, but my next-door neighbor [when I moved to Nashville] was Peggy Lynn [Loretta Lynn's daughter]. I'm married to her now. Loretta loves Todd.[13]

"She's Got Everything It Takes"

LORETTA LYNN

My son-in-law Mark Marchetti pulled up to my home in Hurricane Mills, Tennessee, one day, and I was in my office writing room, which was a mess. I had unfinished songs everywhere. Mark walked in with this long-haired guy who looked half-crazy and high as a kite. Todd came on in in and gave me a big hug. We hit it off right away. He started telling me about his life and playing me songs that were so well written, songs that seemed years beyond his time. Todd got to looking around the mess of half-finished songs laying around. I handed him one I had started called "She's Got Everything It Takes."

Todd loved the song, and we just started writing that thing right then and there. I guess we forgot about Mark even being there because he just let us be. I think it was Todd's honesty that really got to me. I loved that he can be funny in songs, which is very hard to do. Roger Miller could write those witty songs too. Todd was sitting there in my office and looked over at me. He said, "Loretta, do you care if I smoke a joint while we are writing?" I just laughed and said, "You go ahead honey." So he did.

"Don't Tempt Me"

The next time I saw Todd, he asked me to sing on a song we wrote called "Don't Tempt Me." Todd was recording in the same studio Jack White and I recorded *Van Lear Rose*. Our friend Eric McConnell owned this little studio in East Nashville. He engineered both my and Todd's records. I ask Todd, "What part do you want me to sing on this song?" Todd laughed and said, "Hell, Loretta, I don't know. You're the one in the Hall of Fame." A couple years later I recorded the song Todd and I wrote together, and it was the single on my album called *Full Circle*. That album was nominated for a Grammy.[14]

Iconic singer and songwriter Loretta Lynn penned such country classics as "Coal Miner's Daughter," "Fist City," "You Ain't Woman Enough (To Take My Man)," and dozens more.

"Play a Train Song"

TODD SNIDER

Loretta Lynn says the best songs come from really simple [ideas], and you don't need to change the names. "Play a Train Song" came to me really fast. Memory is my talent. I can go right back to that place when a girl hurt me ten years ago. I can tell you about the wallpaper and the weather. Those details work in a song. Skip Litz was my neighbor. He tried to cause trouble every single place he went. Skip was the sound guy at the Radio Cafe and the first to figure out that there was this art scene building. East Nashville was loaded with Americana musicians after the tornado and was awesome. Skip introduced me to Elizabeth Cook. Then he became my main running buddy. We would drink coffee, smoke weed, and I would show him my songs for years. We started getting to know each other during *Happy to Be Here* and were taking lots of drugs together. Boy, we went crazy when he got sick and got them legally. He was a very philosophical guy like Jimmy Buffett and Moondawg.

I collected those guys. There are guys who have nicknames like Moondawg and Skip all across the country. Skip would go into a bar with the intention of starting an argument, but he wasn't a fighter. He just liked to get everybody upset. I don't know why, but I loved it. He would go into a bar, take up the other side in a political argument, and ratchet shit up. Then he got sick when we were getting ready to go to West Virginia. We were all partying over at my house, but he hadn't been there for a day and a half. Our friend Libby was gonna go get some cigarettes and stop by to see where he was. He was dead on his couch. "Play a Train Song" was a good example of how Kent Finlay taught me to have my craft ready for when my life showed up.[15]

"Cheatham Street Warehouse"

KENT FINLAY

I heard "Cheatham Street Warehouse" when I was in the hospital. Todd was in San Marcos for a benefit for me at Cheatham Street, and he played the song. He says he wrote it when he first heard about me being sick. The song is about the old music room at the house. We had all sorts of recording equipment, instruments like guitars and pianos, stacks and stacks of yellow pads with songs written on them, the first two Kristofferson records, all the Bobby Bare, all the Shel Silverstein we could find. Todd's song is all about music and a life in music. I thought, "Wonderful." I always ask what people are working on like Todd says in the song. "What are you writing now?"[16]

"The Ballad of the Kingsmen"

TODD SNIDER

I was writing "The Ballad of the Kingsmen." My goal was to contribute for real to the folk canon with that song. I wanted people to say, "This guy took the talking blues, threw a wrench in it, and the song came out the other side as another thing you can do." I took the meter of a talking blues song and put it over the chords of a Lou Reed song from *New York*. I knew the gist was going to be that there was this song, "Louie Louie," that was an early scapegoat in rock 'n' roll. I wanted to do this big analogy of "Louie Louie" up through Marilyn Manson and how people desensitized and get angry at frivolous things.

I sat down and wrote that like an essay about "Louie Louie," and how I think it relates to Marilyn Manson. There was some stuff about an industrial military complex I wanted in there but didn't make it. The essay was four pages with no rhyming. I got up every morning for like three years and read the essay again to see if I could make it rhyme and have alliteration anywhere. I knew the melody would get chiseled down in accordance with how far I could chisel down those words. How can I get most of these words out? Took a long, long time. I just played this G, D, C, D pattern like "Louie Louie."

Also, I walk a lot every day. Walking is a great way to learn to write. "Damn," Richard Lewis says when I play him a new song, "How many miles was that song?" He knows I try to memorize a song or a story without a pencil while I'm walking. I don't need to write it down at all by the time I'm done. I walk things like the rant in "The Ballad of the Kingsmen." They take longer to write than they sound. I make speeches on walks. Then I think about it over and over again. I also look shit up. I'll be down a rabbit hole and do a bunch of research. Maybe tomorrow I can look up some more shit on the Kingsmen song and get a little deeper on Marilyn Manson and that shit. I found out about all that military industrial complex stuff through that song. [17]

Mike Mitchell

Very cool that Todd wrote a song about our band. We formed the Kingsmen in Portland in 1959 and played high schools around town for several years. We discovered "Louie Louie" through the Tacoma, Washington, band the Wailers one day, but the song had been recorded by a half dozen bands in the Northwest by time we went into the studio. We recorded "Louie" and three other songs in under an hour. The whole session cost thirty-seven dollars. [Everyone] hated "Louie Louie." They said it was the worst garbage they had ever heard, but our friend had a friend in Seattle who had a label. Our friend talked him into coming down and putting us on the label.

They sent the record back east. A radio station in Boston was playing "Louie Louie" on their worst records of the week show, but the kids lit up the phones. The disc jockey called our record company and said they had interest in the song. The man at the label pulled it out of the garbage and said, "I have it right here." Then the song took off. We were contacted by the William Morris Booking Agency and had to join the union, quit the teen nightclub scene, and go out on the road. We had no clue that the song would be a hit. They would play competitions on the radio to see which of the versions people liked the best. We never won. Paul Revere & the Raiders cut it in the same studio we did two days after we did, and theirs was more popular. Somehow our version caught on with people. Someone still plays our version of "Louie Louie" every hour of every day.

Then the FBI came after us. Some kid came home with the record and said he had heard the words were dirty. His mother complained to a friend of the Indiana governor's at the church. The governor told [Former FBI Director] J. Edgar Hoover. Hoover was the most powerful man in the world at one time. We were in Boston at the time and got a knock on the door the next day. Hoover wanted to put us in prison for spreading indecent lyrics to children. The FBI were at every show for about a year and a half, but they were great guys. They used to send us cases of canned green beans and corn because we have a song called "Jolly Green Giant." We would have thrown those cans out to the crowd, but we could have coldcocked the kids.

We became a big family with the FBI guys. Then a picture came out with J. Edgar in a dress, and they were gone. Having anyone right at the speaker listening every night is tough. The crowd was always singing, screaming, and dancing when we played "Louie Louie." We had great fun. The song was recorded more than two thousand times by the end of the sixties. I talked to Frank Zappa about it one time. He hated the song, but he recorded it twice. The song just sold. You know, there was a radio station in the Midwest one time that played different versions of "Louie Louie" twenty-four hours a day.

Richard Berry wrote the original "Louie Louie." Great guy. He had sold his rights to the song to his publisher so he could get married. My partner in the band Dick Peterson helped him get his royalties after the song had been out twenty-five years. So Richard recouped everything from those years and made enough money to support his family for the future before he passed. The song turned us into what they called "America's Party Band." We went through three Greyhound buses touring over the years and were on the road ten months every year. We finally burned out and took a year off, but we're still playing today. We had thirty thousand people come to the show in Deadwood, South Dakota just last March.[18]

Guitarist Mike Mitchell (1944–2021) cofounded the Portland, Oregon, band the Kingsmen in 1959. He played on the group's hugely influential rock 'n' roll classic cover of "Louie Louie" in 1963.

"Blues on Banjo"

RICHARD LEWIS

My best friend was a real rock star when I was at Ohio State University from 1966 to 1969. He knew more about music than anyone I knew. "Come over," he would say. "I want you to hear this guy." He turned me onto everything from rock 'n' roll to folk to jazz. He told me about Todd Snider in the nineties. I fell in love with his work. I get a little over the top with my praise for Todd, but I mean it sincerely. His music, preaching, and storytelling are his feelings about life. I have worked as a comedian that way for fifty years. I felt like doing this was pointless and useless without sharing my feelings. No wonder John Prine gave Todd a record deal. Prine was a genius and knew another when he spotted one.

I found out Todd was a really big fan of mine who had grown up watching my specials. Someone like [legendary drummer] Jim Keltner who had worked with him called me and said I should call Todd. So, I did. He tripped out. "Todd," I said. "I've been a fan of yours for twenty years. Calm down." "How can you be a fan of mine?" he said. I said, "Well, how can't someone be a fan of yours? You're one of the great storytellers." We bonded immediately when we started talking. We would tell jokes and got into some really personal stuff because we trusted each other. We have come through for each other big time and have been best friends over the past seven or eight years.

Todd and I throw ourselves into our work. His lyrics are so loved by his fans. You really have to listen to his songs to get how he feels. We get along because our feelings have been trampled on by people in our lives. We tell these stories about family to each other all the time and became best friends. I told him once, "You know, Todd, I've been such a friend to you. I love you. Why haven't you put my name in a goddamn lyric? Jackson Browne has Richard Pryor in a lyric." I was half joking. Only half. Todd put my name in "Blues on Banjo" on *Cash Cabin Sessions, Vol. 3*, so I added two words to the lyric.

He would always play "Blues on Banjo" when I saw him live. My dream was to tour with him. Todd and I did play a gig together in Los Angeles at the end of my big tour two years ago. He was playing with the Hard Working Americans two weeks before in Los Angeles opening for the Tedeschi Trucks Band. Hard Working Americans only did half an hour, but the powers that be wouldn't allow Todd to advertise that he was playing at the Roxy with me. We were only allowed to say anything about Todd

Snider being there about a day before online. It was all about me, but I didn't want that. I wanted to warm up for Todd, but the show ended up being me headlining. Unfortunately, the show sold out, and it was all about me. They wouldn't even put his picture up.

I was up in the balcony while he was singing. He would look up and was bad-mouthing me for setting him up. I'm up there looking down like Mussolini. It was heartbreaking. That might be my last show after fifty years of touring. He'll always tease me about it because it was embarrassing. I was so proud to be on the bill with him. I destroyed the club, got a standing ovation, and then Todd came out and half the people left. I said, "Todd, you just played a sold-out three thousand seat show in Nashville. Fuck this gig. I wanted to advertise you months in advance, but they wouldn't let me." He will have his point of view if you ask him, but he's so sarcastic and funny. He will bury me.

Todd is in the moment onstage. He's not getting another gig over with. It's so heartwarming to see someone who loves his art so much and doesn't take any show for granted. He leaves it all on the floor. You always see a show that gives you your money's worth and gives you what you want. He doesn't just do the same set every time. He has so much material. That's what made us best friends. I have thousands and thousands of premises on my computer that I'll never use because I'm running out of time. I've written down anything that has struck me funny for fifty years. He writes songs the same way. He will go off on a long-winded rap setting up a song, but he works on those stories like they are jewels. He doesn't just ramble them onstage. He works on them and works on them. I told him about how some great comics like Lenny Bruce or Richard Pryor would work. They would have a bit like he would have a song.

I think Todd was getting a little tired of doing these setups. I told him that the greats like Lenny and Jonathan Winters would get bored too. They would just throw caution to the wind and tell their stories some other way until the audience either left or booed. Then they would switch gears. Todd has been doing that a lot. He'll call me and say, "I think I'm gonna tell it this way." I'm gratified because I told him that his mind is so explosive. It's like what Springsteen said to me one time: Don't settle. You already have a great set-up. See if you can go further with it. Not just because we talked about it. It was already evolving that way.

You ask these famous high-roller musicians about something, and oftentimes they haven't listened or don't want to listen. Todd is one of the few guys I know in the music business who listens to everything. I would send him stuff he had never heard because I have twenty-three years on him. I loved Procol Harum when I was in college. I had a thrill turning Todd onto rock and blues songs. He often would know the blues. I loved blues like Brownie McGee and Sonny Terry when I was a kid. He would send me back even deeper cuts in that genre. We would exchange our favorites, and most of the time we would get a real education from each other about the work of our colleagues. Todd could teach a course in blues and folk music. Todd loves to hear great art and music. Todd embraces all work.[19]

Legendary self-deprecating stand-up comedian and Curb Your Enthusiasm *actor Richard Lewis rose as a frequent guest on* Late Night with David Letterman *throughout the nineties.*

Todd Snider

I've only been in the same room with Richard Lewis six times, but I talk to him almost every day. Richard's such a smart person. I play my new song for him first now. I don't even say things onstage anymore without taking it to him first. He's vicious. I love that fucking guy. He can Don Rickles you, and you will be begging him not to stop. Richard came in and made fun of me at that gig in Los Angeles. Then he made fun of the band. The band was like, "You didn't tell me he was a dick." He finished the joke when he introduced us. He acted like he didn't know who any of them were to their faces. Then he walked onstage and introduced us like he knew us very well. He was definitely giving us a big old hug. He was hilarious. You don't get to totally know if he's fucking with you.

"Sunday Morning Coming Down" (written by Kris Kristofferson)

I think Kris Kristofferson nailed what you give up to be a troubadour. You can go to church, the cookout, Thanksgiving, but you won't be part of them again. You're more connected to the guy with his robe open with blue hair and long fingernails and mustache. I might hate that guy, but my life is over there with him. I make a very honest living with him. I don't really feel it with Christmas anymore. I feel comfortable sleeping somewhere I've never been. I feel comfortable sleeping with somebody I don't really know. I feel comfortable in the same clothes all week.

I tell younger people to watch [the documentary *The Ballad of Ramblin'*

Jack] about Ramblin' Jack that his daughter [Aiyana Elliott] made. You can be a songwriter and live here in Nashville and raise kids, join the golf club with kids on the swim team, but not if you want to be a troubadour. We talk about that movie, and I say, "I'm sorry that hurt, but daughters needed that movie." This kid needs this movie. I'm sorry you had to be exposed for the bullshitter you are, but there's a sea of [Jerry Jeff Walker's son] Django Walkers who need this. I didn't have any kids because I would have left him on the hood of a car like a cup of coffee and drove off. I'm selfish. Very selfish.

"Sunday Morning Coming Down" wasn't just a perfect song. "Sunday Morning Coming Down" was a perfect song about songs. People try to talk about being a songwriter, but [the narrator] blows his brains on cigarettes and songs that he was picking. You don't know that was a vocational party and not just at a house where everyone was rocking out. You're on the wrong side of midnight all the time. I didn't grow up a hippie. My parents were normal. I was popular. One day I was just like, "I'm Hunter Thompson. I'm not going to sleep again." Kris left a really nice life to pursue a muse. The song is about a guy who moved to Nashville and became a poet. Then he realizes that he's writing about the Sunday smell of someone frying chicken. The event is less homey if they bring him in, because now they brought in the biker.

Remember [on the iconic television sitcom *Happy Days*] when Fonzie came to Christmas, and the Cunninghams were like, "Okay, we're having a cozy Christmas, but now there's a biker at the table." There are asterisks by Christmas now. I'm that guy. The kids get to swear when I come over. I don't even drink anymore, but when I get there everybody drinks, swears, and stays up. Dad acts a little differently. We get to see how things might have been a little different when Uncle Todd comes over. They love Uncle Todd. You know, Nanci Griffith was alone crying in a bar when I first moved to town. She was having the "Sunday Morning Coming Downs." She was going, "This is it. There are no sippy cups and babysitters. Ever." You have to [find a balance]. I'm into zen. I sit Indian style and meditate on not having a goal. I usually have a frequency playing, burn sage, and do all that hippie shit.[20]

Bridge: If Tomorrow Never Comes

THE SPIRITUALITY

Todd Snider frequently searches for deeper meaning in songs ("Somebody's Coming," "If Tomorrow Never Comes," "In the Beginning"). He readily admits he knows no answers. "Saying 'I don't know' is the only correct answer," he says. "I wrote, 'Believe, shit, every word I say / But believing and knowing are two different things' when I was coming to terms with not knowing shit [on 'Happy New Year,' the closing track on *The Devil You Know*]. I thought there was a God and his son was Jesus, who they crucified. Well, maybe that didn't happen. There's a pretty valid argument that the story was made up and a very valid argument against." Nevertheless, seeking and spirituality thread a common current throughout his life and music.

Todd Snider

I read the Bible like crazy and started to study Christianity in the late nineties. I had been a very superstitious Catholic altar boy with guilt. Then I read books about the Bible and saw how pretentious I was being as a singer. That knocked me all the way back to being agnostic. I still am agnostic now, but I can honor Jesus. I don't even have to think about him as someone who rose from the dead. I can just believe in Jesus. I believe in God and forgive him if he's not there. Someone asks me why I'm on Earth, and I say, "I don't know."

There's a really good story about Constantine, the rise of Christ, and the way Constantine engulfs him into the Roman empire, reprocesses him, and repackages him. The story is like an indie artist going major label. I'm hip. I saw that a rose is a rose is a rose and don't care what anybody uses poetically to describe those things. Sometimes Christians get mad at you for saying they're just speaking in poetry about forgiveness and love in a metaphor and that they are creating characters who may or may not have existed. It doesn't matter, but some people say I'm losing the game by saying this.

I want mine to be an honest accounting. I'm not gonna stand at the gate going, "I picked B." I'll stand at the gate going, "Man, there were a million choices and no fucking clues. Is that the right answer?" You certainly must get points for honesty. I remember reading in the Bible to "seek the lord God with all your heart." I never once stopped doing that. I say, "As I'm dying I'll probably yell out the same name my dad did." I wouldn't say I have much belief and faith. I'm afraid that when I die there won't be anything. Then again, who knows that nothingness isn't paradise? Who knows that black matter isn't something ten times better than this?

My hopes and ideas for what's on the other side are simple. I want to see my dad, we would walk over to the shepherds, and we would watch baseball. I'm up for whatever the universe holds. We've got planes, spaceships, and everything else trying to find out why we're here. The shit we have managed to do without being able to figure out what we're doing here or where we're going is fascinating. Libraries are full of attempts on that. Look at all the other animals. They're not bothered by it. They're still in the garden.

[Hard Working Americans drummer] Duane Trucks said a great thing one time during my acid phase. I was prepared to move on because it would go too far. I couldn't see sometimes. I could fall off the stage. I didn't use the microphone because I didn't think it was a microphone. Those nights were a bitch on everyone. Duane said, "Earth is easy, man. You can't fall off. Try." I really heard him in that moment. He's right. There's no path. I know I don't even have the first inclination. I only know this much: I'm here to leave at some point. The rest is grab-ass.[1]

(right) Todd Snider (center) rehearsing with Eastside Bulldogs. Photo by Stacie Huckeba.

Todd Snider on a tour bus traveling to Birmingham, Alabama, on his birthday, October 11, 2009. Photo by Stacie Huckeba.

L–R: A Nervous Wrecks reunion with Joe Mariencheck, Todd Snider, and Joe McLeary in Memphis, October 11, 2009. Photo by Stacie Huckeba.

L–R: *Joe McLeary, Todd Snider.*

Todd Snider at home in Nashville, November 23, 2009. Photo by Stacie Huckeba.

Todd Snider at Sound Emporium Studios in Nashville, December 4, 2009. Photo by Stacie Huckeba.

Todd Snider at 3 Crow Bar in Nashville, December 16, 2011. Photo by Stacie Huckeba.

(left) Todd Snider at Sound Emporium Studios in Nashville, December 4, 2009. Photo by Stacie Huckeba.

L–R: Jack Ingram and Todd Snider at the Cheatham Street Woodshed in San Marcos, Texas, April 2015. Photo by Stacie Huckeba.

L–R: Sterling Finlay and Todd Snider at Cheatham Street Warehouse in San Marcos, Texas, April 2015. Photo by Stacie Huckeba.

L–R: Todd Snider and Kent Finlay at the Get-a-Long Ranch in Martindale, Texas, November 6, 2014. Photo by Brian T. Atkinson.

Todd Snider as Blind Lemon Pledge, Nashville, May 3, 2017. Photo by Stacie Huckeba.

L–R: Todd Snider, Ben Kaufmann, Jeff Austin, and Vince Herman rehearse at the Ryman Auditorium in Nashville, November 19, 2008. Photo by Stacie Huckeba.

L–R: Todd Snider and Jeff Austin at the Ryman Auditorium, November 20, 2008. Photo by Stacie Huckeba.

L–R: Vince Herman, Todd Snider, Jeff Austin, and Ben Kaufmann at the Ryman Auditorium, November 20, 2008. Photo by Stacie Huckeba.

L–R: Todd Snider, Chad Staehly, and Vince Herman at the Rutledge Theater, Nashville, November 12, 2009. Photo by Stacie Huckeba.

Great American Taxi rehearsal, February 20, 2010. L–R: Chad Staehly, Vince Herman, Will Trask, Brian Adams, Todd Snider, and Jim Lewin. Photo by Stacie Huckeba.

Todd Snider (center) with Great American Taxi filming The Storyteller *DVD at the Tennessee Performing Arts Center in Nashville, February 22, 2010. Photo by Stacie Huckeba.*

Todd Snider (center right) with Great American Taxi filming The Storyteller *DVD at the Tennessee Performing Arts Center in Nashville, February 22, 2010. Photo by Stacie Huckeba.*

Todd Snider (center) with Great American Taxi filming The Storyteller *DVD at the Tennessee Performing Arts Center in Nashville, February 22, 2010. Photo by Stacie Huckeba.*

Todd Snider, making Time as We Know It: The Songs of Jerry Jeff Walker *in 2011. Photo by Stacie Huckeba.*

(left) Todd Snider, making Time as We Know It: The Songs of Jerry Jeff Walker *in 2011. Photo by Stacie Huckeba.*

Todd Snider, making Time as We Know It: The Songs of Jerry Jeff Walker *in 2011. Photo by Stacie Huckeba.*

L–R: Neal Casal and Todd Snider perform at the Hard Working Americans block party in Nashville, May 30, 2016. Photo by Stacie Huckeba.

Fourteenth annual Targhee Fest artist laminate featuring the Hard Working Americans, July 13–15, 2018. Courtesy Jenni Finlay and James McMurtry. Photo by Brian T. Atkinson.

Todd Snider at home in Nashville, October 26, 2015. Photo by Stacie Huckeba.

A promotional photograph of Todd Snider at his home in Nashville, December 12, 2018. Photo by Stacie Huckeba.

A promotional photograph of Todd Snider at his home in Nashville, December 12, 2018. Photo by Stacie Huckeba.

L–R: Will Kimbrough, Joe McLeary, Todd Snider, Joe Mariencheck, and unknown keyboard player at a Nervous Wrecks reunion at Levitt Shell Auditorium in Memphis, Tennessee, June 2019. Photo by Stacie Huckeba.

L–R: Todd Snider, John Prine, and Cowboy Jim at Ryman Auditorium in Nashville, April 20, 2019. Photo by Stacie Huckeba.

Todd Snider lacing his shoes on his tour bus (formerly owned by pop sensation Taylor Swift) to go onstage at the Devil's Backbone Tavern in Fischer, Texas, February 13, 2020. Snider shared a co-bill with Jack Ingram for three shows over Valentine's Day weekend just before the COVID-19 pandemic. Photo by Brian T. Atkinson.

L–R: Todd Snider and Jenni Finlay at the Devil's Backbone Tavern in Fischer, Texas, February 13, 2020. Photo by Brian T. Atkinson.

Verse: Stomp and Holler

THE HARD WORKING AMERICANS YEARS

Todd Snider salutes nearly a dozen favorite songwriters as lead singer for Hard Working Americans. Snider's supergroup—including Chris Robinson Brotherhood guitarist Neal Casal, Widespread Panic bassist Dave Schools, and Great American Taxi's Chad Staehly—debuts with the covers record *Hard Working Americans* in 2015. *Hard Working Americans* tips its hat toward Snider's friends like Hayes Carll and the Bottle Rockets ("Stomp and Holler" and "Welfare Music," respectively) as well as longtime running buddies Will Kimbrough, Kevin Gordon, and Kevn Kinney ("Another Train," "Down to the Well," and 'Straight to Hell," respectively). The band soars high on hallucinogens and musical freedom until it crashes and burns. "Relationships end with Todd because he's brutally honest, but his incredible honesty makes him a great artist and human being," Staehly says. "Many can't handle that."

Susan Tedeschi

Todd Snider was in the Hard Working Americans with my brother-in-law Duane [Trucks]. Todd is a really great songwriter and performer who is fun to watch. I liked the Hard Working Americans because of energy they had on songs like "Stomp and Holler." My little nephews ate up that song and wanted to hear it all the time. The band appealed to all ages. Todd and John Prine both went through struggles with addiction, love, and loss. Songwriting is a way to deal with all that and put you in tune with your emotions and how you're feeling. Todd writes about real stuff, and his subject matter can be sad sometimes.[1]

Multi-Grammy Award nominee Susan Tedeschi is a singer and guitarist in the headlining jam band Tedeschi Trucks Band with her husband and guitar virtuoso, Derek Trucks.

Hayes Carll

I wrote "Stomp and Holler" mostly in the Carolinas. I had seen a city weekly newspaper that was called something like *Stomp and Holler*. I was walking around with that title and liked those words together. They were evocative and had a theme. I just had to figure out what it was. Then I was in Italy on tour. We were having dinner at a restaurant owned by the promoter, but nobody spoke any English. So, I was sitting there at a table with twenty people and a paper place mat and was trying to rhyme with "holler." I came up with the James Brown line that makes no sense, but I thought was funny and interesting to me ["I'm like James Brown / only white and taller"]. I wrote that on the place mat and took that home with me.

I sat down a few months later and figured out that the song was coming from someone on the fringes who was really struggling and had pent-up frustration. I think Hard Working Americans cut it before I knew. I vaguely remember Todd asking if I had any songs, but he found that on his own. I do remember hearing it for the first time on his tour bus in Indianapolis. I was just visiting to catch Todd's show and jumped on the bus. We smoked a joint, and he put that on. What a really cool moment to have one of my musical heroes doing my song and covering it in such a cool fashion for his new project. Then I heard the harmonica by [Blues Traveler's] John Popper, who I grew up listening to. Really special.[2]

Sharp songwriter Hayes Carll consistently has turned heads with eight studio albums from his debut Flowers & Liquor *(2002) through his breakthrough* Trouble in Mind *(2008) and his most recent* We're Only Humans *(2025).*

Susan Tedeschi

Songwriting helps you deal with life. It's a beautiful way to get the bad energy out and tell the story. Then you can release it like therapy. Responsive audiences also help [validate] that you're writing meaningful songs. Music is a gift we're given, and we have to do the best we can with what we have. You don't just practice and get good at it. I love doing this because it makes you feel good and offers a way to communicate with other people. You can communicate with anyone you're playing with as a musician as well as the audience. You feel alive and in the moment. Life is all about QTL—quality time left—the older you get. You don't know how long you'll have good health to be able to travel and experience all these great things in the world.[3]

Todd Snider

I was taking acid, covering songs I liked, and freestyling with a pen in the Hard Working Americans. We were on acid all the time. I learned new chords and slang. Chris Robinson says, "One day you realize the revolution doesn't go past the front row. So, you just take more drugs and tell yourself that's not true." I agree. Eventually you stay in that mindset. You go crazy, but at least you're playing and traveling every night. You're doing it for a purpose that's not for money. I would rather be that than reasonable. Reasonable is just not what I am.[4]

Chris Robinson

I love freaks like Todd Snider. I met Todd backstage when he came to a Chris Robinson Brotherhood gig at the Great American Music Hall in San Francisco. They were starting to do the Hard Working Americans, and Todd became more in my orbit at that point. Todd is a great performer, but he understands the dark magic of being a songwriter. I liked listening to him because he could do a real talking blues, which is an old traditional thing. I grew up with folk music. My dad was a folk singer on ABC Paramount Records. Todd's talking blues are funny, self-deprecating, and wise.

Todd understands that being a songwriter is a different trajectory than being a performer or a guy in a band. I've attempted to get onstage by myself at times, which is hard, horrible, and terrifying. You don't have your gang. I think Todd's participation in that lineage is so unique in this day and age. Most shit in Nashville is hackneyed and cliched "whiskey frisky" middle-of-the-road. Todd is very dynamic in his creative life. He makes different kinds of records. No one takes those chances anymore, but why wouldn't you if you're an archetypal songwriter like Todd? All the people he idolizes are completely mental cases who really live and die for the poetry.

Todd is a real counterculture character.

Jam bands with the strawberry flip-flops and bubbling cheese manifestos are super cool, but storytelling and having songs in a rock 'n' roll band is what Todd was trying to do with Hard Working Americans. They were a song-oriented rock band. I guess having Dave Schools made them a jam band. Neal Casal wouldn't have been in any of that world if he hadn't been in Chris Robinson Brotherhood. He was coming straight out of making solo records. Neal was another person who understood what it was like to be onstage by yourself. Look at all the great singer-songwriters who have come and gone.

There are some talented motherfuckers out there. I think Neal was a great guitar player, but he understood the songwriting part of musicianship. He could both write songs and play guitar solos. I had him in my band because he wrote songs too. The song is what we're really looking for. The song is the catalyst, but that's the least showbiz part. That's why Neil Young is who he is and why Bob Dylan will always be the greatest living songwriter. There are myriad others. It's daunting to put your songs out there. I would have a different relationship with performing solo if I had grown up doing it. Luckily, people like my songs. They like the Black Crowes, but they also like my solo work. They find it enjoyable, but getting people to shut the fuck up [during a show] when you come from my rock 'n' roll background is impossible. That's what's cool about Todd. People come to his shows to hear what he has to say. That shows the reverence his audience has for him, which is really unique in this day and age.

I'm lucky to have come from a generation where you're allowed to be angry or depressed. Your experience is part of the music that you put out there. I've grown older and am watching rock 'n' roll have a more diminished place in our culture, which is why I told Todd the revolution is only in the front row. It's important but doesn't mean anything the way it did, which most things don't after decades and decades. That wild rock 'n' roll energy that we love and frail moments when things can go out of control are long gone. How do you find a place where you still feel excited about the presentation?

I get if you're a banker. You go to work. You're not the best banker, but you're okay. You put the numbers where they're supposed to be, smile, and take your lunch break. I don't think that you as an artist asking people to listen to you and take part in your music can ever just go through the motions. You realize that people are on their fucking phones. They're looking for some sports score. The Rolling Stones were powerful when they were at Madison Square Garden in 1969 because everyone was focused on them. There was no light show or staging. Mick Jagger wasn't running all over. He was in one place. He was amazing.

I don't get to hang with Todd too much, and he's such a stubborn asshole that he won't get a phone. I went the last time he was playing in San Francisco with Ramblin' Jack Elliott. We got stoned on the bus. Wavy Gravy was at that show. I was super happy about that. I was just thinking, wow, Todd has total command of this room. He's such a master of what he does. I'm always so impressed with his depth and talent. The fact that someone like that has such respect for me and my career makes me feel really good. He gives me a validation that's so much deeper and legitimate than anything commercial or fame-based.

I understand what it's like being the artist as an outsider. The reality is you're like the hunchback of Notre Dame. What's wrong with you that you like music, poetry, and the madness in art, travel, and books? Those things ostracized us from regular life but launched our careers. I still remember having to fight or run because of the way you dressed, or because you were a punk or gay, because of the redneck bullshit in front of you. You have to have the courage to say, "Fuck it, this is what I'm into." My kinship with Todd is that we're both outsiders.[5]

Chris Robinson gained fame as the singer-songwriter behind the Black Crowes' major commercial success during the nineties. He fronts the Chris Robinson Brotherhood today.

Chad Staehly

Our guitar player Jefferson Hamer in Great American Taxi was a big Todd Snider fan, but I don't know that anyone else in the band was aware of him. Jefferson popped in Todd's new record *East Nashville Skyline* when we were on tour in 2006. Our jaws were on the ground as we drove through Nebraska. We listened to that album countless times on that tour. We were asking Jefferson about Todd. We were like, "Taxi would be a perfect band for Todd. We should find him and tell him." Todd had been touring solo at that point. Then we met Todd at the Dunegrass festival in Michigan around 2008. Todd, Taxi, and Leftover Salmon were all playing. Todd watched our set. We watched his.

Our relationship started when we all ended up in this school bus that was like an artist's greenroom backstage and picked tunes for five or six hours. Then Great American Taxi and Todd were both playing Durango, Colorado, on the same night the next year. Todd was playing the Henry Strater Theatre and we were playing the Abbey Theatre. Todd played early, so we invited him to come over to our show after. He obliged and the timing was perfect. We were on set break. "What are we gonna play?" he asked. "Well," we said. "We know a bunch of your songs." "What?" "Yeah, we can probably play a whole set of your songs. He jumped onstage and away we went.

Taxi improvises in the moment instrumentally like Todd does with words. People are ready to dance? All right, let's get dance mode going. The band really understood Snider as far as delivering the songs and what was happening between songs. We as a collective unit were steeped in his live show. I have played onstage with Todd and Dan Baird and have been in the position where Todd is [provoking] the show. He's a chameleon. He wants to challenge himself and the audience. There was a little more setup and thought put into it with Taxi. We really developed a thing together.

Todd says, "Anybody can get up here and play shit they know." He likes to bring danger to the stage and make you feel uncomfortable in many different ways. Good art makes people think and makes them feel taken aback. Todd accomplishes that. There's never been a night when I've been onstage with him and he didn't accomplish that in some ways. That will always happen no matter what the approach is that night. He will play "Beer Run" twice if the crowd isn't paying attention and everyone is talking just to see if they notice. Maybe he'll just split and see if they even notice we're gone. Keeps the audience on their toes.

Boy, it took me a long time to accept that. I'm a Midwestern boy probably with obsessive-compulsive disorder. I'm the oldest of a family of four and like things orderly and in place. I've always been the leader in my bands. I want structure and to nail what we're doing. Todd is the complete opposite. "Let's cause some chaos here and see what we make happen." I eventually saw the magic in what Todd was doing, which was really liberating. Not only as an artist but in life. Let go and don't try to please others, and live in that moment. There's real magic in there. It takes balls to stand up and do that. Todd has a big, giant pair. He wants and needs an audience to have a career, but it's really about what he's setting forth to do. Hopefully, people dig it. He's not a panderer.

Todd's honesty starts with looking at himself. I learned about his honesty in a really intense way. Todd and I started to form a bond after we did the Taxi tours. We were talking about doing other things. I ended up handling some of his day-to-day management stuff. He was disappointed in some things in his career that I saw from working on touring plans with Taxi. I saw where the holes and gaps were. I was taking a break from the road and felt like I might have to get a job. What do I know how to do? Manage musical acts.[6]

Vince Herman

I met Todd at a festival in Michigan. We hid out for a couple hours in a school bus, played tunes, and told stories. His road manager finally found us after causing quite a kerfuffle trying to find Todd. We had instantly disappeared into the music. I remember talking about Jeff Austin. Todd was talking about putting together a band with a bunch of jam band guys, which eventually became Hard Working Americans. Todd goes through these phases of reinventing himself like Dylan with East Side Bulldogs and Hard Working Americans. He's a brilliant guy. What impresses me most is him getting up and writing for a couple hours every morning. He has such an inspiring devotion to the craft.

Todd is fully aware about creating your own mythology like my mentor Col. Bruce Hampton. Todd is living in the shadows of Guy Clark, John Prine, and Townes Van Zandt, all those cats who were so important to him. He found the time to hang with them. I think that put a really big weight on Todd to write at that level. He has always felt that necessity of being a really large, legendary character like those guys, and he steps right up. His writing and lifestyle build that mythology. Todd is the quintessential explorer. He puts his life on the line with the songs and storytelling. He might come across as casual, but his act is so finely crafted. I think there should be a Todd Snider class at Belmont [University in Nashville].[7]

Chad Staehly

Todd invited me to play keyboards on the new solo album he was working on after Taxi had been in the studio with him several times. We did the Jerry Jeff tribute that Don Was produced, which was totally awesome. Then we did the live album [*Storyteller*], and Todd invited me to play on *Agnostic Hymns & Stoner Fables*. I was offering lots of opinions that weren't being asked for. The session ended early. Then I got a call the next morning from [his former tour manager]. "Todd would like to have breakfast with you." We had breakfast. Todd was brutally honest. The things I was saying in the studio were affecting him personally.

That was a hard pill to swallow, but I manned up, owned up, and accepted his truth and honesty. That was a point that really cemented our friendship. We got to a point very quickly where we could be brutally honest with each other, which is what has kept us really good friends. Todd is definitely a leader and not a follower. People are born like that. He has been challenging himself, his friends, his football coach, whoever since childhood. That got him into a lot of trouble, but it also opened doors for him. He was able to push his way into hanging out with John Prine, Kris Kristofferson, and Guy Clark at a fairly young age. He pushed himself forward and went after what he thought he needed and didn't compromise. Todd does not compromise. Not at all.

Todd could spill his guts for months, even a year, writing an album and will have no problem at all in putting it on the shelf and saying, "Nah. Not good enough. Not the right time. Gotta start over." He's brutally honest with himself and expects that from the people around him. I think Todd has been like that from the day he was born. He's always thinking about what he can create that's new and pushes things forward artistically. He had been playing on all these jam band festivals and was seeing the scene from that point of view. He saw these really quality players who cared about what they were doing, but he also saw that the crux of the song was missing from the jam scene. "Boy, there are these great players who have songs, but they get pretty far away from the song. What if someone like me who is nothing but about the guts and lyrics of the song applied that to the jam?"

We talked about that for years. Then we landed on having a date at the Napa Theater in California, and I remembered that Dave Schools lived not far from there. I knew that Todd and Dave had a relationship from way back when Todd and the Nervous Wrecks had opened for Widespread Panic. "Dave Schools lives near this Napa gig," I said. "What do you think about seeing if he wants to play the gig with you?" He loved the idea. It was a way to open the door into the jam world. I got a hold of Dave's manager, and Dave was really open to the idea. Dave invited Paolo [Baldi], who was the drummer for Cake and lived in Sonoma County. They played as a trio and had fun. "We should do a record," Dave said. "I'm thinking the same," Todd said. They both told me that they really loved the idea.

I started to talk with Dave and Todd about the record shortly after that. We knew Dave would help produce with Todd. We talked about who else would be in the band and decided to turn it into an all-star thing that became the Hard Working Americans. Dave had no idea that I was a musician at that point. He only knew me as Todd's manager, but Todd was in favor of me playing keyboards. I told Dave that I would be the keyboard player but also the liaison. We asked Vince Herman and Jeff Austin to be involved. Then we talked to Cody and Luther Dickenson [of the North Mississippi All-Stars]. That was the initial conception for Hard Working Americans. Todd said he had these Americana songs he didn't write but was collecting to put in the jam band context. He made the list in case anyone asked him to produce an album.

Then the Dickenson brothers' manager got involved. Everything got screwed up with them. Cody and Luther really wanted to do it because they had been close friends with Jeff Austin for a while. They knew Vince well and Todd from the Memphis days. I don't remember the details, but things got jacked up. This was maybe January, and we were recording in May. Then Vince's schedule wasn't gonna work out and things were uncertain between Jeff and Todd as far as how this would work. Everything got shaky, but Dave, Todd, and I were committed. I couldn't wait to get it happening. Dave was aware of Duane Trucks and that he had gotten to the age where he could take on a gig like this.

Duane signed up right away, but we still needed a guitar player. Todd had met the Chris Robinson Brotherhood back in the Bay Area in December. He dug the band and what they were doing. I had been a giant Neal Casal fan for years. I literally cold-called him by sending him a message on Facebook. I said, "Hey, man, you don't know me, but I'm putting this band together. We would like to have you involved." He thought it was interesting. We gave him the rundown, and he thought it was wild. He was down to do the recording session in May. Then he called an hour later and said he couldn't commit. He thought he was in over his head, but I talked it through with him, and he was back in.

We showed up at Bob Weir's studio, TRI, in May 2013, and the band literally had never met. Dave had no idea who Neal was. We met at the studio and tracked three songs in the first day. Everything clicked big time after that first record. We decided to film the first show we ever played like the Band had with their last, which really came together in a magical way. We were gonna do like ten shows and that would be it, but Todd had lyrics and riffs. We went into the studio in Chicago. We finished the last show on the tour and went in for five days.

Jesse Aycock was in the band by then. No one had ever experienced what we did in the studio those five days. Lightening was striking left and right. Guitar players were writing these riffs and keyboard were coming in. Dave and Duane were clicking on these grooves. The guts of [the Hard Working Americans' second album] *Rest in Chaos* happened right there in the studio on the fly. Todd had been working on the lyrics and melodies for a while, but the songs came together organically. The band became a first love for everyone involved. Everyone wanted that to happen at one point. There was a very special bromance happening.

Kevn Kinney

Todd and [Hard Working Americans and Widespread Panic bassist] Dave Schools were in Athens one time. "Hey, man, Hard Working Americans recorded your song 'Straight to Hell,'" Todd said. "Check it out." I wasn't sure if they were gonna put it on their record or not, but I thought it was cool. Theirs is the best version I've ever heard, but Todd's solo version is just heartbreaking. He doesn't do songs that he doesn't mean. He's telling the truth even when he does a cover song and always does a very well-thought-through version.[8]

Chad Staehly

Todd understood me better as a musician after the Hard Working Americans. I wasn't just a guy backing him in a band or his manager. We really bonded further throughout the band and developed some collective visions. There was a mutual separation with Neal from the band. We wanted to keep it going, but it came down to a scheduling thing with Neal. His people behind the scenes were making it difficult for us to plan anything with him. They saw the meteoric rise we were having and didn't want that to happen. We were all painted into corners at one point. Neal loved the band and wanted it to move forward. "You guys need to keep this going," he said. "I'm holding it back."

We had a couple very difficult conversations and decided collectively to part ways. We did, played a couple shows, and got into the studio and made a record. We were auditioning guitar players and had set up a week in Nashville. We had about eight to ten guitar players show up. "Hey, I have more song ideas," Todd said. "I've been doing demos out at Johnny Cash's recording studio [Cash Cabin] on his property, a magical little cabin. Johnny recorded there a bunch. What about spending a couple days out there? We can invite some guitar players out if we like them." "Yeah," we said. "Sure." "By the way," Todd says, "I've been having this dream where we're inside the cabin and Johnny keeps telling me that I'm missing a song I have to find." Pretty trippy. Todd's not one to make that up.

We told him maybe he should sleep out there between sessions. Maybe he would find that song. We get in there the first day, everyone took a little acid, and magic happened. You just feel Johnny Cash's spirit in there. There's a vibe unlike anything else. We were all feeling it. Todd didn't end up staying overnight at the studio, but we show up the next day and the vibes were high again. Johnny's son, John Carter Cash, shows up about halfway through. He lives on the forty acres in Hendersonville. We were sitting at the kitchen table, and he says to Todd, "Hey, man, I have this song idea we should write together." He told us about how Loretta Lynn would be out at the cabin recording. Loretta is a friend of Todd's, and they've written some songs.

John Carter Cash is telling this story about Loretta staying over at the studio sometimes and dancing with Johnny Cash's ghost. Our jaws are on the ground. "Well, there's your song. That's the one you're supposed to find. 'The Ghost of Johnny Cash.'" We decided right then to come back and make the next Hard Working Americans record there. We came back in spring 2015. Daniel Sproul from Rose Hill Drive was the guitarist. He fit the bill perfectly. We made an entire album within ten days. Todd arrived the first day before all of us. He got some stuff together and then ran back to his house because he doesn't live far from the Cash Cabin.

Todd was with our tour manager Brian Kincaid, and they almost ran over a guy in the parking lot. Todd didn't recognize him. He doesn't recognize Snider. Then Todd realizes this guy is Bill Miller, who is a Grammy-winning Native American songwriter. He recognizes Todd. They're old friends and start talking. Bill explains that he's going through these real tough challenges. Todd says we're about to record an album and Bill should hang around at least for today. Bill just naturally became the spiritual adviser for the band. Bill ended up being there all ten days. He was doing these chants and prayers some days that literally would leave you with hairs standing up. He was helping us, and Bill himself move forward. Bill sang a bunch on the record. We finished recording the record, but then we were unsure. Then we got back to thinking it was really cool. One person or another would get cold feet.

Then everything came unwound. We were unsure about the record and the future of the band. The album still wasn't out a year later. Hard Working Americans was still touring but it was starting to get into a weird place. People got busy with stuff. We weren't able to line things up. The universe was saying, "You can't put this record out now. This thing has to stop for a minute." So we stopped. Todd was left with these songs that were on the record. He felt like there was still something to be done out at Cash Cabin. He reached out to me and asked me to produce his solo album there. I don't have a ton of production experience but was totally game for that. I encouraged Todd a lot. I knew what his fans love—him and his guitar. I was like, "Hey, man, you're like twelve records in, and you've never done a folk record."

I suggested stripping everything down to be a juxtaposition to what he had been doing with Hard Working Americans. So, we went back to the *Cash Cabin Sessions, Vol. 3* record we made. Everyone in the press was saying, "Oh, typical Snider. He's calling it volume three and there never was a volume one or two." There actually are. That was volume three. Volume two was the Hard Working Americans' album with those songs. Volume one was a bunch of demos and spoken word stuff that he did out there before. The Cash Cabin doors were open for us because Bobby Bare had asked Todd to do the song "A Boy Named Sue" on this Shel Silverstein tribute record there.[9]

Vince Herman

Todd is good at living how Colonel Bruce taught me. He always said to take what you do seriously, but don't take yourself seriously. We were rolling into New York City one time to play with the Aquarium Rescue Unit at the Wetlands festival. We happened to come over the bridge stuck in traffic right next to each other. We were going around in this big traffic circle and big loops on the highway. Bruce stuck his head out the window and said, "Be careful. That's an area in there. Stay out of the areas." Stupid shit like that. Now any time I go around any traffic circle with a big, open space, I go, "There's an area." Bruce just had all these observations on life. He put them in a funny perspective. Todd does that in his writing.

Col. Bruce Hampton

I [was] never discouraged. I [was] honored to play music. Everything collapses into place if stuff goes the way it's supposed to go. There's a different kind of gravity on my planet. Change is the only consistent thing. I do what I do, and I follow my instincts. Music has to come from the church, folk music, or outer space. You can be a sophisticated folk singer, but it's got to come from those places, or I can't listen to it. Doesn't make sense to me. It's gotta have a story and some soul. I want to hear from the people who have nothing to say instead of those who want to say something.[10]

Col. Bruce Hampton (1947–2017) was a founding member of the Atlanta group Hampton Grease Band. He performed with Frank Zappa, Kevn Kinney, Susan Tedeschi, and several others. Todd Snider name-checks him in the lyrics to his song "Turn Me Loose (I'll Never Be the Same)."

Vince Herman

I watched Bruce die onstage. He fell down on the monitor right in front of me. That was a really profound experience that changed my perspective on life and music. Bruce was telling me that he was sore and having a hard time getting out of his chair during the last dinner we had. He didn't think the gigs were that good anymore. He was saying, "I'm getting really tired." That was nothing like anything I had ever heard in conversation with Bruce. He was always positive and saying things like, "Isn't the world fantastic for such a weird place? Check that out." Bruce was feeling like he had done what he wanted to do here. Man, to make that choice and turn yourself off like he did is a true sign of a master.

Todd Snider

I want to go out onstage like Colonel Bruce. I want to live the zambie life. The lifestyle is poetry. You get to make up poems. Go where you want. Write what you want. Follow the muse wherever it goes. Live like a pinball. I love that. I think the gypsy life is what gets Ray Wylie Hubbard, even though he's sober. We steal shit and lie. Throw some rasta stuff in there if you want. I tell stories that aren't totally true. I write songs that aren't totally true. "Here's a song I totally wrote," you say. "It's 'Alice's Restaurant.'" Now here's a story, which may or may not have happened. Now pass the hat and let me get out before you guys realize how easy guitar is.

Vince Herman

I thought maybe I don't want to be on the road and struggling it out at seventy years old after Bruce died. I definitely started questioning what the arc of a life should be. There are certainly a lot of lives to lead. Bruce said always answer the phone because eventually it will stop ringing. Todd is one of the most treasured friends and musicians in my life. He's deeply inspiring just like Bruce. He told me the story about opening for Jimmy Buffett for the first time when he was on Margaritaville Records. Jimmy popped into Todd's dressing room right before he went on. "All right," he said. "Here's your set list. I know this audience and what you should play." Todd told him to fuck off. Todd wasn't gonna compromise or do what someone else wanted him to do.

Another example was when we did the *WoodSongs* radio show in Kentucky. The host had handed out a pamphlet on how to write a song the previous time Todd had been on. You can imagine Todd's response. "The guy gave me a book on how to write a song," Todd said. "I'm out of there if he does that shit again." So, Todd was introduced on the show, goes out onstage, and sits on the stool. He's ready to play. The host talks for a minute then goes on to something else. Two minutes, three minutes, four, five. The host is still going off on something unrelated. Todd got up, walked off, and called me. "I did it," he said. "I'm at the bar across the street. Fuck it." Beautiful. He doesn't put up with shit. I mean, he had a case to sue them when his "Beer Run" was ripped off, but he didn't. "Man," he said. "I'm a musician so I don't have to do that kind of shit. I don't want to sit around with a bunch of guys in suits for hours." He knows how he wants to spend his time, which is one of the best things you can say about a human.[11]

Todd Snider

Col. Bruce Hampton had the Church of Zambie, which was based on a valedictorian kid he knew growing up who aced the SAT. Then he decided he wanted to drive a car backward faster than anyone ever had. He broke every bone in his body. Colonel Bruce said, "This religion probably isn't for you if you can't see the genius in that." I guarantee Jerry Jeff would have said, "That guy knows what I'm talking about." Be in on the cosmic joke. I'm certain he thought I wasn't much of a songwriter. He told me. I remember hearing Willie Nelson being asked what advice he would give a young songwriter. He said, "A real young songwriter would tell me to shove my advice up my ass." I don't think any songwriters think another songwriter has songs better than theirs.[12]

Ben Kaufmann

I came across Todd Snider in the early 2000s. Yonder Mountain String Band was about to headline Red Rocks for one of the first times and were talking about bands that could share the bill with us. Todd's name came up. I had heard about him before and probably had heard "Beer Run." I started listening to his records and really connected with the songs. Seeing him perform brought it all home. The way that he was with the audience and how his personality comes through and his songs made me very much in awe of what he was doing. Todd's voice and phrasing have lots of humanity and honesty. They're utterly compelling to me. What he was saying and the way he was saying it was so clever. Todd is certainly one of the most important voices I've ever heard.

The way he turns a phrase and delivers a message is so smart. He never delivers it in a way that separates you. He thinks about the world in such a greater degree than I ever could and doesn't deliver a hierarchy. Sometimes I feel like artists are talking down to me. Todd's music is always uplifting even if the subject is very [dark]. Todd always offers you a chance to come along with him. We toured with him a couple times, and I've been able to be on the side of the stage watching him do his thing. I bask in it. He is the fullest expression of himself onstage. It's not like every performance is the best ever, but it's always honest.

Look to the songs. The entire *The Devil You Know* and *East Nashville Skyline* are my favorites. Those were concurrent with the touring we were doing with Todd. I can play the bass and sing harmony to every song on those records. Playing with Todd is a really cool experience. There isn't a strictness. Sometimes there can be ebbs and flows in the time signature. He's not as crazy as following Baby Gramps's flow and where he's gonna go, but approaching the music onstage with Todd means following his energetic leadership. One of the cool things about cutting my teeth in the jam band world is having a really wide listening experience. You're not so focused on every beat. Your attention spreads.

You can go in any direction at any time just like with the great jam bands. Any string summits we've been to together are great places to see Todd perform. We would hang on each other's tour buses playing music when we were on the road. He would say, "How about this song?"

That would become our new favorite song. Then we brought a bunch of Todd's tunes into our repertoire with Yonder. "Sideshow Blues" shows up at least once a week. "Sideshow Blues" makes up a super cool modern bluegrass tune. His stuff translates really well to what we do, because bluegrass and folk aren't that far apart.

The last time I saw Todd was at our mandolin player [Jeff Austin's] memorial service in Denver. Todd is one of those weird relationships that you have. I don't call him all the time. You just drop right back into it with such an ease when you see the person anyway. I give him a great big hug and have about twenty minutes to catch up passing at a show. "Dude, what's up? How you been doing?" There's inevitably something to talk about. Classic male friendship. We share music and talk about the different projects he is thinking about doing. That was happening a lot in the mid-2000s. I'm always thinking in the back of my mind when we're talking, "Pay attention, Ben." Todd is the person if there's someone I want to learn songwriting craft from.

Jeff said one time he was going to write with Todd and came back with "East Nashville Easter." I don't know whose idea it was, but I hear much more Jeff than Todd in that song. I'm wondering if Jeff showed up with that one in a more complete state and Todd helped with some lyrics and chord changes. Man, I wish Jeff was here to talk. He would have even more to say. Jeff and Todd were really tight and certainly had a different relationship. Jeff was powerfully influenced by Todd in every way. Todd was a hero. Todd is extraordinarily important as a songwriter and a person in my life. I don't know who I would point to as any other more important modern songwriter. Todd Snider is the gold standard in so many ways.[13]

Founding member Ben Kaufmann has served as bassist for Colorado's wildly popular bluegrass jam band Yonder Mountain String Band for more than twenty years.

Jeff Austin

I believe we get one life. I had this summer where I was hanging out with my daughter while she was crawling and chasing butterflies in the yard. I got to really sit and reflect. My manager told me, "Put your phone in a drawer. Bake some bread. Grow a weird beard." This guy worked for the Eagles and pushed "Bohemian Rhapsody" on radio. He's seen a lot. I grew the weird beard, but my two daughters weren't really having it. I look at [everything] now, and I'm so deeply grateful for this vibe that's happening. It wasn't like my time with Yonder ended, and then I was headlining Red Rocks. I was playing for twelve people in Cleveland, and no one gave a shit. I was hearing everything horrible people were saying.

I never, ever spend one second thinking badly about what happened. I remember to be grateful for the things that we were fortunate enough to have. I [am]grateful that wc got to hang out with last night's crowd five years down the road. I'm grateful twelve times over. Be grateful for what you have. Go forth with your own thing. This stirs my pot and becomes contagious. We're all in this together.[14]

Jeff Austin (1974–2019) was the fierce and fiery singer and mandolin player driving the thriving Colorado-based Yonder Mountain String Band for fifteen years. He ended his career as a celebrated solo artist.

Todd Snider

Jeff Austin and I got into a real argument over [the Yonder Mountain String Band song] "East Nashville Easter." [We fought over whether] lyrics should be linear verses abstract. I was wanting him to just say what he felt, and he was wanting to do something more coded like [the Don McLean classic] "American Pie." We went that direction. Jeff had been awake for a couple of days, and it was Easter Sunday. Jeff was channeling "Sunday Morning Coming Down" in his own way and that place on the road where you realize there is no going home or going back. He might have been going through some buyer's remorse on his lifestyle choices. I encouraged him to say exactly what he was feeling, but he wanted to do more like the hippie word salad thing. He wrote the "engine running hot" line in that song.

Jeff died unexpectedly a couple years ago. He had a show and got booed because he was too fucked up and playing bad. Jeff was lost and probably didn't care enough to play well. We heard that he died when we were on our bus. I had just heard from him. He sent an email one morning that said, "Call me." I called Jeff, and he was crying. We stayed on the phone, and I got him to leave the tour, go home, and go to rehab. He went for five days. They let us talk while he was in there. I was talking to his mom. Jeff came out and he said he had a show on Friday that wasn't very far away. He said it paid tons of money and he needed it. He was gonna go do it. Then he called me. He was drunk and told me that he was sorry and couldn't do it. I was like, "Just go do the show and go home. We'll start over."[15]

Andrew Dansby

People are more comfortable going to talk to others who are survivors. It was easier for me to call [the singer-songwriters] Scott Miller and Chris Masterson than to see a therapist when I needed to get better. Those guys still check in regularly. There is a weird, insular quality there. I'm not surprised that people would go to Todd when they're feeling their lowest. He's walked that road and been through more shit than most people. It has to be a burden on him for people to think that he has everything figured out because he's come out the other end. You know, Todd is in his fifties. Hemingway was sixty-something before he closed the book. Todd's burden is different. People treat Todd like a therapist because he's so transparent.[16]

Andrew Dansby was a longtime arts writer for the Houston Chronicle.

Jack Ingram

Kurt Cobain got too close to the sun and got burned. Todd gets that close to the sun, but he can control things. People like Kurt and G. G. Allin go all the way. [Legendary Texas cult songwriters] Roky Erickson and Daniel Johnston got close and couldn't control it. Todd has control. He just goes as far as he has to go to prove a point. Trust me, what Todd does will make sense to you at some point in the future, but I understand why you and Jenni had to leave the Hard Working Americans show at Stubb's [in Austin] because he looked [strung out]. There are times when I've flown up to Nashville just to check, to go to his house to go, "Are you good?" "Yeah, man, I'm good." Then we hang out, but I have to make sure Todd is all right.

Todd doesn't give a fuck. I don't give a fuck. Some people think we're noble by not giving a fuck, but those faced with it like Todd and me go, "Why can't I just put on a tie and get the job?" Todd and I talk about that. "Why can't you just go with the flow?" "I don't know. I just can't." It's almost not a choice and not a two-way decision. I've gone the other way a couple times in my career, and I feel like a whore. Todd committed to the Hard Working Americans bit like a comedian does.

The band fucking wouldn't have worked if he didn't. Todd has never told me that, but I just know. The Hard Working Americans aren't together anymore because they wanted Todd to write songs. He was like, "The whole thing is that it's not my project. It's not Todd Snider and Hard Working Americans." He could get completely lost and do the funky chicken dance that way and everything that scared you guys. That wouldn't scare me. I would be like, "Yeah, that's how you do it." You commit to the bit. Period. You die if it means you die.[17]

Todd Snider

I have a fleeting thought about Ingram once in a while, "Oh, Jack, don't you fuck this up." I've lost almost all my friends to this dumb thing. You would think I would be the one, but I have lost like a dozen friends instead. Hayes Carll is sturdy as a motherfucker. Same with Jason Isbell. That generation is, but I'm like, "Jack, don't be a phone call." Jeff was a force of nature, but things obviously didn't turn out great. There was a beauty in him. I loved him. There were times when I thought, "Goddamn, Jeff." Vinnie Herman was the same way. I always make it sound so dark, but I always joked, "This is the Manson house, man." I love the freak scene in Boulder because of that. It was almost like Luckenbach.

I have no idea how to pull it all back to Ramblin' Jack Elliott music. I'm feeling compelled to toss all this shit and sing by myself. How can I take all of those records and make a follow-up to *Agnostic Hymns*? That record was getting a little loud but also a little funky. I was so drunk during that record and so hurt. My family hadn't spoken to me in four, five years. I would have rather been dead than make that record. I felt like *The Excitement Plan* was enough. I was over the alphabet and in a really dark, sad place, which led to a divorce. Then we made an even sadder and angrier record with the Hard Working Americans.[18]

I really wanted to quit after doing *The Excitement Plan* with Don. I've been really reluctant to make records ever since. I will if there's some weird conceptual thing behind it that people probably won't even like. I don't care. My friends and people I was close to like Tony Brown knew I wasn't trying to be the Bay City Rollers or Bruce Springsteen on *East Nashville*. I was trying to be Ramblin' Jack Elliott. I wanted the Tom Petty job really briefly and embarrassed myself going for it. I asked God for the Ramblin' Jack Elliott job in genuine earnest. I never asked for anything else again. I've never not wanted it. Even when I wanted it to be there to run away from. Sometimes the move is quitting, but I don't quit the game.

The American troubadour is like sixty years old. Ramblin' Jack told me that after a couple of his albums, this Elvis kid came out and really changed the game. Ramblin' really was the first one to carve out the circuit that Townes Van Zandt fell into. Now we're all rapscallions. All other troubadours call him "The Guest." He carries the smallest bag and goes where the wind blows. He'll come crash at your place for a long time. I love him for that. I think the songwriter and the troubadour are two things.

Anyway, Mercer told me to stop trying to get my life together. I didn't stop drugs as much as I stopped trying to quit drugs. Mercer and Burt played a big role in [letting me know] seeking sanity is not working for me personally or professionally. They got really protective of my insanity. There was a time in my life when I would have given anything to be Nanci Griffith until that night I mentioned, when I walked into the bar and saw her crying by herself. I didn't get it at all then, but I do now. This is an isolating job. The better you do it, the more isolating it is. I haven't figured it out yet. I don't have any idea how I would find my connection back to Sunday morning. I just sit out here alone.

I had a seizure before a Hard Working Americans show, and they started to see that I wasn't a dependable person. I've just retracted and have stayed there since. I'm my best when I'm on the road. I can get off the bus in the daytime when I'm on the road and can go make friends, but they always inevitably end up at the show. I can go meet some people at a coffee shop who won't know me at all, and they'll show me their town. Then I inevitably tell them why I'm in town, and they come to the show. Then they know. I don't have any family, but I travel and get real close to people I don't see again, or they can't get backstage next time.

We wrote [the Hard Working Americans' 2016 album] *Rest in Chaos* together, and that was the rub. The original idea was to be a cover band. Then everyone but Neal wanted to write. I told them that I cease to be easygoing once my lyrics get involved—and I did. We recorded the *Cash Cabin* album, and then I threw it out and did it alone. The difference between the money I made off *Agnostic Hymns* and *Cash Cabin* was just too much. I couldn't afford to write with them. I don't guess that I have enough money to write with anyone let alone a band.[19] Something popped after Neal died. I remembered that I fucking love being a singer and a songwriter.[20]

Chorus: From a Rooftop (Part 2)

THE SONGWRITING LEGACY

Todd Snider signals a sea change with *Cash Cabin Sessions, Vol. 3* (2019) and the pandemic-era *The First Agnostic Church of Hope and Wonder* (2021). The former includes peaks like "Talking Reality Television Blues," "Like a Force of Nature," "Just Like Overnight," and "Watering Flowers in the Rain," while the latter includes "Turn Me Loose (I'll Never Be the Same)," "Handsome John," "The Get Together," and "Sail on My Friend." "*The First Agnostic Church of Hope and Wonder* has a theme that starts with this guy who says he's your preacher," Snider says. "Then later you realize he took your money. He steps down at the end. I tell myself that I have [the Beatles'] *Sergeant Pepper* or [The Who's] *Tommy* going on when I'm [recording]. I get lost in it. Then I'll put out the album and realize it wasn't *Tommy*."

Meanwhile, Snider fulfills a longstanding dream by dovetailing his story as a songwriter. He teams with Jenni Finlay and the author to release Kent Finlay's debut album, *I've Written Some Life* (Aimless Records/ Eight 30 Records, 2020), which was recorded a quarter-century earlier in Memphis. The collection features the Finlay originals "Fat Lou the Tattoo Man," "Citizens for Liberty," Plastic Girl," and the title track. "The character 'Fat Lou the Tattoo Man' was real, but in a Shel Silverstein way," Snider says. "You can learn so much about Kent from the song even though the story is fictional. Kent never said he was in the league of the people he taught, but those of us who learned from him knew that he was. I knew all his songs by heart." "Dad's dying wish was to put this record out," Jenni Finlay says. "He would have been so proud to know it finally was released. Working with our dear old friend Todd just made it sweeter."

Snider's recent albums coupled with the nod toward his first songwriting teacher mark his own emergence as a sage and spiritual mentor for the next generation. He eagerly embraces the role. "We have had another integrity scare today with people like Hayes Carll, Jason Isbell, and Kacey Musgraves," Snider says. "I hope I'm encouraging younger songwriters. I try to bring Hondo Crouch and tell them to have fun with songwriting. I feel less threatened by this whole new generation of songwriters in East Nashville than I was by my peers. I really would try to top a good Kimbrough song when I heard it, but now I can just enjoy a new Hayes Carll song. Also, I remember when I went to Guy Clark's basement for the very first time. He made songwriting seem like a club with rules. I want to pass that on."

Todd Snider

East Nashville almost reeks with talent. Seems like everyone is still there for the right reasons, even now. East Nashville feels amazing and genuine with everyone over there singing and doing guitar pulls. Rorey Carroll, Raelyn Nelson, Hayes Carll, and Allison Moorer all blow my mind. I don't know what my role will be in the world as I grow older. I'll probably sing to something until the end—whether it's to an empty field or a group of people—but it will take place on my porch at night. I can't imagine it not involving a porch at night.

Hayes Carll was the first young guy we all embraced. Jack called me up and said there was a new guy we all had to be friends with. Guy Clark had already given us our lecture on how that all works, so I decided to test out the new system. We took him in as a brother. I love that song "Stomp and Holler." I have a memory of him starting that one at my house. I always thought his songs are really masterful, but "Stomp and Holler" is fun and as heavy as anything else upon introspection. Hayes is really good at those. I don't think he's sure how we did that song in Hard Working Americans to this day. We just put it in half time like the Faces. We took [Bob Dylan's] "Subterranean Homesick Blues" and turned it into "Stay with Me." I think he was cool with it.[1]

Hayes Carll

My first gig in Nashville was when I played a twenty-minute showcase at the Exit/In. I had met Jack Ingram after my first record, and he had been very generous with his time and advice. He started championing me to some folks. My understanding is that he reached out to Todd. I remember being out in the parking lot and Todd came rolling up with no shoes on. I don't even remember what we talked about, but I was pretty green and thought it was pretty cool that he came into town to catch a show. Now that I know him better I know that coming into town is not a nightly thing for him. So, I'm even more impressed all these years later that he took time to do that. I ended up touring with him pretty soon after that.

We toured together around when *East Nashville Skyline* came out. That record is one of my favorites of all time. I think the songwriting, delivery, and sonics are all brilliant. I was fully on the Todd Snider fan bandwagon by then. I can't remember the schedule, but we did a fair number of solo shows together. We got to know each other a little bit. I can't say we got super closely connected at the time, but I was happy to get in front of his audience and to watch him work. Watching how he approached things was pretty informative. We started a correspondence at some point and have loosely maintained that for fifteen years.

We do have similarities, but I'm very aware of the differences between Todd and me. I don't wanna mimic somebody's act. You're ideally working with people you can take from. Todd would say the same thing. You're not stealing necessarily, but you're learning. You think, "Okay, that works, but that doesn't." There are significant differences in our banter, so I could see what worked for Todd but wouldn't work for me. I'm not sure what I took from him other than admiration for what he did. It's like watching Fred Eaglesmith or Ray Wylie Hubbard. It's more, "Okay, he uses a set list." There's obviously a lot of work that goes into the front end to make it seem so off-the-cuff in the moment.

I'm interested in finding out how people arrive at what feels like a finished place and how they make it feel vibrant and alive. Those artists I just mentioned are some of the best I've ever seen. I've studied them. You throw those ingredients into your own style. Anyway, I think the shows opening for Todd went fine. I was cautious to not overstep my bounds into what felt like his territory. He was at a way higher level musically and with his stage persona than I was anyway, but we came up on similar music. Todd was hugely influenced by Dylan and loved his songwriting and the way he approached the folky political thing. Todd has this quote that I still always reference because it's disarming and explains a lot. "I don't write these songs to change anybody's mind," he says. "I write them to ease my own." I thought that was a really smart way to not have an antagonistic relationship with the audience and still get your opinions out. His songs are mostly from the downtrodden point of view and aren't judgmental.

I love his wordplay and that he can also just go Chuck Berry and burn the house down with a band. I felt a kinship with his wordplay with internal rhymes. His syncopation, interesting meter, timing, and way he arranged his words in the rhymes are just as exciting as the subjects of the songs in some cases. They were like vocal exercises or tongue twisters. His songs were challenging. He's funny, which is hard. He's not reliant on a schtick, which might fade over time. For all his humor, rambunctiousness, anti-norm approach, he can be really sweet and put his feelings out there in a way that's relatable. I've always tried to find that balance as a writer.

I've always tried to be funny yet poignant, and political without being heavy-handed. Make something a ballad and a burner. Todd does all those things better than anybody I've ever seen. I feel like he was a little more directly vocal with [his political views] early on. I'm not sure what backlash he faced. Some artists are preaching to the choir. Sometime fans will be outraged if you put something out there that they don't grasp. My sense is that Todd wasn't always the barefoot, stoned, creative preacher living on his own planet. That evolved over time, but I know that many of his fans aren't aligned with him politically. He just puts out his message in a way that's okay. You can say, "I disagree with that, but it made me laugh." It's hard to be mad when someone doesn't beat you over the head.

Todd is very generous in highlighting people he likes in a way that not all artists are. Jack Ingram is the same. Todd has gone out of his way to champion or mention me in the press over the years. He has done the same with many people and is very attentive all the time. I admire Todd and Corb Lund, and I thought it would be good to have their different personalities on "Bottle in My Hand" [the tenth track on Carll's 2011 breakout *KMAG YOYO*]. I thought it was thematically in Todd's wheelhouse. You have this Jerry Jeff Walker and Woody Guthrie-like character bumming around the country observing things. Todd came in and did his Todd thing and nailed it. My takeaway is that Todd is a lot smarter than he lets on and really cares. That can be lost in the personae he has created. Todd is very passionate about songwriting and making music. I love that he can quote Woody Guthrie and also have this jam band doing early rock 'n' roll songs. He is very interested in all kinds of musical styles.

Todd took away his safety net and became a part of a rock 'n' roll group with Hard Working Americans, which is a huge and very scary leap. You're out there naked as a singer. Not literally. Well, who knows with Todd, but I talked to him after and have a better understanding of how far he went in. I have great admiration for the journey he took with Hard Working Americans. He might have been burned out on being a folk singer. Maybe that's why he started a band. I can certainly relate if that's the case. Many people get burned out and don't do anything about it. They don't adjust themselves. Todd is always moving and evolving. It's easy to say, "People like this. It's comfortable. I'm gonna stay here." He strikes me as an artist who has evolved better than just about anyone.

I usually bought a thank you gift at the end of the tour when I was opening someone's shows. I figured out at some point that Todd really liked dogs. So, I found this dog flowerpot and lamp hybrid. I wrapped it up, left it on his porch in East Nashville, and went home. I didn't see Todd for a long time. Then he started talking about me in interviews. His interviews were performance art in that early Dylan way of taking a piss and having fun. They were interesting to read. This story starts to unfold over the course of multiple interviews. They say in the first one, "Tell me about your record." "Well, I'll get to that," Todd said. "First, though, it's just not right what happened to Hayes Carll and his dog." Then he would go on to something else. Then a week later they would say, "Tell us about your record."

"I will," he would say, "but the government shouldn't be able to kick down your door like they did to my friend Hayes Carll." I started seeing this narrative unfold. The story had developed by the fourth interview that the FBI had kicked down my door, raided my house, and stolen my dog. Todd didn't feel that was right. He was upset that the world wasn't as outraged as he was that the government had bullied me and used this abuse of power. I'm sitting there reading this shit saying, "What in the world is he talking about? None of these things happened." The interviewer doesn't know what Todd's talking about. Nobody else in the world knows. Maybe leaving that dog planter on his porch helped him create this whole story.

His own imagination took him from this gift to creating a whole world that nobody understood but him. The point was for him to have fun creating this situation and put it out there. I've always gotten a kick out of watching his mind work and how he views things. He's so creative, funny, and bizarre. Some ways are very clear to see in his music and shows, but other times you have to really get in there to understand. There are lots of levels to Todd Snider, which I'm still trying to figure out. I'm just grateful that Todd Snider exists. He's inspiring to me on a bunch of levels and sure as hell fun to listen to. He seems like this train wreck who doesn't care about much of anything, but he cares about everything.

Todd Snider makes the world a better place.[2]

Jason Isbell

I heard Todd sing for the first time in Memphis when I was in college around 1997. Todd was opening for Willie Nelson on the quad on campus. I went to see Willie and was blown away by Todd's opening set. He was playing solo with a dog onstage. I loved "Talking Seattle Grunge Rock Blues." I was like, "What the hell is this?" I started digging into his records after that. They became a really valuable part of my record collection. The lyrics got me most. He was humorous, witty, poignant, and had something meaningful to say with a sense of humor that was shockingly appealing to me. Todd is good at mixing humor with poignancy.

My favorite example might be "Just Like Old Times." That song is hilarious, but it becomes really dark and sad the second you put yourself into either of the primary characters' shoes. I love the simultaneous extremes in Todd's songwriting. I think that comes from his personality. It's like Voltaire adding comedy for those who think and tragedy for those who feel. Even the saddest things present themselves as hilarious if you view everything as comedy and end up writing songs for a living. Todd's very self-effacing. He doesn't take himself too seriously, but at the same time he does.

Todd knows what he can do at heart. He doesn't hide behind humor, but that's his way of delivering his particular brand of brilliance without seeming like an egotistical bastard. People cannot resist listening to your music no matter how much they want to if your songs are that good. I mean, people aren't gonna stop driving Mustangs if Ford turns into a liberal organization. The Mustang is that good. Hendrix said that if you play the same riff enough times you can hypnotize the audience. You can tell them anything and they'll believe it. Todd does that by getting them to laugh. He can slip in whatever belief he wants when he has people laughing and they don't think, "Well, look at this little erudite asshole." Todd is way ahead of most everybody else intellectually. The way for him to relate to the rest of us dumbasses is to laugh at himself.

He has so many songs that really move me. I have covered "Play a Train Song," and it's really an important song for many people who live in Nashville. The whole *East Nashville Skyline* album gives a snapshot showing how the city was the first times I came up here to play at the Slow Bar and Basement. I also like his work songs like "Looking for a Job" because they're not necessarily celebrating the work. It's easy to fall into the trap of capitalism or equate the value of a human being with the amount of money they can make for somebody else when you write a song about working people.

Todd does a really good job showing the perspective of a working person. His characters struggle because their capital isn't their own. Also, look at the confidence in the character he portrays in "Looking for a Job." He's saying, "I'm worth more than the money that I'm making for my boss." I love that. Even I'm equating the value of the person to the amount of work they do when I write a song. Todd goes past that. His line is, "I don't need the work / Like you need the work done." That's a whole universe of somebody who can't get ahead but still says, "I'm worth more than the shingling that I just did for your roof." Todd shows an understanding of a person who isn't a traveling songwriter.

Todd was the ambassador of East Nashville to the outside world. He bridged a gap between two types of musical creators that didn't exist before. I think people in my generation and the younger one take for granted the infrastructure of the music that lives and breathes in Nashville. It's easy for the kids in East Nashville to bemoan the popular country music industry, but there would not be an East Nashville without that. You get people like [Bonnie Prince Billy producer] Mark Nevers who are able to work in our world because they make a living in the other one. He worked on Music Row and got tired of the artists not remembering his name. He quit, took all his gear, and started his own studio in East Nashville.

Mark wouldn't have had the financial ability or skills to do that if he hadn't been working for the major popular music industry. Todd, Will Kimbrough, Grimey, Bobby Bare Jr., and the other people I hung around with when I first got there understood that. They realized that without all that commerce and ability there wouldn't be a possibility for the underground movement to happen. Todd was somebody who had songs that were cut by major country artists, so he had more money to write more Todd Snider songs. There's a beauty in there.[3]

Jason Isbell and the 400 Unit consistently have topped Americana charts and awards shows for the past decade with albums such as That Nashville Sound *(2017) and* Foxes in the Snow *(2025).*

Todd Snider

I was in a dark spot when we recorded *Agnostic Hymns & Stoner Fables.* I just wanted to drink, but I had to make money to keep drinking. I told Eric McConnell that we would have to find a crew who would help on that chaotic record. Jason Isbell and Amanda Shires helped a lot. I would do guitar parts and then would turn them all loose. Eric said we would need people who didn't keep hours. That's how Jason and Amanda came into my life. Amanda asked if her boyfriend could come over on the first session. I could tell right away how formidable those two were. Eric and I had already made records, but they had an energy that we were losing and rallied us because it was really dark and sad with lots of drinking and coke. There was no rhythm to the recording. We all just jumped in the washing machine for a month. Jason edited a lot of my guitars. I was just starting to learn how to play. I felt like *Agnostic Hymns* was going as far as I could.[4]

Jason Isbell

Amanda was playing on *Agnostic Hymns* with Todd and touring with him. I just started hanging out in the studio and wound up playing acoustic guitar on some things. I think one of those songs made the album. I haven't worked a lot with Todd in the studio because Todd feels like he doesn't want to waste my time. I can't seem to get across to him that the time we spend working together is very important to me. He's like, "This kid doesn't want to come play on my record. He has his own records." Todd is very humble in that way. I have spent a lot of time around him while he's in the studio, though.

Todd has very strict rules when he records. They're not very traditional rules. They're not about when he shows up or how much work he gets done. He has a vision and eschews elaboration at every opportunity. He will do that to my chagrin. I have really tried in the past to produce his tracks more to put guitar, bass, or drums on them. He doesn't want that. I respect his decision because he's not looking to appeal to a greater audience or sound more polished or slick. My natural tendency is to make things sound slicker than they should. Todd is very strict with himself and the people around him on this vision that doesn't sound like anyone could do it.

He's like the Replacements, who tried really hard to keep their work from sounding like [they were] inaccessible virtuosos. Todd wants you to listen to his records and think, I could have done that. A big part of the trick that he pulls is making it sound easier than it is, when in fact nobody else could do that. *Cash Cabin Sessions, Vol. 3* was one where I wanted him to be more elaborate. I brought in an electric guitar and Jerry Pentecost to play drums. In truth, Todd had just asked me to come out and sing, but I wanted to make the song "Like a Force of Nature" sound more like the Rolling Stones. That's not what he wanted to do. I thought "Like a Force of Nature" sounded like the Stones' "Street Fighting Man."

Playing with Todd and hearing his new songs is always fun. His songs sound complete and incredible even if they don't sound finished. The trick isn't him doing more work on a song. It's what you bring. You're coming with the wrong tools for the job if you are looking for a more finished song. You're doing it right if you come ready and hear what Todd has to say. Period. I wound up singing and just playing on one song [on *Cash Cabin*], but I wanted to do all this other shit. I was pissed off for about three days after we recorded because he didn't end up using that version. "Goddamn it, Todd, I want you to do this." I want Todd to be a star, but Todd doesn't want to be a star. I also like playing electric guitar. Wanting to play my black guard Telecaster like Keith Richards probably was at the heart of me wanting to produce it more.

I was backing up Amanda [the night she and Todd played "Mr. Bojangles" with Jerry Jeff Walker] when she was touring with Todd. Todd had us back his set and said, "You know, Jerry Jeff is gonna be here tonight." Sure enough, there's Jerry Jeff standing on the side of the stage. Todd had been such a fan of his. I was just trying to remember as much of that night as possible. That was one of those experiences where you're like, "I never thought I would be onstage with these folks when I was a kid growing up on songwriters." You just stay out of the way and take as many mental pictures as possible.[5]

Amanda Shires

Playing with Jerry Jeff Walker and Todd in Austin was a big deal. Jerry Jeff was very sick but said he would come up to play if he came to the show. I typically don't believe anything is gonna happen until it does. I don't like hope turning into being let down. So I lost my shit watching Todd lose his shit when Jerry Jeff got up onstage near the end of the show. Then the room became a big, really beautiful space with gratitude for music. Also, I like the way Todd handles hecklers. A girl called something to him onstage that night, and he said, "I thought I told you to wait in the truck." Of course, he will just walk offstage if it's a horrible offense. Sometimes it leads to a fistfight. He's figured out a way where people in the crowd can talk but not go too far.

Todd has set lists in his mind every night. He would write the songs down when I was on tour with him, but he wouldn't follow the list. I think it was more like a ritual to get his head in the right space to go play in front of people. Todd gets in his own head sometimes about people looking at him. I do the same. You're wondering what people think but have to think about other things. Set lists for Todd were that hour you spend getting ready to play music. We would make set lists, scribble, and mark, and I would make suggestions even though the list was always his.

Todd knew how much Jason and I love his music and what he does with words. I was the one who asked if he would officiate our wedding. He said he had never done that before but went and got his certification. He came in before we got married to talk to us about being married, and we told him what we were going for with the ceremony. What he said to us was beautiful. He treated us with the utmost care and respect. It was awesome for Todd to be the person to marry us. Todd said, "We're in the music business. Love is awesome."

Having him officiate our wedding was so cool because Todd was one of my songwriting heroes when I was in Texas. He was touring through once when I was trying to establish myself as a songwriter but didn't show up because his house was robbed. My first experience opening for Todd was that night and having to play the same six songs over and over. I started as a side person playing with the Texas Playboys, Billy Joe Shaver, anyone that would hire me. Billy Joe told me that I was a fine songwriter, and I should write my own songs. I thought he was firing me very nicely at first, but he really did think I was a good songwriter. I moved to Nashville a year later because I was having trouble getting booked as an artist.

I met Todd when they rescheduled that show in Dallas. I was young and probably drinking too much, but I guess he remembered me. I eventually had the same drummer as him named Paul Griffith when I moved to town. Todd can be careful about who he lets in and around, but I think

Paul vouched for me. I was playing on *Agnostic Hymns & Stoner Fables* soon after that. Then I started opening shows for Todd and playing with his band. My first bus tour was with him.

Todd has a way of working in the studio that I admire so much. He throws everything away for the creative process. He runs with that all day long. Everything is to serve the art and creative process. So much so that it's hard to find him in a moment where he's just Todd Snider. He's so embodied in this other part of the brain that most of us only access a couple hours a day. He's been practicing being in that space for years. The experience itself was all about feeling. The notes didn't have to be in tune as long as the feeling was right. Todd was very open to ideas. The process was almost democratic because he wasn't precious about what ideas were his.

He is secretly methodical and knows what sounds he wants to hear. He thinks on songs and poems and uses the players he knows. He picks people he has played with who don't get in the way too much of the right or wrong ways to play. You don't want to ever get in the way. Todd plays the songs in the keys that feel good to sing in, and sometimes he will let you play solos as long as you want to play them. That's pretty fun. He can challenge you to think even farther than your normal eight to twelve bars. Sometimes he will just talk instead of going into the next verse, which makes for a different show every night. He keeps you interested in playing. Plus, a good boss like Todd makes you want to play with him every night. Super fun.[6]

Singer-songwriter and fiddler Amanda Shires came into her own with albums like Carrying the Lightning *(2011) and* My Piece of Land *(2016). She frequently has toured with her ex-husband Jason Isbell and his band the 400 Unit.*

Elizabeth Cook

Todd rents a beautiful, sweet house out on [Old Hickory Lake] now. One side pretty much has all glass, so he wakes up to the lake every day. It's been really funny to watch Todd learn how to homestead. He honestly didn't know how to clean. I would have to show him simple things like how you use a broom and a dustpan, and how you might mop. He literally did not have those adult skills. He has way more rooms there than he needs. One just has a stuffed elephant in it. You know, the elephant in the room. One has a treadmill with an exercise bike in it. He has gotten way into gardening and has championship roses that piss me off. I love seeing him enjoy that.

Anyway, we have known each other for a while. I first heard Todd's music as a young woman when I moved to Nashville. I didn't realize there was a creative underbelly to the music scene at that point. I learned about Lucinda Williams and John Prine and would hear Todd's name came up in those circles. Then I was put on a show opening for him at a little shed in a park in Wilmington, North Carolina, after my *Balls* album came out around 2007. That show changed my life. I couldn't believe I was seeing this guy with an off-brand acoustic guitar throwing a party for about five hundred insane people. I was worried about him by the time we left. People were standing by the foot of the stage yelling, and there wasn't any security.

I didn't know this was something that was possible to pursue and achieve. I had a major label record deal and had had no exposure to his world. Warner Bros. wanted my first gig to be the CMA Awards. They weren't interested in me touring, but I knew I needed to in order to get better. Todd was on the road all the time with Skip back then. He had a successful path in music that didn't have ball gowns, arenas, and dumb songs. I had been invested in this game for years, and this was the route I wanted to take. Todd was doing it in such grand fashion. I mean, there was an ice sculpture at this Wilmington gig that said, "Fuck Luckenbach. Drink with us." He was doing his thing, being real, and having a good time.

Todd encouraged me to write whatever the fuck I wanted to write and tour at a more economical level. He was authentic and important. I probably would have gone back to whatever fucking job, but he changed my perspective. I already had a booking agent that had more of a bluegrass and folk background, and I was ready for the change. My old agent was only interested in booking me on package arena tours as I was brought up through the Music Row system. Then Todd started an early version of the East Nashville Bulldogs, and I married my boyfriend. We lived about a mile from Todd and Melita. We were all in East Nashville super early on.

I was so enamored with Todd. My husband would get frustrated when we would get a call to do something. Plans often fall through with Todd, but I looked at it like I'm gonna say yes if there was a 50 percent chance of something happening that Todd asked me to be involved with. Pray for the best, expect the worst. I never had a problem with that, but other musicians grumble about it. "Oh, he's just on a whim today. He's gonna fuck with a lot of people, and it's not gonna happen." There certainly was grumbling in my house. I was like, "This guy is a fucking genius who is winning the folk lottery."

I had that big-eyed little sister view of him. Then I had a nervous breakdown before making the *Balls* album. I do not understand what happened to me for about a decade, but Todd started letting the girl artist hang around after *Balls*. I became more than my guitar-playing husband's wife. Todd started viewing me as a real artist—a baby artist, but a real one. That was super encouraging. Todd made a few nice comments about the writing on *Balls*. Then I wrote *Welder* and started doing more shows and tours with Todd.

East Nashville was pretty barren when we got here. Dave Rawlings and Gillian Welch were at Woodland Studio. The studio was condemned after the tornado in 1998. Then they got movie money from *Oh Brother, Where Art Thou* and bought the studio. I think they still live there. They're always walking around. So, there was them, my husband and me, Todd and Melita, Chuck Mead at some point. There was Mike Grimes's Slow Bar. Todd started leading the pack in that he would talk about East Nashville. "Yeah, we have a neighborhood. We have a club. The real artists are on this side of the river." I feel like Todd manifested it.

Slow Bar later turned into the 3 Crow, which was right at the corner [of Woodland and South Eleventh streets] in Five Points. There really wasn't much going on with the music scene in East Nashville besides jams here and there back then. Slow Bar had rock bands. Brad Pemberton, who played with Ryan Adams and Steve Earle, had a wife who was a bartender there. Mike Grimes was playing with Bare Jr. at the time. Slow Bar was the first brick and mortar place with music for our crowd. It was a super cool, grungy dive. Lucinda [Williams] would go in there. Slow Bar was the spark in a physical sense for music on the east side.

I feel like many artists are singing bullshit for their own self-validation and branding, but the guy singing "Alright Guy" is the guy in the song. You can tell Todd's songs are based on his life and actual conversations. Music Row had homogenized stuff like Kenny Chesney and songs that are manipulative. Todd is not. I know he was on major labels like me early on, but his real self kept poking through with songs that had all those quirky specifics like "Talking Seattle Grunge Rock Blues." Todd relates to the flunky, the hobo, and the gypsy. He sings the underdogs' songs and is their voice. Todd is always defending his position about the little guy. Our conversations have always been very deep. We almost talk on a bigger and more philosophical scale than social issues and the mechanics of songwriting. Our conversations hit the runway and take off into la-la land. Everyone else falls away when we start talking.

Todd fearlessly stands up for himself. That hasn't always been easy with the personalities around him. He has become more of a force and has settled into himself from having to fight for himself, which is practically unheard of in Nashville. That's why when I saw that show in Wilmington, I was like, "No shit." Going on the road with Todd is great. I really value time with him and getting to travel together. We'll have hangs that bookend the day. His audiences are incredible. They're there to listen and have a good time, which is difficult to find. People usually talk all over you if you're a party band. A strict folk audience is boring as hell. Todd married the two, which is a dream for me. "Fuck yeah, this is like serious music but also a really good time."

I say yes every time Todd asks to go on the road if I can. There are always random people he knows from years of traveling coming on the bus, and always watermelon, Twizzlers, and weed. I remember Pamela Des Barres coming on the bus one time. Same with the guy who invented Crocs. I'm naturally fascinated with the people in this really interesting circus. I learned from a musical point that touring and performing isn't about technicalities or slick playing and singing but about finding a vibe and an intention and getting everyone on that page with you. I also learned a lot about handling crowds.

Todd demands respect. He gets pissed plenty. That's good for me to see as a woman in this business. He always has treated me like one of the guys, which I couldn't believe. My appreciation of Todd includes and expects all that like what I was saying with the Bulldogs. That's who Todd is. He's highly sensitive, smart, and dealing with his own shit. He's raw. Feels like you're looking into the sun when he's looking into your camera. He's very intense. He has to make decisions based on what he can handle. Somebody who can explain you to you in the way he does has a really high antenna. There's weather up there.

I'm more concerned about his self-care when he feels the need to bail on whatever we're doing than about him messing with my schedule. There is a circle of us—people like Kevn Kinney and Aaron Lee Tasjan—who are checking on each other constantly. Doing this is hard and lonely, with high pressure and stress, but the chains and expectations are off now that I'm older. I can do whatever. Making art that way is the only way anymore. It feels like I'm just manipulating people to sell something if I don't. There's a spirit of service. Your music helps people. We want to help people and get better. We always want the next album to be better than the last. It's still fun, and hopefully you get to a place where you can make travel easier by spreading out the dates and getting nicer hotels.

I was so sheltered when Todd asked me to sing "Little Bird" on his Jerry Jeff Walker tribute album [2012's *Time as We Know It*]. They didn't like Texas music where I grew up in Florida. We only had one mainstream country station and a rock station out of Orlando. Todd totally introduced me to Jerry Jeff. It meant a lot to me to be on something that I knew meant so much to him. We recorded with those sweethearts in Great American Taxi at House of Blues where I made *Welder*. Todd had all his Jerry Jeff Walker vinyl spread out on a table the whole time. I didn't even understand the weight of what I was doing. That's just one of the many ways Todd has mentored me. Todd's like my way smarter big brother.

There's no pressure with me and Todd. I'm not ever not gonna understand him. He's a good person, always has your back, and will fist fight anybody that picks on you. He's incredibly encouraging. I was really blindsided when I was asked to do the David Letterman show for the first time. It happened fast and I didn't understand why. My career was not at a level to be on late night shows. I wasn't even playing. I was just gonna sit and do an interview. It was very, very rattling. I went on that, and then I was in Los Angeles and there were big agents and all this shit like a sitcom deal with CBS going on.

Todd saw it all going on from a bird's-eye view. He sent me a very long email that included a metaphor about Tom Cruise and Johnny Depp. He said, "They're trying to make you Tom Cruise, but you're Johnny Depp." He meant that Tom Cruise is a massive action movie star, but Johnny Depp has more artistic integrity. God, I needed that. Nobody I knew had experience in that world. I'm a girl from a trailer park in Florida. So overwhelming. Todd was a lighthouse during that time. I forever will feel connected to Todd. I'm proud to call him my friend.

I was not in good mental or physical health that fateful week when we played the Americana awards in 2014. This girl who worked for me called in tears because of stuff she was hearing. It was so far-fetched. We were shocked. Dave Schools and Todd both knew that I was in trouble. They talked about going to [Thirty Tigers President] David Mascius about how to help me. I'm sitting at what's basically an intervention with my manager and am put in a rehab that almost killed me next thing I knew. Todd was always there. He knew the rehab deal and was always asking, "Okay, how can we get you out of here?" Everybody thought Todd and I were together because our divorces went down at the same time, but commiserating did push us closer together.

I had told my boyfriend that I would get to call him from rehab in seventy-two hours. I was scared to death. I was institutionalized. You have to give up everything—your credit cards, your ID, your money, your iPod. They thought my toothpaste was drugs. Really rattling. My boyfriend didn't answer when I was able to call, so the next call was to Todd. He picked up. He was the first human I got to talk to in rehab. I think that was a gift from God. He's always been there by my side even when I didn't ask him to be.

Todd not suing anyone over "Beer Run" is a karmic decision. You put a lot of effort, energy, and intention into suing someone. We take that as the automatic thing you would do in our American culture, but it's not the only option. You're gonna reserve that energy sometimes to aim it in a different direction. I know artists in Nashville that have been so screwed in the industry that they're so sour and bitter. Nobody wants to work with them because they're miserable people. Todd refuses to get in that zone. The sheer power of whether you direct your energy toward the light or not is so important. Todd doesn't like a bad time. Suing somebody sounds like a bad time. Money doesn't have a role in his lifestyle or personality.

Todd has done well living like he wants. He doesn't own a car. He did buy Burt's truck, which, of course, immediately wouldn't run. The truck just sits there with a Kevn Kinney cassette tape in it. We drove to get tacos in that truck with that tape one day, but Todd rented a car all year. He could have bought a car for what he paid to rent, but he doesn't want to own one. I think there's something about not completely going along with the system where you have to have rugs and Tupperware. Todd keeps it breezy and not mired down with responsibilities. I'm too chickenshit to do it. He's inspiring—to see someone not play into the herd mentality and capitalist system with everything they've got. He learned that from Jerry Jeff.[7]

Elizabeth Cook stirred waves with her albums Balls *(2007) and* Welder *(2010). The frequent David Letterman guest hosts* Elizabeth Cook's Apron Strings *on Sirius XM's Outlaw Country channel.*

Todd Snider

I did learn from Jerry Jeff. He and I stayed together a lot on trips, or I would go to Austin and stay with him for a few days. He gets up in the morning and sings to no one for no reason for a very long time. Every day. Beautifully. He sings like it's a concert. He's often singing a song that's rolling off him in the moment. You can tell it's not done, but he sings them like they are. He commits. He lets it out and fixes it next time he sings it. I have seen notepads in his room, but his singing was his healing, meditative process. I've always hoped that people his age still could use singing that way. I had this feeling that I would always love playing and singing when I first heard him singing in the morning. I knew it would never get away from me.

We went down to Belize one time when I was out of control. I left on my own, but I thought that was my end with Jerry Jeff. Keith Sykes told me that wouldn't happen. Jerry didn't work that way. I didn't know Jerry was in the crowd next time I played the Cactus Cafe [in Austin]. I was there alone without my band doing an hour show. He didn't know that was something I could do yet. It was the first time I had seen him outside his birthday parties. He yelled from the back, "You're free. You're a free man." I knew what he meant. Everyone heard him. He meant that you can always throw your hat on the ground and get free food. No one can ever tell you what to do again. It was like tattooing my face.

Then we went back to his house and talked—not about the songwriting, but the principle of being free. We sat around and sang his songs. That's my greatest memory. He was such a singer. He was relaxed. He could always keep it like a campfire. It was never like the Bluebird [Cafe in Nashville], but everyone still would shut up. I admired that. I think he got that from Hondo. I feel so much more appreciative of everything now that I'm older and have seen all the cats. I got a letter from Jamie Lin Wilson when Jerry Jeff died. I was gonna take her on tour with me last year. She and Hayes, Chicago Farmer, Sierra Ferrell, and Aaron Lee Tasjan give me goosebumps.

Jamie Lin Wilson

My brother had learned how to play guitar by the time he came home from college. He came into my parents' house, sat down, and played Todd's song "Alright Guy." He gets to the part about tearing up pictures of the Pope and smoking dope, and I was like, "What is happening right now?"

My parents are super conservative small-town people. Todd was already gone by the time I got to San Marcos, but I became friends with Kent and the Finlays. They were all so close to Todd, which I thought was so cool. Todd came in for Songwriters Night one time when I was a brand-new baby songwriter. Kent was on my team and said, "Hey, Todd is our special guest tonight. I'm gonna put you on right before him to make sure he's in the room when you're playing."

I don't know if Todd really watched my set that night. I was too nervous and didn't open my eyes, but I sat down later and watched him play. I remember being in such awe. I've learned from Todd ways to keep people interested in your show and how to be funny and tell stories. Also, I learned how to have a little depth and humor and how to write sad songs. Kent sometimes would play songs they had written together. Todd and Kent really loved each other. Hearing Kent talk about Todd was like hearing him talk about his own kid. His eyes would twinkle. Kent talked about him with such admiration and pride.

I know every note on *East Nashville Skyline* like some people know Robert Earl Keen's *No. 2 Live Dinner*. Somebody asked me at a show the other day if I could play Todd Snider songs, and I almost played "Iron Mike's Main Man's Last Request." "Iron Mike" so perfectly captures this character. "Hey, little buddy"—he's calling Mike Tyson "little buddy"—"Don't get angry. God please at least not at me." Just funny. Then he talks about all the cars in his driveway and gets mad about carrying the boom box. The song is a trip through this peon's thought process. He presumably pays for it at the end. How do you think of writing that? "You know who needs a song? Mike Tyson's personal assistant." I love when he says "Me, Mike. Goddamn it. Me."

Todd makes writing sound so easy, like the way Billy Joe Shaver wrote. Seems like he just sits down with a guitar, and all this information comes out. "That was cool. Let's record it." I'm sure it takes much more work than that. We all try to use the simplest words. You can't relate to a song if you don't understand what's happening. The way Todd does that and the stories he uses to connect the songs [are unbelievable]. His stories go halfway into the songs, which seems like the last half of the story. Laid-back. He's just talking to you, and it happens to rhyme. *East Nashville Skyline* is full of songs like that. "Tillamook County Jail" is like a Tom T. Hall song with the easy humor. I don't write like that often because it's so hard to do well.[9]

Jamie Lin Wilson emerged as a singular songwriter with the Sidehill Gougers and the Trishas. Her solo albums include Holidays & Wedding Rings *(2015) and* Jumping Over Rocks *(2018).*

Andrew Dansby

My wife and I flew into Tacoma a few years ago. We went to see Prince shows there and in Victoria, but we mainly went to road-trip around the Northwest. We were coming back down from the Prince show in Victoria and passed Tillamook, Oregon. I thought, "Let's call it a day. It's late." We visited a cheese factory, checked into our hotel, and went to this pizza place. We were eating our pizza with nobody other than these three families at this table adjacent to us. They kept apologizing for their kids. We were like, "Your kids are fine. Our kid's not here, but she would be making a racket too if she were."

We eventually struck up a conversation. They were all in law enforcement. I was still drinking back then, but I wasn't so drunk that my antenna didn't go up. "Wait, you're in law enforcement here in Tillamook?" "Yeah." "Have you heard a song . . . ?" These three cops and their spouses start singing "Tillamook County Jail." They were really drunk but invited us to the jail the next day. "We can show you where Todd got fucked up." My wife and I are the people who ring the doorbell the next day when we're invited to shit like that. We showed up, and they are red-eyed but recognized us. Todd told me a couple weeks ago that he notices every year there's a merch order from the Tillamook sheriff's office.[10]

Jamie Lin Wilson

Todd's songs feel like he's talking only to you like with "The Ballad of the Kingsmen." Again, who thinks of that? "The Kingsmen came together in a garage . . ." People are like, "What is he talking about?" Todd makes me want to try harder and be more inventive in my songwriting. You write then revise, revise, revise. He has political songs that make people go, "Hey, I'm a conservative Christian, right-wing Republican." They still love Todd because at same time he's going, "Pot-smoking, lazy-ass hippies like me." He dogs himself as he dogs them. He has that way of shrugging things off so everyone else does the same. They love him for it. He's just speaking a little bit of truth, and everybody can recognize the truth.

Todd was gonna produce [Wilson's former group] the Trishas' record. We had the same manager before we had even made our first EP. So, we loaded up our van to head to Nashville to make the EP with Todd. Our manager called [Trisha singer Kelley] Mickwee and said, "Hey, y'all need to turn around and go back to Austin. Todd can't do it anymore. He's headed to Texas to be a character witness at Billy Joe Shaver's trial." We were like, "Well, shit." That was our only window of time with him. So, we got stood up by Todd Snider because he had to be in the courtroom for Billy Joe Shaver when he shot that guy in the face. I wasn't even mad about it. It's actually awesome. "Huh. This will be a fun story to tell later."[11]

Jonny Burke

I went to prison a few years ago. The prison investigator, who inspects all your tattoos and reads all your mail to make sure you're not in a gang that will threaten the general population, told me when I came in, "I know who you are. I can get you a guitar if you want." "That would be great." I ended up playing a show every Friday for the sixty-six-man dorm that I lived in. I mostly played stuff like "Folsom Prison Blues." People in jail love prison songs, but then I tried to play my own songs once or twice. Didn't work. They didn't like them. I tried out Todd Snider's "Alright Guy." People fucking loved it. They yelled for it from then on.

That song works for a bunch of locked up motherfuckers. It's a great song to sing along to. They eventually found out that I was a songwriter, and people would think that I wrote that song. "No, man, I didn't write that song. A guy named Todd Snider wrote that song." They wouldn't believe me. "You're in here for drinking and driving. You wrote that song." I couldn't convince them otherwise. I would play that song every week. Eventually I was like, "Yeah, man, I wrote that song." I told Todd this. My girlfriend said that Todd sent me an email when I was in prison. He wanted to give me a gift when I got out. I'm still waiting.

I have known Todd's music forever. I had a brother growing up who was seven years older than me. He had *Songs for the Daily Planet* playing in his car right when it came out. I would be riding in the back seat of my brother's car hearing "Easy Money," "My Generation," and especially "Talking Seattle Grunge Rock Blues." We all listened to Pearl Jam and Soundgarden, so I thought "Seattle Grunge Rock" was the most hilarious thing I had heard. Then I was twelve years old in middle school, years later, and heard Todd was playing at Gruene Hall. I had my mom drop me off. I was standing on one of the tables. I thought it was incredible that he was playing solo with just an acoustic guitar. Everybody around me was older, loud, and partying.

Todd's crowds are always so eclectic. You have frat boys and businessmen like my brother who fell in love with Todd's songs. You have your hippies, miscreants, vagabonds who are all so intelligent and laugh at the right time. They're all people Todd has somehow gotten to be his. Everybody enjoys a good story while being entertained. Todd's shows are entertaining, and his songs are so smart. People appreciate that. Some songs are silly. You know that you're gonna be entertained when you go to his show.

The fact that Todd has the balls to start a show with a ballad like "Lonely Girl" sat with me. I used to have a band called the Dedringers that opened for Todd on several tours. Todd had me open up a tour a month after we broke up, but I didn't realize that he wanted to produce my album. He sat me down the first night in the green room. "Yeah, man," he said. "I would love to go in the studio with you." "Yeah," I said. "You should hear these demos." I don't know what mood he was in, but he told his manager to tell my manager to kick me off the tour tomorrow.

He said he didn't know why I was on the tour if he wasn't gonna produce my album. That was very hurtful. I remember sitting in a Starbucks parking lot in Colorado being like, "Well, am I going to the next show or am I going back to Texas?" Everybody settled things eventually. "No, no, Todd's keeping you on the tour." I told them that I didn't realize he wanted to produce my album. Todd gave me the best apology that I had ever heard the next day in the green room. "I'm playing the rest of these shows, right?" "Yeah, man, I'm sorry." The only thing I could say was, "Well, man, seems like you have done this apology before."[12]

Jonny Burke led his group the Dedringers into regional popularity around the South before staking claim to a solo career that has seen him open for Americana royalty James McMurtry.

Bob Schneider

I played a show with Todd Snider in Corpus Christi and shared a trailer dressing room, which is the only time we really hung out. I was a huge fan by then. Honestly, I was a little starstruck. *East Nashville Skyline* is one of my favorite records of all time. I really wanted Todd to like me, but I didn't want to bother him. I remember talking about drinking and drugs because I've been sober for twenty-five years. Todd was telling me about his drinking regimen. He would have a beer like thirty minutes before the show so he wouldn't get too fucked up. I said, "How's that working for you?" "Pretty good," he said, "but I'm not happy." The way he said it was funny, dude. That dude is as funny as anyone I've ever seen play music.

"Mike Tyson's Main Man's Last Request" is so funny, but at the same time there is so much going on about the relationship between Mike Tyson, the other guy, and their world. So profound and sad. So much underneath the funny stuff. The guy has a longing to be loved and will do whatever it takes to get there both with Mike and this other guy. Writing a great song is tough, but writing a really profoundly good song isn't mysterious. I understand how. It's a subconscious, intuitive process, but the way Todd does that is real genius.

I am not impressed often. It doesn't do it for me if I see a song that I can write. It's like watching a magic trick when you know how the trick is done. You can appreciate it if they have great sleight of hand abilities, but I get impressed when I don't know how it's done. Todd creates these magic tricks I don't know how to do. I'll create magic tricks every once in a while. I'll say, "Wow. I don't know where or how that was made." My subconscious is working with my conscious brain and letting it flow. Then it comes out. It's in my brain moving underneath the surface. Todd does that incredibly well. He does that as good as anybody writing songs.

"The Ballad of the Kingsmen" is such an amazing, beautiful, perfectly crafted song. I always think of songs like solvable equations. The best are short, simple, and fully solved. My least favorite songs are really intricate and never solved. Rush is a prime example. They're not solving shit. They're just making nonsense noise all day long. Todd is deceptively simple. You don't have to explain things. Kurt Cobain wrote these songs, and you were like, "What the fuck is he talking about?" You don't know. Nonsense. Todd doesn't adorn songs like "Play a Train Song" with bullshit. He's telling it like it is, like a great storyteller. You leave out the bullshit and tell what needs to be told. You don't know what's going on at first, but then the song reveals itself and reveals itself, and you go, "How amazing is that?"

Todd probably couldn't believe the song was turning out so well when he was writing "Play a Train Song." The best songs I've ever written immediately present themselves as to what they are. Then you're just writing down the words. They come almost complete. "Play a Train Song" must have been one of those. I can look at my songs when I write them and know which parts are weak and shitty or strong. I tend to be like, "Well, fuck it." I'll leave the shitty parts on there because I want to write the next song. I'm not very disciplined. It sounds like Todd takes the extra time to keep working on his songs until they're actually solved.[13]

Singer-songwriter Bob Schneider pays bills simply by playing residencies around his hometown of Austin. Lonelyland *(2000) and* Lovely Creatures *(2009) have cemented his capacity crowds.*

Steve Poltz

Todd Snider was in the Nervous Wrecks when I was in the Rugburns. I was turned on to him with "Talking Seattle Grunge Rock Blues." I thought that was a funny fucking song, which was like an updated Arlo Guthrie song with a little Mark Twain. We both would play *The Bob and Tom Show* [on WBFQ in Indianapolis]. Todd and I painted each other's toenails the first time we hung out. We were at an outdoor festival in Indianapolis, and I thought he was so cool. We played wiffle ball inside the venue with Will Kimbrough. I loved watching his shows because you don't always see someone who can own a crowd when they want.

I watched his solo troubadour vibe when I was starting to go solo myself. The Rugburns were fun but hard to keep together. I remember seeing Todd at McCabe's Guitar Shop around then, which was when Jewel's ["You Were Meant for Me," which Poltz cowrote] was happening. I was really inspired. Todd was staying in a little hotel right down the street from McCabe's. This was before I got sober, and we were smoking weed and drinking whiskey at a bar. I remember he had his guitar in the room and two porno magazines. I loved that he had those two magazines. The room was disheveled the way you would expect.

People were on their feet at the show. So good and inspiring. Todd's music inspires and moves me to be better at my own craft. "Oh yeah, I see where they're going with that." I never get tired of seeing people play live shows. I'm not the guy who goes to a show and says, "Oh, that sucks." I could go see Justin Bieber and learn something. He's obviously got talent. Then you see someone like Todd. He walked out onstage barefoot before his doctor told him to wear shoes. I like studying another songwriter and seeing how they go about their craft, which I always do with comedians and musicians. I look at it with an eye as someone who has played ten thousand hours everywhere and played festivals, going, "How is this person going about it?" I'm not thinking, "How is Rodney Crowell going about it?"

I find beauty in what Todd does. He's able to bring together all these misfits who definitely have different political views, but they somehow all fit together. Todd is unapologetic and unabashed about who he is onstage, yet he's also super sensitive. I've seen him walk offstage when something spooks him. He says, "This is not right." We both played River Roots Festival in southern Indiana about two years ago. I played my set and wanted to see Todd the next night, but I had another show and was so bummed. The promoter and I went to a late-night diner. I told him, "Tell Todd I said hi." He said, "It was weird. He showed, but they wouldn't strike the drums from this guy who was a Nashville songwriter going on after Todd. Todd said, "I'm not going on unless the drums are struck." He wanted the stage clear so he would have his stuff set up.

I remember thinking that I can respect that. He knows what he wants. I always appreciate people who have their quirks. His quirk was that he didn't want to get up there with drums behind him. The promoter was such a huge Todd fan and finally struck the drums, but Todd was like, "Clear all the merch. We're out of here." Todd's Midwest fans had driven far and wide and were like, "Come on, play." The bus was gone. I was like, "Whoa." So fucking random. He just walked offstage another time at the Mint in Los Angeles when the crowd was being loud. I like him so much probably because my favorite band is the Replacements. You would see them one night, and it would be a shambolic mess. The next show would be the greatest in the world.

I always like characters who can have things go sideways one night and then pure brilliance the next night. I remember seeing Todd once at an outdoor street festival in Nashville where he killed. Destroyed. Todd went on after Lucinda Williams. "I'm really glad she wasn't 'on' tonight," he said. Saying that was so honest. I'm really close with Bob Schneider, and Bob will flat out tell me that he doesn't want to do a show with me. He won't even watch me if I go on before him. "You're gonna have the crowd," he will say. "I want you to do horribly." Bob will tell me this, so I thought it was funny that Todd would say that.

I have seen him play so many shows. The last time was at the Ryman Auditorium in Nashville. I played the night before at the Purple Building. Dude, it was mass mayhem. His fans are insane. I had all these new fans overnight who were such nice people. Todd's fans are out of their minds the way Rugburns fans were. Todd's Ryman show was one of the greatest ever because of how he puts stories together. He tied together the story at the beginning to the end. His dog Cowboy Jim was still alive, and my friend Stacie Huckeba took the most beautiful photo of them walking offstage. My buddy Tim Easton and I were arm in arm backstage. That's what a show was supposed to be like. Then we all went to Acme Feed and Seed after where my friend Allen Thompson's Grateful Dead cover band was playing.

Todd walks that fine line being a shaggy dog who admits his own faults. You want to take him in. He admits who he is with no apologies, finds the warmth in someone's heart, and reaches that point that makes you feel something and go, "Wow. I want to take some friends to see this so we can share." Music should do that. You have right and left wingers at the show. Todd encapsulates that perfectly in "Conservative Christian, Right-Wing Republican, Straight, White, American Males." He talks about being a porn-watching, tree-hugging person and using all these pejorative terms to describe the image right wingers have of him, but he's making them laugh about it. Genius. He brings it all together.

Todd's fans are all joining in over their love of him. There are circles where we call each other names, yet all these circles come together at his shows. Todd brings them together so they can laugh at the absurdity. Also, Todd has found a balance between fucking up and not fucking up too much. He knows not to fuck up the big Ryman show. It's interesting and admirable in some ways that he wouldn't play that one time when there was a drum riser onstage. Can you imagine if I did that? That's not how I am. Stacie always says I represent the light side, and Todd represents the dark side.

Dark and light are good together, which is why I love to be around Todd and Bob Schneider. There was a guy coming up the ranks years ago when I was playing at Java Joe's in San Diego, and we both were wearing a trucker hat. I would come out and tell stories. He would come out and tell stories. He ended up becoming really big. His name is Jason Mraz. People were like, "Fuck that guy. He stole your thing." I was like, "No, he didn't. He's fucking awesome. That guy can sing and play guitar." He doesn't play my kind of music, but he's fucking great.

I felt the same way the first time I saw Todd as when I saw Loudon Wainwright. I was like, "Whoa." There was a feeling more than jealousy or competitiveness that I could do this. This is cool. I told Loudon he inspired me to think that I could go solo and make a living playing onstage. I didn't mind seeing Todd do well because I like seeing people who are really good. You don't want to let people affect your schtick. You just want to be yourself. Todd had me open a few shows at City Winery in Atlanta, and it was a no-brainer that they were gonna be cool. It could have been like when I opened for Ozomatli, and someone threw a beer can at my head. They were there that night to see Ozomatli.

You might think that Todd and I are too similar to play the same show, but it was like how John Prine would have Todd open. I would ask Al Bunetta, "Does John get bummed?" "No," Al said. "John wants people to kill. He loves it." I don't know if he gets worried about that, but I prefer having a girl open my shows because it's different. Then I found out that John Prine liked having Todd open. I would go see Todd anytime on a night off. I will go get his record when he puts one out and will be excited the way I would when Prine or the Replacements would have a new album. I like to study the twists they take and go, "Oh. Cool." Going to see Todd is like getting a booster shot or how some people would see [life strategist] Tony Robbins.

We're all these manifestations of God, and Todd is a beautiful flower the same way Mark Twain was Mark Twain. Everybody has their own strength all based on love. Love is the key to everything. That sounds so hippie-dippie, but it's true. Really meditate on love. Seeing Todd makes me happy. Sometimes I think he needs to be loved. We're all insecure, which is why we got into this business. We're always comparing ourselves to other people. I can listen to a Guy or Townes record and say, "I should have written that." What makes it so good? What made Townes write, "He wore his gun outside his pants for all the world to feel" instead of "outside his pants for all the world to see"? My mom used to always ask, "How did that make you feel?" Todd makes me feel things, and for that I'm grateful. He's a gift worth celebrating.[14]

Steve Poltz might be best known as cowriter of Jewel's hit "You Were Meant for Me," but the folk singer's albums like the Will Kimbrough-produced Shine On *better capture his sharp wit.*

Tim Easton

Todd Snider and I were at Las Manitas in Austin one time during South by Southwest. He sat down next to me at the counter and said, "Hey, what's your stuff sound like?" We discussed what we were doing. Todd said he had been hanging out in Texas for a while. I didn't see him again until we played a couple shows together in Ohio. Then he canceled a couple shows that I was on with him. We played the Rolling Stones song "Far Away Eyes" when they put Chris Smither and us onstage together with Levon Helm's daughter Amy's gospel band at the Winnipeg Folk Festival one time. I wrote "Festival Song" [from Easton's 2011 collection *Since 1966*] that weekend.

We played a gig at a Catholic church in Kentucky another time. I went backstage, which was the rectory in the guy's house, and the room reeked from weed. Todd was sitting on the couch. "Dude," I said. "This is the priest's house." "Whatever," Todd said. "Jesus smoked herb." I have a true-story song ["Broken Brain"] on [2019's *Exposition*] that says, "I married a redhead, she's a fighter / Smokes more weed than you or Todd Snider." That's an easy comic line, but I delivered it with timing each night on a run we did recently with very much success.

[Easton's ex-wife Katie Shaw] doesn't like the song too much, but she laughs about it. Some Keith Richards types are constitutionally able to truck it all down. Then they need more the more they do. I can't imagine being as baked as Todd gets and walking out onstage. The Sadies do the same thing. They would smoke a huge joint and go onstage. I thought, "Well, that's just a different skill set that I don't really have or want to have." I've smoked weed and played before, but that was around the house. I was in a jam band in Joshua Tree that would smoke and play every Sunday, but there were eight people in the band. You had to get into their wavelength.

Weed calms people down and makes them feel more free and open, but I prefer not to be so spaced-out onstage. I'm doing too many things and can't have interference. Todd has made a career out of it. He talks about it onstage. He just acknowledges it when he has a weird moment onstage. I'm always like, "Yeah maybe it's because you just blazed a ton of weed. Maybe it wasn't the right strain." He's very similar to Mitch Hedberg. Some people wouldn't be able to function without weed. They prefer to go through life absolutely tilted. I've tried. I was a weed farmer for a while. Didn't work out. I was smoking all day eventually. Smoking before I got out of bed. Smoking to go to the Kroger. Smoking to go to the bank. Everybody's different. I might have pointed fingers before, but I can't really point fingers anymore.[15]

Traveling troubadour Tim Easton honed his chops busking streets in Europe for seven years before turning heads stateside with Break Your Mother's Heart *(2003) and* You Don't Really Know Me *(2021).*

Todd Snider

Mitch Hedberg and I knew each other from *The Bob and Tom Show*. People were telling me I talked like Mitch, but I came before him. I know I didn't get my [delivery] from him, and I don't think he got his from me. I kept working harder on it. Mitch and I had the exact same drug regimen in the last years before he died. Sounds dark. I always wondered if drugs had something to do with his rhythm. He was on pain pills, was stoned, and had had a few drinks, which gave him a weird rhythm.

Aaron Lee Tasjan

I discovered Todd's music when I was fifteen and just starting to write songs. An older friend who was playing guitar in my band gave me this tape called *Prime Prine*. I wore that out. Then I took it to Magnolia Thunderpussy Records in Columbus, Ohio, and was like, "Hey, man. I really like this. Do you have anything else like this?" "Yeah, man." He gave me *Songs for the Daily Planet*. I thought Todd was doing what Prine was doing for my generation. Then I saw him open some Thanksgiving shows for Drivin N Cryin solo at the Roxy Theater in Atlanta and one at the Georgia Theatre in Athens, Georgia.

I felt like the way Todd describes watching his first Jerry Jeff Walker shows when I saw Todd. I didn't know it was possible to open for an incredibly loud rock 'n' roll band in a giant theater just playing acoustic guitar and saying really funny shit. Todd became my new gold standard for performing. I had been a fan of his music, but seeing those gigs sealed the deal. I became a huge, obsessive fan and listened endlessly. I listened to pretty much nothing but Todd Snider, Guy Clark, Jerry Jeff Walker, and John Prine. John Prine is cool. Todd is cool, but in different ways. He has this cool rock 'n' roll Keith Richards vibe.

Todd has this devilish grin that gives a certain quality to his work even when it's Mark Twain funny. The only other person I can think of who has that same dark rock vibe is Nick Cave. Listen to how Todd describes waiting in an alley and hearing footsteps in "Highland Street Incident." His songs are dark even though they're funny. Prine songs are more sad and funny. I love the darkness in Todd's songs, but he also has very beautiful sentimental moments in his early albums. He has solidified that edge he has in the last few records.

Todd lives on the edge. I love "Just Like Old Times." Remember that movie *Searching for Sugarman*? I went to a premiere and sat by Craig Finn from the Hold Steady. He was like, "Hey, man, what have you been up to?" I said, "I just played a couple shows with Todd Snider." He was like, "Is that the guy who wrote the song 'Just Like Old Times'"? I thought that was amazing because people usually say "Beer Run" or "Talking Seattle Grunge Rock Blues." "Just Like Old Times" is a timeless song. The lyrics are so specific and come with Todd's dark humor. Todd talks about these seedy characters from disparate parts of society, but they're the heroes in his song. What a beautiful twist. He allows us to celebrate a side of humanity that we don't usually talk about. His songs are cinematic.

Todd calls up the local gang to make musical mayhem with the Eastside Bulldogs. He's the perfect ringleader with the right top hat for the job. It's really cool that he uses stuff like a cool neighborhood band as a way to build community. Anybody can have a lame night when people get together and talk about how hard the music business is. Todd builds community around the art. He's the consummate artist. He finds ways to include all these great singers and musicians in a band with him to capture the moment in time. We all played on the record, and now we have that moment in time forever.[16]

Aaron Lee Tasjan has performed with folk legend Pete Yarrow, Americana all-stars Drivin N Cryin, and punk icons New York Dolls. Silver Tears (2016) established his songwriting chops.

Todd Snider

My favorite record is *Eastside Bulldogs*, which is music I grew up on. I don't overthink or wonder if the words aren't good enough. They're about fighting and fucking, driving a car and rocking out. Partying balls. I was thinking I was this guy Elmo Buzz who hated Todd Snider when I created the Bulldogs. I hated what was happening in East Nashville. Like the guy in leather pants who I saw down at the 3 Crow one time. I knew he was an A&R guy spying from the wrong side of town. He came over and talked to me like he didn't know who I was, but I know for a fact he knew. "Hey, fuck you, pretty boy. Go back to Franklin. I didn't come here to listen to music. I came here to look at some boobs like an adult."

Elmo Buzz loves Hank Williams Jr. He's almost "Louie Louie" if you take out the words. I tried to get Hank Jr. in to sing on "Bocephus," which probably has the best lyrics I have written. I wanted him to walk down Second Avenue and let me feel him in slow motion, but he wouldn't do it. He probably felt like he was getting picked on. I don't mind Republican singers. I love them actually. I think, "There's a guy letting it all hang out." Toby Keith is showing me his whole fucking heart. Cool. I don't give a shit what he does in his spare time. Same thing with this cat Casey Beathard, who made a solo record once that was the opposite of me. I thought, "This guy is fucking great." He's like what I'm trying to do, except I don't wanna be a good guy.[17]

Aaron Lee Tasjan

The Bulldogs get to hang out with Todd Snider and have a musical communion. We're all ambitious in the sense that we all want to write good songs. Sometimes we spend days out on the lake on the boat bullshitting about ideas for songs. Other times those days will turn into songwriting sessions. Kevn Kinney, Chuck Mead, and I got together at Todd's house one day and ended up writing a couple songs. You never know what interesting thing to expect when you go to Todd's. My fondest memories are when Todd plays pieces of new songs that he's working on. We get to hear how he shapes what ultimately will be on the record.

Agnostic Hymns & Stoner Fables is great with songs like "In the Beginning," "Too Soon to Tell," and "Brenda," which is Keith Richards's nickname for Mick Jagger. Todd continues to reinvent what I thought was possible in a song. He offers different sides and takes. Each new thing that he offers up is actually good. It's probably maddening because he works so incredibly hard for those songs, but his batting average as a songwriter is pretty remarkable.[18]

Darrin Bradbury

Todd Snider's *Storytellers* and *Near Truths and Hotel Rooms* live albums were the first ones I bought. I became enamored by his ability to tell underdog stories and be arrogant and humble at the same time. I was in an indie rock band at the time and tried showing his music to the guys.

They were like, "Is this a comedy record?" "No," I said. "This is amazing songwriting." My relationship with that music, along with John Prine and other artists I really liked, became how I got to Nashville. Todd's songs became really personal to me. I lived the life Todd was singing about in songs like "Greencastle Blues." He was singing the life I was living right then, and I fell in love with his studio records when I moved to Nashville.

You understand why Todd is the way he is when you see him play in an intimate setting like the 5 Spot in Nashville. Todd doesn't even need a guitar onstage. You can't take your eyes off him. I don't know how he does it, but it's even more so when he's onstage. You don't even have to be a fan. You will become one when he gets onstage because there's something so enigmatic about whatever tortured, twisted illustration is in that guy's soul. You have to look at him like a piece of art in a gallery. His songs are just him cracking a smile. Everything he does is art. I picked up pretty quickly that he's elusive. I played a song for him the night we met and thought it was the coolest thing in the world that he laughed at one of my lines.

Todd preaching about East Nashville is exactly why I moved down there. I wanted to know what the East Nashville skyline and all the liquor and tobacco stores looked like. I know that Todd, Sturgill [Simpson], and Jonny Fritz lived there. "I need to be there. That's what's going on." Todd had a huge impact. I think he's a better energy to be observed than to be known. I just prefer to know his work rather than the man. I don't know why. He's a good dude who I like just fine, but there's something maybe like a starstruck thing I have. It's not that there's a bubble to burst. Nashville bursts all those already.[19]

Darrin Bradbury well represents East Nashville's quirky outlook. He has developed a significant regional following with offbeat albums like Talking Dogs & Atomic Bombs (2019).

Brian Wright

I was in Ireland on tour when my friend Catherine Feeney played me *East Nashville Skyline*. I was a big fan immediately. Songs like "Age Like Wine," "Tillamook County Jail," and really that whole record blew my mind driving through the Irish countryside. I felt like I was discovering John Prine. I saw Todd play one show during his residency many years ago at the Mint in Los Angeles. I didn't go for a few weeks, but a good friend kept telling me, "You have to go see this guy Todd Snider. You're gonna love it." Of course, I fucking loved it. Best thing I have ever seen. I saw him a year or two later at the El Rey, which was about a quarter full, with Elizabeth Cook opening. I was so embarrassed my town didn't know this incredible dude.

I felt a personal connection to Todd's attitude then and can relate even more now. "Seven managers, five labels, a bunch of picks and patch cables, three vans, a band, a bunch of guitar stands, and cans and cans of beer" [from "Age Like Wine"]. That was me to a T. I wish I would have written that song. I liked how clever and funny he was and how he didn't seem to give a fuck. He didn't try too hard, but he was still winning. The best storytellers plan it all out but seem off the cuff. No accident. It would be scary if anyone was that good without planning ahead. Then there's "Just Like Old Times" about the hooker. His banter is funny as shit, which is the hardest job in the entertainment industry in my estimation.[20]

Singer-songwriter Brian Wright tours as guitarist in Aaron Lee Tasjan's band and has carved his own niche with influences from Townes Van Zandt to the Velvet Underground.

Jon Latham

I knew Todd from when *Songs for the Daily Planet* came out, but the first record that really made me aware of him was *The Devil You Know*. That came out when I was the age of going to Bonnaroo. Also, my dad had gotten a subscription to Outlaw Country on Sirius. They were playing "Looking for a Job" pretty heavily. Then I went back to get records like *Happy to Be Here*. I finally got to see him live at Bonnaroo in 2007. He was doing his thing solo in the tent in front of however many thousands. His crowd control in a festival setting with the stories was what made me fall in love with what he did and how he did it.

Even his darker songs have a subtle humor. He wrote songs about serious things that weren't being taken too seriously. You could tell what he was saying, but he was telling you in the way that a friend would tell you at the bar. Todd got across his beliefs without becoming preachy. He introduced me as a songwriter to the idea that you can be direct with your opinions if you deliver them in a song-and-dance way so no one's feelings get hurt. Todd's always been very inclusive, but he's not afraid to tell you where he stands. He has lots of life experience in his pocket. He got that by being open to the adventure even though he doesn't know how the story would end or how he would get out of it. He wasn't like, "Jesus, how will I get out of this pickle?" More like, "Let's see where this goes."

Look at the pantheon of rare-bird songwriters he's put into. I think back to a video of a Bob Dylan press conference in 1966. Dylan had a sit-down press conference at a poetry convention. You can tell the press is trying to pinpoint exactly what makes him Bob Dylan. I think the question asked was, "Do you consider yourself a poet?" "No," he said. "I'm a song-and-dance man." I think of people like Jerry Jeff Walker, John Prine, and Todd Snider when I think of song-and-dance people. Snider was the next generation. They all write great songs, but his purpose in life is to travel from town to town and tell these stories to a group of folks. Some have heard them and love them. Some are just discovering him. Todd has a minstrel thing that goes back to Chaucer and *The Canterbury Tales*.

I'm trying to commit to the lifestyle. I'm green to touring and have expanded the past couple years as my fan base expands, but I have held down a job at a retail drug store for fifteen years. I think part of the lifestyle is being honest with yourself about whether you can sustain yourself with it. Rent prices in Nashville when Todd did it were such that you could throw yourself to the wolves. He could go out for a couple weeks and make enough bread to put groceries on your table for a while. You have to have a willingness to realize that this is absolutely fun even with the rigors of the road. Getting into a van to go to a town you don't live in to play a gig and miraculously find people showing up never gets old.

The work is the rush. You're constantly tired, eating crap food, sleeping on couches when you're on the road. I don't mind working a job at a drug store as a supplemental income to make sure I have a roof over my head when I come back home, but it's not like I'm looking to Walgreens for a career opportunity. Walgreens has the ways and means to make sure I can make the music I need to make. That's scratching the back there. I think if someone came to town who thought they would put out a record independently in East Nashville and go rent a tour bus and go out and play listening rooms would find out very quickly how much money they would lose. Also, there's no creature comfort in that. You have to be open to the adventure of it all and not mind sleeping on a couch or floor. The adventure is what it's all about.

Todd's "Hey Pretty Boy" is hilarious. He wrote that as an Elmo Buzz song way before I came to Nashville. You pick up on Todd's experience in Nashville from the stories he tells. I originally was playing open mics more in places on the west side and midtown like Belcourt Taps and Bobby's Idle Hour. They throw you into these writers rounds with kids who are writing pop songs. They're fishing for publishing deals writing songs about whiskey, tailgating, and trucks, and hope to God that song gets cut by Kenny Chesney. They will make millions and be set for life. I wish I could write songs like that.

You come to Nashville if you're them. Write your hit song. The song gets cut. You can afford your luxurious house in Franklin and never have to come back to town again. "Hey Pretty Boy" has taken on a life in East Nashville. My friend Darrin Bradbury and I met at an open mic. He came over to the west side where I was doing mine and we did our songs. He introduced me to Tim Carroll and had me do some writers rounds with him. Swapping songs with Tim Carroll was some rock star shit for me. Darrin eventually dragged me kicking and screaming to East Nashville. He booked a gig for me at the 5 Spot. Tim Easton, Allen Thompson, Jack Schmidt, and Darrin were on the bill. Everyone from that group was there. I met Aaron Lee Tasjan there.

Aaron and Darrin changed my life. They championed me before I was even across the river. "Hey Pretty Boy" pops up at nearly every Aaron Lee show I have ever done because it's a fun, dumb rock song to end a set with. That's exactly what makes those Elmo Buzz songs so fun. They're two or three chords and a bunch of dumb shit. "Hey Pretty Boy" hits on all cylinders. Sit with anybody who says they're anybody in the industry, and they're name-dropping like motherfuckers just like I am in this interview. A level of bullshit comes with that. I tell my friends who come here from Atlanta that they need to pack a toothbrush and a good bullshit detector. Keep that thing calibrated. The deal probably is too good to be true.

East Nashville is just your neighborhood if you live there. You'll talk some other time if someone comes over to East Nashville while you're watching your friend's gig and offers you a publishing deal. You're like, "I just came here to drink a beer and hear my friend's band play and maybe go home with somebody." Nobody here wants to talk about publishing here. Don't be that dude at the bar. Don't bother Gillian Welch if you walk into Five Points Pizza and see her sitting there. Tourist shit. "Hey Pretty Boy" is the unofficial anthem of East Nashville in a two-minute song. It gets across our mentality, which is that we're gonna do this whether we make money or not, in a humorous way. Go back to Franklin if you're so worried about the money part. They have plenty there.

Todd put out a single just the other day on social media called "L. W. D. (Little White Dick)." His brain is always working in that way even when he's fucking around. He finds a shortcut way to get right to the point. Todd can be entertaining and meaningful at the same time. That entire *Eastside Bulldog* album and Elmo Buzz material is like that. *Eastside Bulldog* is regionally based, but it's interesting to see how many songs on that album are still great. That's a very underappreciated Todd record. People think the songs are silly. That album hits close to home if you live here.

"Come on Up" is an interesting bookend to "Hey Pretty Boy." He's talking to the very same kid and saying, "Hey, you go get your shit together. Find yourself in East Nashville with a lawnmower that has been stolen, fuck it. Come on down to Drifters and get some barbecue. Let's play some tunes." Pretty amazing. Todd's inclusive all the way to the end. I met Todd for the first time at a Darrin Bradbury gig at the Basement East a few years ago when he was hanging with Steve Poltz. I talked to Elizabeth Cook. "I'm out on the lake with Todd," she said. "Would you be able to play guitar for an Eastside Bulldogs show?"

Todd had booked a gig at this place called The Shed in Maryville. I think he decided to make it a Bulldogs show at the last minute with no rehearsal. The gig was the Bulldogs songs, a few Todd songs, and a laundry list of songs like "Louie Louie." I guess I did good on that show because he called me up to do another gig at the Moontower Music Festival in Lexington. "You're a Bulldog," he said after the gig, "until you don't wanna be a Bulldog anymore." Todd's thing when I took the Shed gig was, "You gotta play the show drunk." I told him I don't drink, but with no rehearsal I'll sound like I'm drunk. "That's it," he said. "Don't learn the songs and you'll be in good shape."

Sometimes that's where it shines. It was nerve-racking but also like you prepared your whole life for it. Todd's hand started cramping at one point. He put his guitar down. "You know how to play 'Play a Train Song,' right?" he said. It wasn't on the set list, but I did know how to play that. No pressure whatsoever. I had to play "Play a Train Song," which is one of his hits, to his massive fans. I had to retrain my head to play it properly and luckily I nailed it. It was one of those things as a fan that was an out-of-body experience playing one of Todd's songs for Todd as he delivered it to the crowd. That's a moment that I'll carry with me forever no matter what else happens in music for me.

Same for standing side stage with John Prine at Todd's Ryman show before he went out to play "Illegal Smile." Small gifts from Todd. I think everyone from that Shithouse Wire group flew in for the show. It looked like East Nashville invaded the Ryman. I was standing there with my girlfriend, Elizabeth Cook, Brian Wright, Aaron Lee Tasjan, and Tim Easton and felt a hand patting me on the shoulder. Prine standing there. It was the ultimate Nashville moment—standing there side stage at the Ryman watching Todd play to a sold-out crowd between John Prine and all of East Nashville's up-and-comers. Then there was an after-party to see Allen Thompson's band Lady Couch at Acme Feed and Seed. Almost everybody went across the street for that show including Todd. He was hanging out with the masses.[21]

Atlanta, Georgia-area native Jon Latham has shared stages with Elizabeth Cook, Aaron Lee Tasjan, and several others. His recent album Lifers *was released on Cafe Rooster Records.*

Allen Thompson

Todd is ubiquitous in East Nashville. We didn't get to know each other until we met through my good friend Elizabeth Cook in summer 2015. I put together this Black Crowes cover band for an East Nashville beer festival, and Todd showed up. He said, "I wanna play 'Remedy' with y'all." I'm a jam band kid so I knew Todd through Hard Working Americans more than his folk singer stuff. That isn't really my bag, but I really fell in love with it after we became hang-out buds and I was part of the East Nashville Bulldogs. Neal Casal's playing in Chris Robinson Brotherhood and Hard Working Americans is what really drew me to the music. Plus, it was improvisational playing with literate songwriting.

[Grateful Dead lyricists] Robert Hunter and John Barlow were both brilliant writers. The Allman Brothers and Widespread hit that mark sometimes. CRB and Hard Working Americans really inspired me to move away from the Americana thing and forge my own path in that world as well. The songwriting and lyrics are what got me into those bands before I really started to appreciate the improvisation. Think about the Allmans' *Eat a Peach.* Killer songs top to bottom. You listen to that and then you can ingest the thirty-three-minute "Mountain Jam." I would never jump into "Mountain Jam" or "Dark Star" without hearing [the lyric-based] songs first.

You begin to understand when you fall in love with the songs that someone like Neal or Derek Trucks is telling as much of a story with their notes as Todd is with his lyrics. It's more fun for the audience and performers when the band knows where it's going in improvisational music but doesn't know how they'll get there. Life keeps things from being boring at the very least and makes things exciting at the best. The Allmans and the Dickey Betts instrumentals like "In Memory of Elizabeth Reed" are perfect examples. There's a very defined beginning, a very defined second piece, and then it breaks wide open until they decide to get out of the mess they've made. Then there's a cue to make that happen. Structured chaos. Also, the psychedelic drugs don't hurt in making that connection.

I knew Neal from being around CRB and Hard Working shows. He was a very sweet guy who always was very cool to stop, talk, and give advice. He was friendlier than most people. I had been watching him since he was with Ryan Adams and the Cardinals. That band was a turning point and influence in me deciding whether this would be a hobby or my life. I watched them make the transition from a folk group into something much more exciting and jammy. I loved watching Neal's sensibilities evolve from being the Ace Frehley pentatonic scale picker to getting into folks like Jerry Garcia and John Coltrane. He was moving the needle in a different direction in the time I was doing the same as a guitar player.

People don't think about jam bands in East Nashville, but Marcus King, Billy Strings, and Nikki Blume are here. Margo Price and Maggie Rose do different things with Widespread or Disco Biscuits at any given festival. Some of us are actually making decent money doing this, but we're completely under the radar. No one pays attention to it. People think more about the Americana troubadours when they think about East Nashville. We've gotten a lot more freedom to explore what we want to do here than the midtown machine types. There were other people making the same headway at the same time, but Todd was super integral in making that happen. You would always see him in Five Points. Todd was the mayor of East Nashville.[22]

East Nashville hippie songwriter Allen Thompson fronts Lady Couch and tours as a solo artist with the Stolen Faces.

Chicago Farmer

My wife and I went to see Yonder Mountain String Band at House of Blues in Chicago because she's really into bluegrass. Somebody told me that the opener was a folk singer. I thought, "Man, this could be rough." The kids are already all jacked up for Yonder, but then Todd come out with no shoes, his guitar, and a harmonica. He started "Can't Complain" and immediately had the crowd in his hand. My wife and I were hooked. You could tell that he loves what he's doing. What a presence. He's been doing it so long and is so into it, but it's not like a huge country star stage presence. Todd has his own thing that pulls you in.

He has a slacker confidence so I think people wouldn't guess exactly how hard he works on his albums and how much time he spends working on his live show. He's always involved in some other project, like working with me, when he's not on the road. He has an incredible work ethic and inspires me. I was just listening to "Long Year." I love that song so much. We have a connection there. We focus lyrically on people on the outskirts. I've always wanted to be a free spirit, someone who lives on the outskirts. Not many artists tackle that angle. Todd hits home with me so much. He's definitely influenced me as a writer. I want to go write and play and get better at my guitar, songs, and stories for the show when I hear Todd.

I started opening a show here and there, which is the greatest job in the world, then it was three shows, then one January we did ten shows together. I'm always grateful for the opportunities. I learn more from opening for Todd for seven nights than I do touring on my own for seven months. Todd's show is an experience like the Grateful Dead was, but he's just one guy. People drive from all over the country to see Todd. They get hotels and hang out all day. They listen to his music and go over what songs he might play before the show. These people just live for it. Playing in front of them is all I wanted to do for the longest time. I didn't even care about my career. I wanted to open up for Todd full-time. Then I got greedy and thought it would be nice to have my name on top once in a while. The first time I ever really hung out with Todd, he said, "Pull up a chair." I thought that was the coolest thing to say.[23]

Illinois native Cody Diekhoff adopted the stage name Chicago Farmer twenty years ago and has since established a reputation as a big-city songwriter who dutifully nods to his small-town roots.

Joe Pug

I was getting my start playing in Chicago and was opening gigs for national artists coming through. Todd was playing a gig at the Old Town School of Folk Music, and I landed the gig as the local opener. That was the first time I heard his music. Needless to say, Todd blew my mind. I became a fan. I was too green to know that it was unusual for a headliner to invite their opener to hang out at that time. Todd did that. Really cool. He's always made an effort to remember me and be kind. Todd is a very pure soul. I was reminded when I finished a tour later and had to drive the van back from Seattle to Austin.

The best place for me to stop one night was Salt Lake City. I booked a room about two blocks away from the State Room. I pulled in and said, "All right, wonder if there's any music at the State Room." The marquee said, "Tonight. One night only. Sold Out. Todd Snider." Are you kidding me? Totally serendipitous. I texted his guy Brian and said, "Hey, man. I'm in town. I would love to see the show and see Todd. Let me know what's up." They got me tickets to the show, and I got on the bus with Todd after. He had a smoke, and I had a beer, which is more my vibe. He said a couple things that stuck with me.

"You know, Joe," he said. "How many people are there out there who get a ticket to this dance? Five hundred of us? Six? Maybe it's less. Two hundred? I'm talking about guys like us who get to go out and play our songs exactly how we want to do it. We're not getting rich, but we make a living. How many do this?" That really made me reflect on what a privilege doing this is, and how few people really get to do this for a living. Times might get tough, but I always remember that question Todd asked and remember how lucky we are.

Todd said another time, "I almost died in a car accident a month ago. I was in the car with [my former tour manager]. Something happened and we were driving right toward a brick wall. I knew for a second I was gonna die. The coolest part was that I wasn't scared at all." He was at peace with something. He wasn't worried about driving into that brick wall. He's so idiosyncratic like his songs, but that wouldn't matter at all if they weren't so well written. They're better than everybody else's. The details are better. The comedic timing is better. The balance between characters is better. Todd is the full package.

Our whole job is to take our influences and pass them on. We're not making deconstructed postmodern sculptures out of hair and toothpicks.

We have an oral tradition. You should innovate to the degree that you're inspired to and speak with your own voice, but all these songs are coming out of a particular context, which is what gives them meaning. I don't think there's a real tension between taking something from someone else like Kris Kristofferson and John Prine and putting it into your own voice. You learn the boundaries so you can have your own voice.[24]

Joe Pug became a rapidly rising songwriter with his early collection The Messenger *(2010). Albums such as* The Great Despiser *(2012) and* The Driving Sun *(2021) confirmed his promise.*

John Craigie

I moved to Santa Cruz from Los Angeles when I was eighteen in the nineties and was really interested in songwriter music. I didn't know any of that music scene. I was into Pearl Jam and Nirvana. I found the station KPIG in Santa Cruz. I initially was turned off because the PIG made me think it was country, and I wasn't interested in country music. I started listening at some point because they played some classic rock like Tom Petty. Then I started getting exposed to people like Greg Brown, Robert Earl Keen, and Loudon Wainwright. Todd was a big deal on KPIG. They really loved him. I went to all the shows that Sleepy John put on for them. He's the one mentioned in "Beer Run" and Robert's "I'm Coming Home."

Sleepy hosted Todd a bunch, which is how I got interested in his music. I was just getting interested in the guy with a guitar who was telling stories. There really weren't many people doing that. Maybe Arlo Guthrie. Todd was huge in that sense. I wasn't just a fan. I wanted to learn from him because I never wanted to be Adam Sandler. That was a fear and is for anyone who wants to bring humor into music. You really can't be serious if you do that. Any comedian will reach a threshold where you're the jester. I was always the class clown, but I also had that softer side like any burgeoning artist.

You hear about all these scenes like San Francisco in the sixties. They're all about parties. It's hard to think about a songwriter scene other than maybe Greenwich Village in the sixties. The KPIG thing definitely had a scene. I could go see any of these guys like Todd, Loudon Wainwright, or Robert Earl Keen any given weekend. They were intelligent, had good taste, and were politically minded. "Woke" would be the current term. They were really exciting for me coming from the more pop, watered-down atmosphere in Los Angeles with bands like Hootie and the Blowfish, Everclear, and Matchbox Twenty. So it was really cool to hear well-crafted songs like "Conservative Christian, Right-Wing Republican, Straight, White, American Males."

Sleepy John is very significant as far as us knowing Todd. It was clear that he was cataclysmic in these guys' careers, not only because he would get you a gig in Santa Cruz but because he was well connected in the scene. Sleepy John got me my first two gigs opening for Todd. John said, "We have to get you opening for Todd Snider." I think it was in the same way he got Todd to open for Robert Earl Keen. John was the gatekeeper for this Americana music that was slightly humorous but slightly serious. I was a nobody. John had the idea to get me to open for Paul Thorn and the Waifs, but the big get was to open for Greg Brown, Robert Earl, or Todd. The first we got was Todd at the Rio here in Santa Cruz during a time when Todd was doing a rock show. That was great, but I think the people of Santa Cruz missed the folky storytelling guy. I opened that show and think it went well. We might have said a hello, but I didn't really connect with Todd that night.

I opened for Todd about a year later here at the Catalyst. He did a rock set again. Our friendship began when I almost stole his weed. Then I did a Midwest run with him about two years later. We played around Ohio. Todd was great. I had my song about almost stealing his weed and was a little nervous because you hear all these stories about him being volatile and canceling shows. I caught him on a good run, and he was really sweet to me. We weren't like Jerry Jeff and him going out on the town, but he would let me on the bus and we would share a joint. He told stories. I was in the process of learning what I do then and picked up on the influence of him.

He felt like an Obi-Wan. You're out there, do your thing, then get taken to school every night. I learned more about marrying stories and songs. It was really cool to follow someone like him around to see what stays the same and what fluctuates. I think there's a myth that everything's so spontaneous with humor at the shows. People always come up to me at the merch table and go, "Oh man, was all that stuff off the cuff?" It's cool to see what is off the cuff and what isn't. Experts like Todd helped shape me into understanding what makes each night unique. I'm very grateful for that. Todd and I have always had a very professional relationship. We never got too close to butt heads. He always inspires me.[25]

Southern California folk singer John Craigie deftly carries on the legacies of Woody Guthrie and John Prine as well as comedian Mitch Hedberg in equal measures.

Chelsea Lovitt

I lived with a very kind artist named Molly Thomas from my hometown when I moved to Nashville in 2008. Her dad was a minister who married my parents. Molly was on the road playing fiddle with Todd. She introduced me around town and also to Todd's music. I found he was an influential realist songwriter who says it like it is and have loved him ever since. He's hilarious and sings like he talks. I play songs and tell stories about them, and you unintentionally have your influences there. I have been working on a cover of "Conservative Christian, Right- Wing Republican, Straight, White, American Males." That song is liberating as a woman trying to keep up with the man's world. I like it because I cover it from a male's perspective and don't change pronouns.

Todd is good about keeping that song unisex. He's ballsy and puts forth his ideas but is moderate and addresses both sides of an opinion. A good songwriter puts forth a message that makes people feel good and they can relate to. Todd addresses that delicately and in a funny way. I feel like I share a general sense of humor with him as a writer and purveyor of the world. We're trying to express an idea in a lighthearted way. Ain't that the trick? Todd has a longstanding history in that town. He's an example of someone who really has owned his craft. People will say that here. "You have to show me that you've owned your craft." The big-business people often say that even if they don't know what that means.

Todd is a cornerstone. I remember going to some party Todd was playing at the 3 Crow Bar in Five Points with Molly one time. The 3 Crow never has music, but the show was packed. East Nashville had more affordable rent and was the place to be for songwriters who were not on Music Row ten years ago. East Nashville is opposite of [Nashville suburbs] Belle Meade and Green Hills where people like Taylor Swift live in this opposite [world] where creative types are. Todd made East Nashville. He put the neighborhood on the map either with *East Nashville Skyline* or just the writers who live over here. It's still pretty chill. I live on Eleventh, right up the street from Todd's Purple Building.

The boom in this town is unbelievable. Nashville is a destination place now. Nashville has always been the place to make it in country music, but now it's a place for bridesmaids and bachelor parties on Broadway.

People come here just to get drunk. Every goofy bro country artist like Jason Aldean, Luke Bryan, Dierks Bentley, and Blake Shelton has a bar now. Big Machine Records has put their mark here with that and shitty cover bands that play Poison. Todd is such an influence when you think about the way he would say something about that. I think Todd's personae onstage is real. You're gonna be honest if you're worth your salt. You get these nuances like when I was driving around this old drunk guy from Boston the other night. He was out of his mind drunk and wanted to listen to the Stones. I played him my record. "You know," he said. "I'm gonna give you advice. You're gonna blink and get old. You gotta wake up. Don't lose your dignity. You're fucked if you lose your dignity." You see some kind of linear correlation between this and the whole heart-breaking aspect of the business.

Todd is persistent. He probably got shot down tons, but then he ended up opening for Jerry Jeff Walker. Todd has consistently and persistently done his thing. He owns his craft. There are days when you feel like it's right and you know what you're doing. Then there are days when it's a shitstorm and shambles. Then you stand back and remember people like Todd Snider and realize it's all about the song. You have your dignity if you can write good songs like therapy. You seek the truth.[26]

Chelsea Lovitt blends country, soul, and bluegrass with influences of Johns Keats and William Faulkner into her own style, which is well represented on her album You Had Your Cake So Lie in It.

Raelyn Nelson

Todd came up to me backstage after my band's set at Farm Aid in 2014. "I just wanted you to know," he said, "I liked your songs and really enjoyed your performance." I was like, "Oh my God, you guys. That was so cool. Who the fuck was that?" "Todd Snider." "Oh. Uh, who is Todd Snider?" They showed me all his songs and videos on our trip from Raleigh to Nashville. He reached out to me later to write a song through email. We still haven't done that, but we're friends, and I dog sat for him when Cowboy Jim was alive. The humor and great messages in his songs draw me to them. "Conservative Christian" is my favorite. He makes "Conservative Christian" a party song even when he's making a statement.

You would think he leans left, but it's very clear when we talk that he's in the gray like everyone else. There's no black or white. Todd is for everyone's rights, and he's hilarious. I'm a big fan of comedy. We always send each other comedians to watch. Todd should be a stand-up comedian. One example is when somebody called and asked for an interview about Todd. The guy said that Todd had told him that we had eloped. I was like, "No, that's not true." It ended up being printed anyway. Todd's crazy and unpredictable. Sometimes we'll get in a fight and not talk for six months.

Todd bases his humor on ridiculousness. Have you ever seen that Blind Lemon Pledge game that he made up? He said they couldn't release it. They played the game, and it didn't work. Also, he tells me a new story every time I see him. Then he'll tell me the same story next time I see him, and it will change. His stories get bigger and better. Charming. It's interesting that he has female openers at his shows 90 percent of the time. He told me that he wouldn't feel as bad being upstaged by the girl as he would by a guy. I don't know that that's the best reason, but I still think it's cool that he has girls open for him. I mean, he tours in Taylor Swift's old bus.

Todd is all about ideas, but then he will be done. We were at my house talking with a friend of mine one time, and he just left. He called me when he got home. "Hey," I said. "Where did you go?" He said, "Is she still talking?" "No, she got the point and fucking left." Then he called last October. "I'm sick of living like a bachelor," he said. "Come in and put a woman's touch on my place while I'm on tour." I went out, stayed on his couch, and gave it a hippie and bohemian vibe. He came home and told me he loved it. Next time I see him, it's completely different. All the stuff was there, but he had moved it around the house. Still looks like a bachelor's house. Just a hippie bachelor's house.[27]

Country legend Willie Nelson's granddaughter Raelyn Nelson has shared stages with superstar Tim McGraw, indie darlings Drivin N Cryin, and rock supergroup Hard Working Americans.

Sierra Ferrell

Todd found me busking on the streets when he was in West Virginia to play [the long-running public radio show] *Mountain Stage* [in Charleston]. He loved my music and was like, "We're gonna go to Nashville, and you're gonna record a record." Yeah, right. You know how people always talk. Then he hit me up after about a year had gone by and said,

"Hey, come to Nashville. We're gonna record you." "Cool." I don't have a car. I just have my dog, so I hitchhiked here to Nashville, showed up, and we ended up recording with Eric McConnell. Todd's an early riser, so we showed up at Eric's probably around seven in the morning. Eric was like, "Who is this girl?"

I didn't know him when he found me in West Virginia, but I got into Todd's music after I saw him play. He's phenomenal. Honestly, I went to his gig for the first time and was like, "Oh, here we go." There were all these seats where you had to sit down, but I wanted to dance. I didn't know what to expect, but he started playing and I loved how he can use his anxiety and nervousness to his advantage. He's an amazing and hilarious genius. His stories always take you somewhere else. You're really there with him. Of course, everybody loves "Beer Run." Who doesn't love beer? I love that story about how he met up with that guy who wrote the other "beer run" song. "Yo," he said, "that's my song."

Todd has helped me so much and has taught me that you can write a song about anything as long as the delivery is right. You're onto something if you can make people believe you. It's hard to hear someone today and believe what they're saying. I create characters in my songs and write from their point of view. Todd helped me explore that more instead of just writing from my own experience. I'm observant and pick up pieces of what's going on around me. I had to work my way in here because I wear black and chokers and look different, but people [welcomed me to East Nashville] after they heard me play. I have such a great community of people here who I love. Todd is phenomenal. He absolutely created the East Nashville community.[28]

*Todd Snider discovered Sierra Ferrell busking on the West Virginia streets. She won four Grammy Awards in 2025 including Best Americana Album (*Trail of Flowers*), Best American Roots Song and Best Americana Performance (both for "American Dreaming"), and Best American Roots Performance ("Lighthouse").*

Coda

JACK INGRAM

Todd and I took the bottle of tequila from the Rockbar and went out walking after that show in Scottsdale. We went swig for swig straight from the bottle and were singing songs off Kris Kristofferson's *Jesus Was a Capricorn*. We were laughing about how fucked up the night was. We knew the hotel was this way, so we started walking toward it and ended up being right in front of the police department. There was a fountain out front, and Todd started washing his face. I pushed him in the fountain. Todd looked at me like, "What the fuck?" Everything had just gone badly that night. Todd is like six foot four and pulled me in with him.

We sat there in the fountain in front of the police department drinking tequila from the bottle for an hour. We're like, "We can't even get arrested in this town drinking liquor in the police department fountain." I woke up the next morning, and my belt, my wallet, and my shoes were in the hotel swimming pool. We apparently went swimming after we left the fountain. What a cliché. We were being idiots and saying to each other all night, "I'll do it if you do it." We packed up and went on to the next gig.

Acting like that is such stupid, alpha male bullshit in some peoples' minds, but in another respect we both understood that we would go as far as the other would. We don't have to do that every night, but it's always been comforting to know that someone else out there will go as far as you want to go. Todd wants to chase whatever cliffs there are to jump off together when this business gets really strange. It's really nice to have a friend to go, "You're good. Calm down." The point is Todd is not like a brother to me. He is my brother.

Todd is a star shining at me, and I hope I'm the same way for him. I was soaking in how Todd gets so gone when we were touring together early on. He wears his influences from Dylan, Springsteen, and Jagger on his sleeves. I was a young guy trying to figure out how to get there. I've told him this. I wanted to be clear what I was doing. People would be like, "Hey, man, you're copping Todd Snider." "Fuck yeah, I am." I got to sit at the side of the stage and be friends with someone I think is brilliant. I've laughed with Todd about it. I used to tell him, "Hey, Todd. People will say I'm stealing your shit. I am." He was my gateway into becoming like my heroes.

Todd knew it and would laugh. Guitar players get to cop Eddie Van Halen and their heroes until their licks don't sound like him anymore. They start sounding like Slash or whoever. People thought Richard Pryor was just another Bill Cosby when he started. He was until he wasn't. Same way with me coming of age with a buddy who was ahead of me in shows and years. I'm so grateful that he took it as the same compliment he would give to Dylan. Getting permission to learn from someone like that was great. He was like, "Yeah, man, I see what you're doing." He let me find my own voice. Especially on nights like Scottsdale.[1]

Todd Snider

Yeah, that was one of the greatest nights of my life. Nothing like bombing together to make a couple guys friends for life. We scaled the side of the hotel after the fountain. The police came. Everybody came out of their rooms. We thought, "Fucking finally."[2]

Big Finish

TODD SNIDER

I've always thought that you'll eventually shut up if you're really a poet. Shutting up has to be the point, right? Has to be. Aren't you seeking silence? Aren't you seeking the last word? [Western Zen guru] Alan Watts spent the last ten years of his life not talking. He only laughed and made animal sounds. That's where I wanna go. I don't see myself doing this gig until I'm really old. I can see myself vanishing. Going to some other country and get a job. My fantasy is to take four years off and go to college. Then maybe be a professor. I'll probably always sing. I know a million songs, but I would love to teach the history of music. I just don't want people talking about me and my legacy in a hundred years. I would hope my name would be gone by then. I've always had this basic approach: "You can't prove I'm here. Where are we going after here? Fuck, where are we to begin with?" I'm just not very concerned with having a legacy. There was never a point to that. I just want to be a gypsy.[1]

"FROM A ROOFTOP"
East Nashville?
Shit, man, we're living in a dream world over here
Born on a full moon's what I heard
Turned over drinks from a neighborhood
Into a full-on goddamn dream world
By two guys if you ask me
Mike "Grimey" Grimes and Skip Kenneth Francis
"Play a Fucking Train Song" Litz
The spirit of whom many still claim to see on full moons to this day
Swerving up Woodland in that ghost of a Cadillac he drives

Of course, a lot of us smoke more dope before nine a.m.
Than most people do all day
Saturday nights at the 3 Crow
Sundays, Alley Cat
We're that guy from your town that would rather pick than eat
We usually got about half a tank of gas
And we don't feel like crossing the river
But we will, we will for a song we like

Nobody else in the world knows when Mac's gonna open the Radio Cafe
But we do, and we tell each other
We stand around down there and smoke during Dave Olney's break
Just like we do outside the Family Wash during Tommy Womack's
On the Fourth, we have the best illegal fireworks show on earth
Last year, we even got it together to organize a non-flyover
By the United States Air Force
It was beautiful
We were all pretty high
Our skyline
It ain't very high
But we love it
It says, "Discount Cigarettes Liquor and Wine" across it
I think our neighborhood's a lot like our skyline
We've got great news
And we're shouting it from the highest rooftop we got

Todd Snider, "East Nashville Skyline," from *Peace, Love, and Anarchy (Rarities, B-Sides and Demos, Vol. I)*
Shad-N-Froyd-A Music, 2007

Appendix

SELECTED TIMELINE FOR TODD SNIDER

1966

Todd Daniel Snider is born on October 11 in Portland, Oregon. Snider and his brother, Mike, grow up in Beaverton, Oregon.

1985

Snider exits Beaverton High School. He moves to San Marcos, Texas.

1987

Snider meets Cheatham Street Warehouse owner Kent Finlay at Songwriters Night. He writes his first song, "Bus Tub Stew," while working as a busboy. Snider moves in with the Finlay family for nearly three years. He studies songwriting and songwriters under Finlay during this time.

Snider records the demos collection *Early Daze*. Highlights include "Happy Hour Hero," "Who Says It's Lonely at the Top," "Look Back Kindly on Me," and "Feeling at Home." He develops an enthusiastic fan base performing around the area.

Snider discovers Memphis-based songwriter Keith Sykes's music. He mails Sykes his demo tape. Sykes sees potential.

1989–1993

Todd Snider moves to Memphis.

Sykes becomes his new mentor.

Snider quickly lands an open-mic-night gig Thursdays at the Daily Planet.

He develops his signature storytelling style while packing the club each week.

MCA's Margaritaville Records President Bob Mercer seeks out Snider at a Daily Planet gig.

He soon signs his first record deal with Margaritaville Records.

1994

Iconic MCA Records producer Tony Brown oversees Snider's debut, *Songs for the Daily Planet.*

Key songs include "Alright Guy," "Easy Money," and "Talkin' Seattle Grunge Rock Blues."

"Talkin' Seattle Grunge Rock Blues" becomes a minor radio hit.

Snider and his band the Nervous Wrecks establish a national while touring the record.

The official video for "Alright Guy" spreads word farther and wider.

Meanwhile, Rick Treviño gives Snider his first album cut by recording "She Just Left Me Lounge."

1995

Snider and the Nervous Wrecks perform "Alright Guy" on *Late Night with Conan O'Brien.*

Meanwhile, Mark Chesnutt takes Snider's "Trouble" to number eighteen on the country chart.

Snider moves to Nashville.

1996

Mike Utley, Brown, and Snider produce *Step Right Up* for Margaritaville Records.

Key tracks include "Side Show Blues," "Tension," and "Late Last Night."

Snider and the Nervous Wrecks makes their first appearance on *Austin City Limits.*

Joe Ely and Snider cut "Oh Boy!" for *Not Fade Away: Remembering Buddy Holly.* They sing the song on *The Late Show with David Letterman.*

Snider knocks out a tooth during his tequila-fueled thirtieth birthday show.

1998

Snider records his third album, *Viva Satellite.* The scattershot collection redeems with classics "Can't Complain" and "Doublewide Blues."

Snider's drug and alcohol consumption reaches new heights.

He insults MCA Records executives onstage at a private showcase in Los Angeles. MCA drops Snider from the label.

The Nervous Wrecks soon disband.

2000

Snider signs with new mentor John Prine's Oh Boy Records. He debuts on the label with his fourth album, *Happy to Be Here*. Key songs are "Forty Five Miles," "Long Year," "D. B. Cooper," and "Lonely Girl."

Meanwhile, country star Gary Allan records "Alright Guy" as his album's title track.

Additionally, Jerry Jeff Walker cuts "Alright Guy" on *Gonzo Stew*.

2002

Snider releases his fifth album, *New Connection*. Highlights include "Beer Run," "Statistician's Blues," "Rose City," and "Waco Moon."

Snider performs "Beer Run" solo on the *Late Late Show with Craig Kilborn*.

2003

Snider releases his first live album, *Todd Snider Live: Near Truths and Hotel Rooms*. The album showcases Snider's savvy and singular showmanship. Key stories include "The Story of the Ballad of the Devil's Backbone" and "Typing Gibberish." Standout tracks include "Tension," "Long Year," "Easy Money," and "Doublewide Blues."

2004

Snider releases his masterwork *East Nashville Skyline*. Standouts include "Age Like Wine," "Tillamook County Jail," and "Play a Train Song." The collection becomes his final Oh Boy studio album.

"Conservative Christian, Right-Wing Republican, Straight, White, American Males" foreshadows his increased leaning toward sociopolitical songwriting.

2005

MCA Records releases the greatest hits compilation, *That Was Me: 1994–1998*.

Popular Red Dirt band Cross Canadian Ragweed covers Snider's "Late Last Night" on *Garage*.

Snider opens the Americana Music Association's awards show with "Nashville."

2006

Snider releases his eighth album, *The Devil You Know*, on the Universal imprint Hip-O. Highlights include "Looking for a Job," "Just Like Old Times," and the title track.

Snider performs "Looking for a Job" on *The Tonight Show with Jay Leno.*

Rolling Stone magazine ranks *The Devil You Know* among the year's fifty best albums.

Snider becomes a beacon for East Nashville's creative community.

2007

Oh Boy releases *Peace, Love and Anarchy (Rarities, B-Sides and Demos, Vol. 1)*. Highlights include "East Nashville Skyline" and "Cheatham Street Warehouse."

New Door releases *Live with The Devil You Know at Grimey's Nashville 10.20.06*. Standouts are "If Tomorrow Never Comes" and "Happy New Year/All That Matters (Reprise)."

Meanwhile, Cross Canadian Ragweed covers Snider's "I Believe You" on *Mission California*.

2008

Snider forms his own Aimless Records. The concept album *Peace Queer* marks his Aimless debut. Key tracks include "Is This Thing Working?," "Is This Thing On?," and "Fortunate Son."

2009

Snider signs a one-off deal with Yep Roc Records for *The Excitement Plan*. Rock star producer Don Was (Bob Dylan, the Rolling Stones) guides the journey. High points include "Greencastle Blues" and the Loretta Lynn duet "Don't Tempt Me." *Rolling Stone* magazine gives the album a four-star review.

2011

Snider and backing band Great American Taxi record *Todd Snider Live: The Storyteller*. Key stories include "The Bill Elliott Story," "The Mushroom Story," and "K. K. Rider Story." Standout tracks include "Tension," "Looking for a Job," "East Nashville Skyline," "Rose City," and "The Devil You Know."

Snider releases *The Storyteller* and all subsequent albums on Aimless Records.

Meanwhile, Robert Earl Keen covers “Play a Train Song” on his album *Ready for Confetti*.

2012

Snider releases *Agnostic Hymns & Stoner Fables*. Standout tracks include “In Between Jobs,” “Brenda,” and “Too Soon to Tell.”

Was returns to produce *Time as We Know It: The Songs of Jerry Jeff Walker*. Great American Taxi serves as the backing band. High points include “Sangria Wine,” “Pissin’ in the Wind,” and “Mr. Bojangles.”

Rolling Stone ranks *Agnostic Hymns & Stoner Fables* among the year’s fifty best albums.

2013

Snider and Widespread Panic’s Dave Schools form the supergroup Hard Working Americans. The band records cover songs by favorite songwriters at Bob Weir’s TRI Studios. The film *The First Waltz* documents Hard Working Americans’ early adventures.

Snider delves deeply into psychedelic drugs during this time.

2014

Hard Working Americans’ self-titled debut hits shelves early in the year. Highlights include Hayes Carll’s “Stomp and Holler,” Drivin’ N Cryin’s “Straight to Hell,” and the Bottle Rockets’ “Welfare Music.”

The band tours consistently during its short lifespan.

Da Capo Press releases Snider’s memoir, *I Never Met a Story I Didn’t Like: Mostly True Tales*.

2015

Snider releases the digital album *Cheatham Street Warehouse* as a fundraiser for Kent Finlay. Standout tracks include “Hill Country,” “Plastic Girl,” and “Cheatham Street Warehouse.”

2016

Hard Working Americans releases its second album, *Rest in Chaos*. Snider writes all songs besides Guy Clark’s “The High Price of Inspiration.”

Creative tension between band members builds. The group dissolves before the live album *We’re All in This Together* comes out a year later.

Meanwhile, Snider releases the ramshackle garage rock album *Eastside Bulldog*. Players include East Nashville pals Elizabeth Cook, Aaron Lee Tasjan, and Robbie Crowell. Key tracks include "Hey Pretty Boy," "The Funky Tomato," "Bocephus," and "Come on Up."

Loretta Lynn and Elvis Costello duet on her Snider cowrite "Everything It Takes" on *Full Circle*.

2019

Snider releases *Cash Cabin Sessions, Vol. 3*. Key tracks include "Like a Force of Nature," "The Blues on Banjo," and "Talking Reality Television Blues."

Snider name-checks legendary comedian Richard Lewis in "The Blues on Banjo."

2020

Snider and Jack Ingram book a three-day run at the Devil's Backbone in Fischer, Texas. The old friends swap songs throughout Valentine's weekend at the historic venue.

The World Health Organization declares COVID-19 a pandemic less than a month later. The world shuts down.

2021

Snider rebounds with wildly popular Sunday morning live streaming shows.

He releases *The First Agnostic Church of Hope and Wonder*.

Meanwhile, Tom Jones covers "Talking Reality Television Blues" on *Surrounded by Time*.

2022

Snider begins touring full-time again.

He releases his third concert album, *Todd Snider Live: Return of the Storyteller*.

2023

Snider finally releases the long-shelved album *Crank It, We're Doomed,* which was recorded during his creative high point in the mid-2000s.

Notes

Introduction

1. Craig Marks, "The Balladeer of Just Getting By," *The New York Times*, June 12, 2009, https://www.nytimes.com/2009/06/14/arts/music/14mark.html.

2. Loretta Lynn, interview by Peggy Lynn, text from an email sent to Brian T. Atkinson by Mark Marchetti on December 30, 2020.

3. Andrew Dansby, interview with Brian T. Atkinson, November 24, 2020.

4. Todd Snider, "Play a Train Song," from *East Nashville Skyline*, Oh Boy Records, 2004; Todd Snider, interview with Brian T. Atkinson, November 14, 2020.

5. Jason Isbell, interview with Brian T. Atkinson, November 8, 2020.

6. Todd Snider, interview with Brian T. Atkinson, December 15, 2020; Kent Finlay, interview with Jenni Finlay, October 26, 2014, in Brian T. Atkinson and Jenni Finlay, *Kent Finlay, Dreamer: The Musical Legacy of Cheatham Street Warehouse* (Texas A&M University Press, 2016).

7. Damian Jones, "Tom Jones announces new album with Radiohead-esque single 'Talking Reality Television Blues,'" *NME*, January 15, 2021, www.nme.com/news/music/tom-jones-announces-new-album-with-radiohead-esque-single-talking-reality-television-blues2857910

8. Todd Snider, interview with Brian T. Atkinson, November 6, 2020.

9. Hayes Carll, interview with Brian T. Atkinson, October 14, 2020.

10. Richard Lewis, interview with Brian T. Atkinson, September 29, 2020. In an email sent to the author on October 2, 2020, Snider wrote: "For the record and the book, I wildly contest Richard's word salad explanation of our legendary show at the Roxy. What he did to me that night was nothing short of a Larry Holmes vs. Tex Cobb-style beat down on purpose for good times. (Actually one of my top ten favorite gigs ever.) We joke about that night constantly. I would do anything for Richard. He sent Steven Tyler to my house. I don't make a move without consulting Richard even with songs. Smartest person I know."

11. Don Was, interview with Brian T. Atkinson, November 9, 2020.

Verse: Cheatham Street Warehouse

1. Todd Snider, interview with Brian T. Atkinson, October 26, 2020. "Call the girl by her real name in the song," Snider says. "John Lee Hooker did a great video where he explains the blues. 'If you got your heart broken, does it really matter what name you say for the rest of your life?' he says. 'There's a real girl's name in there. You can always access that.' Kent Finlay said the same thing."

2. Todd Snider, interview. "Worked like magic. I had parents, but my dad went bankrupt when I was a sophomore [in high school]," Snider says. "I guess

I could have worked for my dad, but there didn't seem to be any roads out of town. I didn't think "Bus Tub Stew" was a real song. Then my friend told me when I walked into Cheatham for that first open mic that he was gonna do art for my first album. He did the second album. He said, 'Great painters paint two hundred paintings, throw them out, and start over.' I thought, 'No, no, no, don't say that,' but it's the truth."

3. Mike Snider, interview with Brian T. Atkinson, December 4, 2020.

4. Kent Finlay, interview with Jenni Finlay, October 26, 2014, in Brian T. Atkinson and Jenni Finlay, *Kent Finlay, Dreamer: The Musical Legacy of Cheatham Street Warehouse* (Texas A&M University Press, 2016). Todd Snider, interview with Brian T. Atkinson, November 16, 2020. "Now I get a little money every year for the songs I write and other people sing," Snider says. "It's weird to make a living at this. It's all hook or crook. I just assume it's gonna end under a bridge or end in a dark hotel room. I know a guy who went to Harvard and writes books [for little pay]. We're brothers because of it. Brian, that's why you and me are brothers and kind of why [others are] not. It's why [others] offend people like you and me. This is it for us. This is the end. This isn't some hobby for a couple summers before I go back to the wonderful life that's been carved out for me. I wrote my book [*I Never Met a Story I Didn't Like*] to eat. I don't even know if I wanted to share all that, but I gotta eat and don't have a job. I separate that totally from the work. It's easy to turn off commerce and write songs.

"All Jerry was was an aftershow, but when he was hitting that on the sweet spot he wrote 'Mr. Bojangles.' Shaver too. Reckless abandon. Prepared to be a total loser. Who gives a rat's ass? That's where it was headed anyway. I've thought about all the stuff I've done that's taken years off my life. I was earnestly getting in those cars for songs. I really was. Maybe two out of ten adventures [would pay off]. I don't really do that anymore. I write them at home. Now my songs are speaking with authority, which I've never really done. This is what I think. The first line of the new record is, 'If I'm not mistaken, and I may well be / There's a fine line between reason and absurdity.' It's unique at the very least. It might be a piece of shit you can't listen to, but it's unique."

5. Jenni Finlay, interview with Brian T. Atkinson, October 4, 2020.

6. Diana Finlay Hendricks, email interview with Jenni Finlay, October 17, 2020. Finlay Hendricks is the author of *Delbert McClinton: One of the Fortunate Few* (TAMU Press, 2017).

7. Jenni Finlay, interview.

8. Scott Beckwith, interview with Brian T. Atkinson, September 1, 2020.

9. Todd Snider, interview with Brian T. Atkinson, September 19, 2020.

10. Scott Beckwith, interview.

11. Terri Hendrix, interview with Brian T. Atkinson, September 22, 2020.

12. Todd Snider, interview with Brian T. Atkinson, October 22, 2020. "My very first song [cut by another artist] was "She Just Left Me Lounge" for Ricky Treviño," Snider says. "Terrible song and recording. I've had a bunch of cuts from guys like Jack Ingram, Pat Green, and [Cross Canadian] Ragweed, but I don't keep up with it. I was living here in my house a few years ago when Ingram

did our song "Barbie Doll" [at the Academy of Country Music Awards in 2010] with Dierks Bentley and went to get the money. He found out that I hadn't collected any of my money from all the songs I had written for other people, which was just sitting there. BMI owed me a shit ton. Burt Stein formed this company called Nobody Collects on These Songs and got me the money. I needed it because I had just been through a divorce. I didn't know where to go to get the money and figured they had given it to me already."

13. Scott Beckwith, interview.

14. Greg Ellis, interview with Brian T. Atkinson, December 9, 2020.

15. Jimmy Collins, interview with Brian T. Atkinson, November 1, 2020.

16. Todd Snider, interview with Brian T. Atkinson, September 4, 2020.

17. john Arthur martinez, interview with Brian T. Atkinson, October 14, 2020.

18. john Arthur martinez, interview.

19. Terri Hendrix, interview.

20. Joe Ely, interview with Brian T. Atkinson, December 1, 2020.

21. Cody Canada, interviews with Brian T. Atkinson, September 17, 2020, and June 28, 2014.

22. Jack Ingram, interview with Brian T. Atkinson, December 4, 2020.

23. Todd Snider, interview with Brian T. Atkinson, November 7, 2020.

24. Greg Ellis, interview.

Verse: Can't Complain

1. Todd Snider, interview with Brian T. Atkinson, September 4, 2020.

2. Keith Sykes, interview with Brian T. Atkinson, September 9, 2020.

3. Todd Snider, interview.

4. K. K. Rider, interview with Brian T. Atkinson, September 1, 2020.

5. Mark Marchetti, interview with Brian T. Atkinson, October 20, 2020.

6. Joe McLeary, interview with Brian T. Atkinson, November 14, 2020.

7. Stacie Huckeba, interview with Brian T. Atkinson, October 7, 2020.

8. Eric Lewis, interview with Brian T. Atkinson, December 16, 2020.

9. Kevn Kinney, interview with Brian T. Atkinson, September 15, 2020.

10. Dan Baird, interview with Brian T. Atkinson, September 27, 2020.

11. Eric Lewis, interview with Brian T. Atkinson, December 16, 2020.

12. Mike Snider, interview with Brian T. Atkinson, December 4, 2020. Todd Snider, interview with Brian T. Atkinson, December 2, 2020. "My brother, Mike, was there when this guy punched me right in the face around 1996," Todd Snider says. "We were in Milwaukee, and there was this line to get stuff signed. Some guy waited in line and then jacked me in the mouth. My brother and I looked at each other and thought it was funny for some reason. I don't do that anymore. I hate getting hit. I never found out why that guy did it. He took off running after. Isn't that wild? There's been weird shit. Some guy came up on a beach one time and said, 'Todd?' 'Yeah.' He pulled out a huge knife and said, 'Come with me.'

"Some lady broke into our home another time. She said I told her to come there, and her parents were trying to kill her. She said I knew what I was talking about. Melita and I weren't home. The police came and got her out of the house. She tried to drive her car into the president the next day and made national news. Then it made the Nashville news that she had been to my house the night before. She got out of jail two years later. I was at the Golden Nugget in Reno in my room. The police knocked on my door. 'Mr. Snider, will you come with us?' I thought I was in trouble. Melita was like, 'Goddamn, what did we do?' They said that woman had just checked in across the hall from us. They had been keeping tabs on her all the time since she had tried to hurt the president. She had blue hair."

13. Keith Sykes, interview.

14. Todd Snider, interview with Brian T. Atkinson, December 12, 2020. Tony Brown, interview with Brian T. Atkinson, December 8, 2021.

15. Will Kimbrough, interview with Brian T. Atkinson, September 9, 2020.

16. Keith Sykes, interview.

17. K. K. Rider, interview.

18. Tony Brown, interview with Brian T. Atkinson, December 2, 2021.

19. Joe McLeary, interview. Joe Mariencheck, bassist for the Nervous Wrecks, email to Brian T. Atkinson, January 23, 2021. Mariencheck offered the following statement after being approached several times for an interview for this book: "Todd Snider is the greatest storyteller of our generation. We had a good rock band that played like every gig and every night was our last and most important of our lives. I was so privileged to meet many amazing musicians, fans, and people all over the world. Those were wonderful experiences, but I made a decision to make a career in another business and haven't looked back except to improve myself, my life personally and my playing/singing professionally—though only part-time—for the last twenty-five years."

20. Mike Grimes, interview with Brian T. Atkinson, November 24, 2020.

21. Tommy Womack, interview with Brian T. Atkinson, November 17, 2020. "You have to watch Todd like a hawk when you were onstage together," Womack says. "He sometimes would just skip a chord and go into the chorus. He pushed the band over once in front of thousands of people on the riverfront in Louisville. The band was just me and Molly Thomas, and he didn't show us the set list until we went on. I think he was trying to pull a Bob Dylan where you get onstage, play, and the band has to follow. I discovered that I'm not very good at that. That was a shitty gig, but the next week we were on *The Tonight Show with Jay Leno* and on fire for three minutes. Todd always gets this deer-in-the-headlights look when he's on television. He gets nervous.

"I was in one dressing room, and they were in the other. They were doing the best they could to make sure they were not gonna be nervous. I was already trying not to drink by that point in my life, but they were dipping into the Johnny Walker Red by noon to get ready for the show. They smoked a lot of pot. I smoked pot after the show. I thought, 'This is my one time on national television, and I'm not gonna fuck this up.' Leno was great because they have a stage to the left of where the host and celebrity couches are. The stage where Jay does his monologue is not where the band sets up. It's a whole other stage, so we were able to set up and get our sound and play the song a few times. The guys who work there are really cool, and we were really comfortable.

"They lead you down to the stage at the very last minute as a ploy to keep you from getting nervous. They came for us in the dressing room and said, 'You're gonna play in three minutes.' Cutting it pretty close. All our instruments were in tune, Jay introduced us, and we kicked ass. Leno was a good experience. The next week we did the Letterman show at the last minute. We had the three-minute commercial break to run our amps out there, get our sound, and get in tune while the loud-as-fuck Paul Shaefer orchestra is playing the whole time. We were ready just about in time for David to throw it to us after the commercial break. Paul just stared us down without a smile or a frown.

"The show went okay, but Todd still looked a little like a deer in the headlights. I think I did too because I was playing a guitar in a special tuning, which was a bitch to tune. We had to do that behind the curtain while Al Franken was talking to Dave, and Dave keeps the studio at forty-seven fucking degrees. Trying to tune the guitars in that temperature when you're also nervous about going onstage in front of a national audience was the beginning of the nightmare, but we did the Ed Sullivan Theater. I had a moment to myself when everyone was doing other things, and I thought about how I was at John Lennon's spot onstage. This is where John Lennon, Mick Jagger, and James Brown all stood. Nice moment."

22. Will Kimbrough, interview.

23. Paul Griffith, interview with Brian T. Atkinson, November 19, 2020.

24. Jason Rigenberg, interview with Brian T. Atkinson, December 8, 2020.

25. Will Kimbrough, interview.

26. Todd Snider, interview.

27. Dan Baird, interview.

28. Peter Cooper, interview with Brian T. Atkinson, November 8, 2020. Todd Snider, *I Never Met a Story I Didn't Like: Mostly True Tall Tales* (Da Capo, 2014).

29. Kevn Kinney, interview.

30. Kim Richey, interview with Brian T. Atkinson, December 4, 2020.

31. Marshall Chapman, interview with Brian T. Atkinson, November 2, 2020.

32. Jimmy Collins, interview with Brian T. Atkinson, November 1, 2020.

33. Keith Sykes, interview.

34. Pamela Des Barres, interview with Brian T. Atkinson, November 20, 2020. Interview with Jason D. Williams, October 8, 2021. Todd Snider, interview with Brian T. Atkinson, November 7, 2020.

35. Joe McLeary, interview.

Chorus: East Nashville Skyline

1. Jenni Finlay, interview with Brian T. Atkinson, October 4, 2020.
2. Todd Snider, interview with Brian T. Atkinson, November 7, 2020.
3. Dan Baird, interview with Brian T. Atkinson, September 27, 2020.
4. Will Kimbrough, interview with Brian T. Atkinson, September 9, 2020.
5. Todd Snider, interview with Brian T. Atkinson, December 12, 2020.
6. Will Kimbrough, interview with Brian T. Atkinson, September 9, 2020.
7. Todd Snider, interview with Brian T. Atkinson, November 7, 2020.

8. Chad Staehly, interview with Brian T. Atkinson, September 14, 2020.

9. Mike Grimes, interview with Brian T. Atkinson, November 24, 2020.

10. Peter Cooper, interview with Brian T. Atkinson, November 8, 2020. "'Hey,' Todd said one day. 'Do you want to play Leno with me?'" Cooper says. "You don't get do-overs when you do that show. It can cost the crew money if you have to do it over. 'Okay.' We did 'Looking for a Job,' which begins with a bass run. I'm passable as a bassist at best. I spent so many hours practicing that to make sure I stopped at the right place. Todd brought his friends to do that show. Look at the video on YouTube. Solo artists like Todd call in the top gun slinging guys in town for gigs like that. Todd picked his friends. Todd calling me in for that meant a lot and was very scary. You record early in the afternoon.

"We went back to the hotel after and had to wait until late that night to see it on television. So, we had a very Todd Snider event—a party on the rooftop of this West Hollywood hotel. They had a pool up there. Todd brought up a jam box and put on Delbert McClinton's 'Two More Bottles of Wine.' We got kicked off the roof by the police for playing Delbert too loud. Todd could have gone to dinner with the record company folks, but he wanted to hang out with his friends. I call it a 'Very Todd Tonight Show.' Todd always seems like he has a casual approach to everything, but he doesn't. He knew exactly what was gonna happen and why. He knew where everyone would stand on stage. He said he was disappointed in himself because people said his eyes were too big on the screen. I thought he did great. Then he called two days later. 'Hey, guys," he said. 'We got Letterman, too.'"

11. Justin Corsbie, interview with Brian T. Atkinson, November 24, 2021.

12. Stacie Huckeba, interview with Brian T. Atkinson, October 7, 2020.

13. Kevin Gordon, interview with Brian T. Atkinson, December 4, 2020.

14. Peter Cooper, interview.

15. Mike Grimes, interview.

16. Patty Griffin, interview with Brian T. Atkinson, December 16, 2020.

17. Don Was, interview with Brian T. Atkinson, November 9, 2020.

18. Otis Gibbs, interview with Brian T. Atkinson, October 13, 2020. "I don't want to devalue Todd," Gibbs says. "He must get tired of being thought of as a guy who can make you laugh, but being able to make people laugh is a beautiful thing. You take away a little bit of their burden when you do that and then sing them a beautiful song that has some meaning that maybe someone hasn't thought about. You're working a job that you know you'll be working your whole life and then hear some guy who's funny as all hell on *The Bob and Tom Show*. You're gonna pay twelve dollars to go see him at the Vogue on Saturday. Todd always delivers. His shows are always fun and uplifting. That's a big part. Show up and the show sucks and people aren't gonna come see you again, but he's more than funny.

"I opened for Todd at the Patio in Indianapolis in 1995. There were more than three hundred people there. I remember he asked me if I had a G harmonica at sound check. I lived about three blocks from the club, so I walked home and got one. He played it that night, handed it back at the end of the gig, and said, 'Thanks.' 'No, man,' I said. 'That's all you.' The audience loved him that night and was different from what I usually saw in the rock clubs in Indy. I sold over a hundred CDs. Todd would go on *The Bob and Tom Show*, which was a nationally syndicated morning radio show in Indianapolis. They spoke exactly to that suburban factory worker guy who's slinging a sledgehammer on a construction site. Classic rock station. Those were their listeners, but Todd could go there just being Todd. They loved him.

"Todd was able to speak to these folks who might not have otherwise heard a voice like his. Todd would be talking about Bush cleverly in his songs years later on the show and reached those people. I'm sure some hated him for it and stopped listening to his music, but others kept listening. That's a talent not many people have. Todd had the platform for it at the time [with *The Bob and Tom Show*]. There are probably a whole lot of people who enjoyed "Beer Run" and wanted to hear him play that instead, but there was other stuff. You could draw a straight line from Woody Guthrie and John Prine to Todd. They can make you laugh and then bring the truth that comes along with it that might not have made it to the construction site or auto plant.

"I always thought that was great about Todd. The people who would show up at his shows would be a really neat mix. There would be a Grateful Dead fan and someone who obviously loves Guy Clark and John Prine. Then there would be someone who liked Bob Seger and wanted to come have fun with that guy who sounded fun on *The Bob and Tom Show*. Straddling those lines is a rare thing, but Todd does it effortlessly. I grew up with these folks. My grandfather worked on the assembly line. My dad worked at the factory. I think it's Todd's humor that attracts that crowd. You can make people listen to things by making them laugh that they would never listen to if you were preaching."

19. Stacie Huckeba, interview.

20. Peter Cooper, interview. Justin Corsbie, interview with Brian T. Atkinson, January 7, 2021.

21. Robbie Crowell, interview with Brian T. Atkinson, December 16, 2020.

22. Todd Snider, interview with Brian T. Atkinson, December 12, 2020.

23. Robbie Crowell, interview.

24. Peter Cooper, interview.

25. Don Was, interview.

26. Vince Herman, interview with Brian T. Atkinson, December 12, 2020.

27. Don Was, interview. Todd Snider, interview with Brian T. Atkinson, November 22, 2020. "There's nothing good that can come out of forming a sentence," Snider says. "The first song [on *The First Agnostic Church of Hope and Wonder*] is about a guy who tries to quit his job to find something more meaningful. He decides meaning is dumb and goes back to work as a hustler. He starts his own church. He starts milking everybody and gives all these sermons that are actually pretty good, but then he gets caught stealing and claims it's a hoax. It's kind of funny. I made it all up this year. I think people are pretty forgiving with whatever kind of artsy fartsy thing I do. Some is better than others. Some you like better. Usually, one or two songs will make it into the toolbox for the show.

"I had just figured out how to write about my life in time for my life to get really exciting. Don Was says you can't hold those things. You can dissect them, but they'll be dead like a frog when you're done. You keep going. I do benchmark that as something that everything I was doing was leading up to. That's what I've been trying to do again. I at least want to have that same genuineness, but my life isn't always going to be that interesting or my pencil isn't always going to be that sharp. I'll take time off sometimes. I feel like I've made a ton of records and see them all as okay."

28. Ramblin' Jack Elliott, interview with Brian T. Atkinson, September 28, 2020. Todd Snider, interview with Brian T. Atkinson, October 26, 2020. "We [artists are] a family who risk failure and public humiliation on a regular basis," Snider says. "We've all read that we suck. The real bond is that we just love songs, but there's this broader bond that we just know what it means to be good. It's a load of shit, but we've thrown ourselves into that vacuum. You're not just a poet anymore. You've entered the contest. Strippers before tippers. Whores before bores. We're an allegiance with the lead singer to the band, to the crew, to everybody who works past midnight. The thing Kent showed me is real up at the Kristofferson level. Kristofferson is like my brother. We're close because I dated his daughter for a while, but Ingram doesn't know Kris. Jack could lead a police chase to Kris's house anyway. I like watching Hayes. He's maybe my favorite. Think about it: Woody Guthrie didn't tour. The real father of the guy who writes songs and tells stories is Ramblin' Jack."

29. Todd Snider, interview with Brian T. Atkinson, December 12, 2020.

30. Pamela Des Barres, interview with Brian T. Atkinson, November 20, 2020. Todd's story about the Los Angeles show is from his email exchange with Jenni Finlay, November 24, 2020.

31. Peter Cooper, interview.

32. Bruce Robison, interview with Brian T. Atkinson, October 12, 2020.

33. Kevin Russell, interview with Brian T. Atkinson, January 12, 2021.

Verse: Play A Train Song

1. Todd Snider, interview with Brian T. Atkinson, December 12, 2020.

2. Anita Webb, email interview with Brian T. Atkinson, October 22, 2020.

3. Jack Ingram, interview with Brian T. Atkinson, December 4, 2020. Todd Snider, interview with Brian T. Atkinson, October 26, 2020. "There are some songs that come out as a drip and I force them out over time because I have an axe to grind," Snider says. "Others you check the faucet, and it's already pouring. I played 'Can't Complain' for Kimbrough and told him that was the song I was gonna anchor *Viva Satellite* around. I shaved my head around then and was heading toward a bad bipolar downside. So, it was weird. I had that song and 'Doublewide Blues,' which are two really good ones, and then I wrote like ten really self-serving, fight-winning, narcissistic songs. The record sounds good because of Will, but he had some songs at the time that had way better lyrics than mine.

"Will was my main muse at the time, and I was trying to write songs as good as the ones he was playing me. We should have made a record of his songs if we had it to do all over again. He was on fire and understood the band. I didn't. I'm a talking blues guy. That record could have been really good, but the script wasn't up to the sounds. I can't listen to that whiney guy who has the world by the balls and thinks he got screwed over."

4. Jason Rigenberg, interview with Brian T. Atkinson, December 8, 2020.

5. Todd Snider, interview. "I almost called 'Is This Thing Working?' 'The War on Terror,' but I wouldn't have liked it as much," Snider says. "I was writing a parable. I went out to a Mexican restaurant with Burt [Stein], and he asked if I was working on anything. I told him, and he said, 'We have to make it right away.' So I made a whole album called *Crank It, We're Doomed*. I don't know where to get that record now. I kept trying to make 'Is This Thing Working?' into a song. We did thirteen takes and tried every radically different musical way. I thought none were good. Almost all the songs on *We're Doomed* made it onto other records like *Peace Queer* and *The Excitement Plan*. I don't think any stayed on the floor. Those songs and 'Is This Thing Working?' are fun to play live.

"My live show was very natural from the very beginning. I talk when I get nervous. You can tell I have an idea because I get quiet. In fact, talking is what I like the least about myself. I would like to turn off the talking, but it works at the gig. Talking serves me for an hour and a half as this instinctual thing. I feel more comfortable onstage for some reason. I knew who I was when I realized who Ramblin' Jack Elliott was and that Jerry Jeff was being him. I have been that my whole life. That's the easy part, but I honed it over the years. I started taking pride in that part once they let me tour all over the country."

6. Bob Kevoian, interview with Brian T. Atkinson, September 20, 2020.

7. "Sleepy" John Sandidge, interview with Brian T. Atkinson, November 11, 2020.

8. Kent Blazy, interview with Brian T. Atkinson, October 6, 2020.

9. Kent Blazy, interview.

10. K. K. Rider, interview with Brian T. Atkinson, September 1, 2020.

11. Todd Snider, interview with Brian T. Atkinson, September 15, 2020.

12. Todd Snider, interview with Brian T. Atkinson, September 19, 2020.

13. Mark Marchetti, interview with Brian T. Atkinson, October 20, 2020.

14. Loretta Lynn, interview by Peggy Lynn, text from an email to Brian T. Atkinson sent by Mark Marchetti on December 30, 2020.

15. Todd Snider, interview with Brian T. Atkinson, November 9, 2020.

16. Kent Finlay, interview with Jenni Finlay, March 5, 2014. Todd Snider, interview with Brian T. Atkinson, October 26, 2020. "I like to seek adventure and make it interesting," Snider says. "That's what Kent was saying. He was really good at that. Jimmy Buffett was making Key West something. Jerry Jeff and Willie were making Texas music something. Check into a hotel and try to create. Everybody's somebody in Luckenbach. That applies to songwriting. If the whole key to it is opening your heart and showing people what's in there—and that is what it is—without trying to filter it for them or wondering what they want—I'm just gonna open my heart. If I'm singing about being frustrated with gardening I'm probably not gonna interest a lot of people, but that's what there is today.

"Look at Willie. His songs are so good because he's just a good, deep, caring, sweet, adventurous man. Bitter music crap never comes out when he opens his heart. It feels like the Stones are getting even with some girl sometimes. That's become its own thing, but that's a hard way to live and walk around. How are you gonna be mad at your dad when you're sixty? How are you gonna hold that as your muse? It was more like if you seek the bright side, seek adventure, and hope that the homeless guy is there because he thinks that's hilarious—it probably isn't the case, but keep that on the menu. That was something about Kent as a person. Be kind. That reflects on you as a person. Kent and Bob Mercer were the most influential on me for sure.

"Mercer was more about not letting anybody change that. He was telling me stick to what I came from and do what you have to do to save that. He was of the mind that you're not on the road to be liked. Be not liked if that's your destiny. You're not gonna clean up and go to town. Nobody in this town wants you to be like Kent Finlay. No one. That's slowly turning. Jason Isbell and Chris Stapleton have had an effect on this town as far as trying to open your heart and let people see what's in there. I feel like what Kent taught me was the words to the songs. That's still the thing. Sometimes I write songs that are melody driven.

"I felt like I harnessed my vision for the two records after *The Devil You Know* into a way that felt like art, and I wanted to do it again. I had Kent to call, but I wanted to do it myself. I remember feeling like I was writing too many songs, and it was beneath him. I felt like I lost the plot. I had thirty-five songs and felt like I lost them all. I took them and split them into *Peace Queer*, *The Excitement Plan*, and *Shit Sandwich*. The way I got out of that hole was picturing myself going back to Kent. That was *The Excitement Plan*.

"I told my manager that these political songs were stupid, and the garage rock was a palate cleanser. They're not really songs. I really, really like my manager Burt. We don't even really talk about my career. We just talk about the songs. That's all he cares about. He's very Kent-like. He understands. He said the political songs are really valid. 'They feel very Steve Earle-y,' I said. 'I feel funny playing them for Kent.' There are good songs like 'Stuck on the Corner,' which I think he would have liked, but I felt like they were pretentious. Everybody was doing them at the time. I stuck with the heartfelt songs and story songs. That was *The Excitement Plan*. I recorded the garage rock songs for my birthday and didn't think I would ever play them for the world until I got divorced and needed money."

17. Todd Snider, interview with Brian T. Atkinson, December 2, 2020.

18. Mike Mitchell, interview with Brian T. Atkinson, December 18, 2020. For more on Mike Mitchell and the Kingsmen's significant impact on rock 'n' roll music, see Madison Bloom, "The Kingsmen's Mike Mitchell, Guitarist on 'Louie Louie,' dies at 77," *Pitchfork*, April 18, 2021, https://pitchfork.com/news/the-kingsmens-mike-mitchell-guitarist-on-louie-louie-dead-at-77/; and Daniel Kreps, "Mike Mitchell, Guitarist on the Kingsmen's 'Louie Louie,' Dead at 77, 'I learned how to play the guitar because of Mike Mitchell. I know every one of his solos, mistakes and all,' Joe Walsh says of founding members of garage rock icons,"

Rolling Stone, April 18, 2021, https://www.rollingstone.com/music/music-news/mike-mitchell-guitarist-the-kingsmen-louie-louie-dead-obit-1157393/.

19. Richard Lewis, interview with Brian T. Atkinson, October 1, 2020. Todd Snider, interview. "I have acres of notebooks around here, but those are almost in code," Snider says. "I'll have the word that reminds me of the whole line. Now things end up in 'mail waiting to be sent' ever since I got a computer. That's the last place. There are three in my mail to be sent right now. One is a mix of a new song. Another is a song called 'Filthy Rich Dirt Poor.' I forgot that I got up this morning and took another shot at that this morning. I learned another thing from John: Make a record, take a week off, record another song. No matter what. It might not be good enough for the record, but so what? Don't put it on."

20. Todd Snider, interview with Brian T. Atkinson, December 2, 2020, and email to Atkinson on February 27, 2021. "I always make people mad talking about Christian stuff," Snider says. "I am not degrading any god when I compare [spirituality] to Santa Claus. Only a fool wouldn't believe in Santa Claus, and I mean that. There's proof of Santa Claus everywhere."

Bridge: If Tomorrow Never Comes

1. Todd Snider, interview with Brian T. Atkinson, December 18, 2020.

Verse: Stomp and Holler

1. Susan Tedeschi, interview with Brian T. Atkinson, September 4, 2020.
2. Hayes Carll, interview with Brian T. Atkinson, October 23, 2020.
3. Susan Tedeschi, interview.
4. Todd Snider, interview with Brian T. Atkinson, December 18, 2020.
5. Chris Robinson, interview with Brian T. Atkinson, January 14, 2021.
6. Chad Staehly, interview with Brian T. Atkinson, September 20, 2020.
7. Vince Herman, interview with Brian T. Atkinson, November 17, 2020.
8. Kevn Kinney, interview with Brian T. Atkinson, September 15, 2020.
9. Chad Staehly, interview.
10. James Calemine, "Walking with Zambi: The Colonel Bruce Hampton Interview," Swampland.com, http://swampland.com/articles/view/title:walking_with_zambi_the_colonel_bruce_hampton_interview, accessed January 24, 2021.
11. Vince Herman, interview. Todd Snider, interview with Brian T. Atkinson, October 26, 2020. "I keep getting sued," Snider says. "I was supposed to be on the Don Imus show a couple years ago. I was sitting at the table getting makeup. 'When we come back from the commercials, Todd Snider.' I turned to Don when they went to commercial, and I told him, 'I don't know what to tell you, but I'm leaving.' I went to a doctor after that one. Burt said, 'Man, you were there.' Sometimes I'm there and just don't want to do it. That happened in the Hard Working Americans twice. I go to a doctor because it's deep. It happened on Imus. That's the one thing I've actually gone to a doctor about. How come sometimes I just don't go? I got scared on the Imus show because there were nine shows left on the tour, and I had just seen a photograph on the sidewalk that confused me.

"I couldn't stop thinking about it. I got on the show, and it got away from me. I feel like I'm gonna tear up just talking about it because it's really embarrassing. I just knew I wasn't supposed to be there. I just left even though it was a really awful time. I wasn't even on drugs. I got on the bus and canceled the tour. Brian knew it was futile to try to save the tour. I went home and like a week later I was like, 'How come everyone is mad?' 'Well,' he said. 'You canceled a TV show and nine gigs.' 'Tell me about that.' I think maybe I've been on the road too long. The doctor said it was just OCD or whatever. Sometimes if I don't like something I just go, but I don't mean to be Ryan Adams. It's like I can tell before I start crying. I need to get out of here. It's overwhelming.

"My manager says, 'We have to be a bad wrestler because we can't control it.' So, we have to be a bad wrestler. It's not that I haven't tried. It comes off as really arrogant sometimes, but it's insecurity on [level] fifty. It's that same faucet, but this time it doesn't have a song in it. You just drown in it. It happened on the last tour. I got into an argument with Chris Knight and left a show, but I was present and very aware. I called and answered the phone. I told my manager that I didn't want to be with Chris Knight and wanted to go home, but I didn't vanish. That was a step forward. Then there was a show in Chicago with other people. It doesn't make sense. I had something in my head about Lukas Nelson trying to take my girlfriend.

"Last year was really good. I went everywhere I said I was going. Eddie Vedder missed a show last year, and I was like, 'That was my first year to go to every show.' I don't think Kent ever knew about that part. I had that when I was back in school. I wonder if Ryan Adams has what I have because I identify, but Neal always said, 'No, no, he knows what he's doing.' Neal said he's mean. He doesn't vanish like I do. He stays there and is mean, but he's doing the same thing. He's exhausted with trying to feel confident, and the balloon is pissing out around the room. He's been carrying around that false confidence all day."

12. Todd Snider, interview with Brian T. Atkinson, September 15, 2020.

13. Ben Kaufmann, interview with Brian T. Atkinson, October 15, 2020. Todd Snider, interview with Brian T. Atkinson, November 16, 2020. "I would never kill myself," Snider says, "but it would be more like, 'Careful, you've taken too much of that.' 'Oh, I've had a good run.' I remember saying to my mom after Neal, 'I'm not going down easy. No more walking around whining on the yacht. Even if it means no more songs. Sing, travel, be happy.' I feel really, really lucky, but on my shitty days I didn't. I was divorced and was being divorced from my family. It wasn't really about drugs, but that was a hard time. It's not even better now, but I'm happy. I like working on my songs. I moved into a studio and made a record when my wife kicked me out, but it was too much. I was trying so hard to be unique that it was barely music. I felt like I did everything no one normally does—and I figured out why. No wonder everyone has choruses. Songs without them suck. I was trying to break all the rules. I did. Unlistenable. I have reined in all those ideas.

"The thing I'm working on now is trying to be original. I have no idea what it will sound like when we're done. I move the other way if it sounds like one thing. We're not gonna play a great rock chord through an electric guitar. We're not gonna play a funky beat the [typical way]. Run the other way if it starts to sound like the Stones. Usually, you have a couple records you can show a producer what you're going for, but now I've done it so much. I don't have a record I'm going for. I want to make music that sounds like nothing we've ever done before. I doubt I will, but I'm hoping to do something original sonically. There's no one-four-five going on. It's just one right now, but who knows? I do this stuff a lot and throw it away. I keep waiting for it to show itself."

14. "Coast to Coast—Talking with Jeff Austin," Wintergrass festival website, 2018, wintergrass.com/coast-to-coast-a-conversation-with-jeff-austin, accessed January 24, 2021.

15. Todd Snider, interview with Brian T. Atkinson, October 26, 2020. "Coast to Coast—Talking with Jeff Austin," Wintergrass festival website, 2018, wintergrass.com/coast-to-coast-a-conversation-with-jeff-austin, accessed January 24, 2021.

16. Andrew Dansby, interview with Brian T. Atkinson, December 30, 2020.

17. Jack Ingram, interview with Brian T. Atkinson, December 4, 2020. Todd Snider, interview with Brian T. Atkinson, November 22, 2020. "I'm gonna make another country record," Snider says. "I have a whole bunch of country songs I wrote with other people like Jack, a couple with Billy Joe, one with Loretta, two with Johnny Cash that his son gave me the lyrics to, a couple with John Carter himself. Jack and I and his friend made one up called 'Here Comes a Cowboy in a Pickup Truck with a Kickass Country Song Jacked Up.' I would love for a big star to cut that, but I want to cut it, too. Jack told me some big star cut it, but I don't know. The names always sound like Luke Bryan or Bryan Luke. Luke Shelton Daniel. I can't keep up with it.

"Jack and I are talking about making a record now. I'm trying to get him to sign with my label. It's not like he needs it, but I'm like, 'Dude, I just built a studio. Guess what the budget is? Nothing. Come down and make a record. Produce yourself. Let me put it out if you don't like who else wants to put it out.' I think that would be a great idea. He's my main brother. He goes to bed at five in the morning, and I get up at five. We say we're gonna start a security company. Almost every fucking morning that thing rings, and it's Jack. He's pie-eyed, reading poetry, and getting ready to go to bed. I'm up stoned doing the same thing. We have a little powwow when we're working. He works right before bed. I work when I get up. We check each other's temperature. I root for him as hard as I root for myself.

"Same with Hayes. They're two people I've really bonded with. Also, Kevn Kinney, Aaron Lee Tasjan, and Elizabeth Cook. There are more, but those are my main blood family. Melita and I did great work. We were in our prime. We really got along for a really long time. Then my family stopped talking to me, and I turned into someone else. She didn't love that guy. I hope she's doing good. I'm really proud of that time."

18. Todd Snider, interview with Brian T. Atkinson, November 6, 2020.

19. Todd Snider, email exchange with Jenni Finlay, January 15, 2021. Tom Jones released his cover of Snider's "Talking Reality Television Blues" as his new single that morning.

20. Todd Snider, interview with Brian T. Atkinson, October 26 and November 6, 2020. "I like both solo and band shows, but the solo troubadour thing feels like an extension of who I am," Snider said in the October 26 interview. "I don't feel like I'm auditioning or have anything to prove when I'm doing the troubadour shows. You can go fuck yourself if you don't like it. I've been feeding myself with this for years. This is just this thing I do. I have to go do it tomorrow, and I like it that way. Everything else I do is a fun lark. I don't feel like I'm doing what God put me here to do when I'm playing with a band. I feel like I'm doing what I can do because I work hard at what God put me here to do. Like sailing. I do my calling so I can go on a sailing trip now. People go watch Woody Allen play clarinet because he worked so hard at his movies. I see myself like that. I worked so hard as a troubadour that the world let me sing in a jam band for three years as the payoff. I made a garage rock record because of 'D. B. Cooper.'

"I work hard at being Ramblin' Jack's son. I take it seriously. If I was on some team and a coach told me to improve, I'd say, 'Fuck off, coach. I got this.' I'm not doing this for you. I can't see myself starving. I can't even see myself not getting a place to stay. I know so many songs that aren't even mine. If some guy has a boat and I want on it, I feel good about my chances. I know some songs that guy wants on his boat. I can grift that guy. I can get anybody as a troubadour. Point out a house, and I'll go, 'They'll let me stay over there tonight. I guarantee it.' I'm just gonna stand in the yard, and this guy will give me the key to his car. I know some songs he likes and some stories about places you can go. I wrote a mediocre book and got to be a pretty mediocre jam band singer because of all that. Made a couple mediocre movies.

"I was really proud of how bad our films came out because I know how to busk. I like doing all the other stuff, but they feel like a prize, the glaze on the donut. They're pay for being a troubadour, just like being able to go to Key West. I get to go arrange my songs in the studio like I'm Brian Wilson. Nobody's waiting around to say, 'I can't wait to hear what sounds Todd Snider goes for,' but I get to do it. I get to pretend like I'm a producer and make records because that's part of being a troubadour. I meet actors and interesting people like politicians and sports stars because of that. You have a life of perpetual childhood if that's what you want. I would tell [young songwriters] that's what it's all about, because if you switch it to money you won't be able to switch it back. We're getting away with something hilarious. Period. Try to make it like something your dad did and you're gonna lose it. I say to the kids that everyone will say this is a business and you have to stay grounded, but I disagree. This isn't for you if you're not ready to get a tattoo on your face.

"Don't do this if it's something someone said you're talented at doing. That's not what this is. Talent in music is a small part. That's something you teach other kids. Talent at being adrift isn't something you can teach kids. You don't have schools for how to live like a millionaire with no money. Kent Finlay can teach you. I was ready to learn that when I met Kent. You couldn't give me a shirt that was gonna make me feel better then. I saw through that. There's a part of this that your parents won't understand, but Ramblin' Jack will. Run through the shit field, son. I always thought Kent saw me as wayward. That part was there before I met him. I ran away at fifteen and was a misfit and got expelled.

"I wanted to be like, 'Yeah, Christmas is coming up and the big game . . .' I just never gave a fuck. You got a strip poker game going on down the street at the house where the dad left because he's an alcoholic. Ooh. Sounds fun. Hunter Thompson was my thing. Now, his son [Juan] and I talk all the time. I feel like his son is a real liaison for someone like me to have a front seat to watch his dad make decisions based on something entirely hard to predict. [Juan] is really good at saying, 'You don't have to stop.' Sometimes I get caught up with gambling, or a girl, or drugs, but these days I try really hard not to let the crowd down because there are so many more. I figured that they would get over it when it was like a hundred or three hundred people. Now, there are like a thousand people at the show. My crowd just built over the years."

Chorus: From a Rooftop (Part 2)

1. Todd Snider, interview with Brian T. Atkinson, October 26, 2020.
2. Hayes Carll, interview with Brian T. Atkinson, October 23, 2020.
3. Jason Isbell, interview with Brian T. Atkinson, December 3, 2020.
4. Todd Snider, interview with Brian T. Atkinson, November 16, 2020.
5. Jason Isbell, interview with Brian T. Atkinson, December 3, 2020.
6. Amanda Shires, interview with Brian T. Atkinson, October 14, 2020.
7. Elizabeth Cook, interview with Brian T. Atkinson, November 10, 2020. Todd Snider, interview with Brian T. Atkinson, October 26, 2020. "Jerry Jeff and I talked in his last days," Snider says. "I think he had similar regrets. I don't like cocaine. There just aren't that many Willie Nelsons. I'm not saying I've thrown tantrums. I'm just saying you can't not admit your own odd behavior when people show it to you. Then what do you do when you're fifty-something? You don't know how to act anymore. I keep to myself. I've been doing really good lately."
8. Todd Snider, interview with Brian T. Atkinson, November 16, 2020.
9. Jamie Lin Wilson, interview with Brian T. Atkinson, November 12, 2020
10. Andrew Dansby, interview with Brian T. Atkinson, December 30, 2020.
11. Jamie Lin Wilson, interview.
12. Jonny Burke, interview with Brian T. Atkinson, November 24, 2020. In an email exchange with Jenni Finlay on October 3, 2020, Todd Snider commented on removing opening acts from touring while on the road: "[I threw the woman opening the tour off the bus because she] kept getting too drunk and trying to tell me what I should do. I couldn't help her to see that I don't try to win or go for them or any of that. She'd be like, 'It would go over better if you did this or that. You'd be bigger.' I get that a lot. My only goal at my gigs is to do whatever I want, whenever I want, however I want. Nobody can help. I'm not trying to go over better or get bigger. I don't perform from there. Keith Sykes got thrown off for the same reason. It's obvious to me. Why do I get them every time? I can tell them that once, but I can't have it around if they don't get it. I can't have that desire to be liked around me. It's what kills people on the road. I let it go in the nineties."

13. Bob Schneider, interview with Brian T. Atkinson, September 18, 2020.
14. Steve Poltz, interview with Brian T. Atkinson, September 15, 2020.
15. Tim Easton, interview with Brian T. Atkinson, September 12, 2020.
16. Aaron Lee Tasjan, interview with Brian T. Atkinson, December 4, 2020.
17. Todd Snider, interview with Brian T. Atkinson, November 26, 2020.
18. Aaron Lee Tasjan, interview.
19. Darrin Bradbury, interview with Brian T. Atkinson, September 15, 2020.
20. Brian Wright, interview with Brian T. Atkinson, December 16, 2020.
21. Jon Latham, interview with Brian T. Atkinson, September 29, 2020.
22. Allen Thompson, interview with Brian T. Atkinson, October 19, 2020.
23. Cody Diekhoff, interview with Brian T. Atkinson, November 6, 2020.
24. Joe Pug, interview with Brian T. Atkinson, December 7, 2020.
25. John Craigie, interview with Brian T. Atkinson, November 6, 2020.
26. Chelsea Lovitt, interview with Brian T. Atkinson, September 27, 2020.
27. Raelyn Nelson, interview with Brian T. Atkinson, October 23, 2020. Todd Snider, email to Jenni Finlay, February 5, 2021. "We usually get a different bus every leg," Snider says. "The drivers change. Whoever was in it last changes. So, the driver always has a story from his last trip. Sometimes now people get the first one Taylor Swift [toured in]. I fucking love it. Oddly, it has a trophy case. I only have that one golf tournament trophy from Ingram's tournament, and I stole that then broke it. I went through a phase of stealing trophies. People said it wasn't the same as winning, but they don't know."
28. Sierra Ferrell, interview with Brian T. Atkinson, October 20, 2020. Todd Snider, email exchange with Jenni Finlay, October 14. 2020. "Sierra is as real as they get, and she is about to be huge," Snider says. "She was in bad shape when I met her and in a crud scene. Eric [McConnell] and me moved her here, made an album everyone wanted, and she vanished. Came back a couple years later ready to rumble and cleaned up. She really is my favorite young troubadour. I am like her Kent."

Coda

1. Jack Ingram, interview with Brian T. Atkinson, December 4, 2020.
2. Todd Snider, email exchange with Brian T. Atkinson, November 26, 2020.

Big Finish

1. Todd Snider, email exchange with Brian T. Atkinson, January 3, 2021, and interview with Atkinson, November 16, 2020. "I read something one time that Woody Guthrie knew how to punctuate and spell, but he didn't," Snider said in the November 2020 interview. "That wasn't who he was. I don't do that, but I was a really uneducated person when I started. I like to think I've read a lot because one thing you get with this life is free time. I wanted to go to college. I feel insecure about not going, so I've tried to educate myself in my adult life. My new heroes are Alan Watts and Terence McKenna. I read a book if a singer writes it. I have all Mark Twain's books. I started trying to read stuff on physics classes

online when I got into my forties. I would have liked to have a college education. I think it would have helped with songwriting. I was gonna make a bunch of money as a singer in my early days, go to college, and then go back to singing after. I got sidetracked loving being on the road.

"I read lots of history books, but I mostly stay tuned into the world because I want to write songs about it. I skipped high school then started getting my education from Kent and learning the history of music. Songs about different battles. I started studying music like crazy after I got a record deal. I still do. I have a ritual. I get up and write poems for a few hours. Then I work on playing music for a little less time. I used to go to the record store, but these days Spotify recommends stuff from what you've listened to, and there is a ton of music. I study it all. I just went through a deep Norwegian metal dive but found nothing of any use."

Selected Discography*

Todd Snider

1. *Songs for the Daily Planet* (MCA Records, 1994)
2. *Step Right Up* (MCA Records, 1996)
3. *Viva Satellite* (Geffen Records, 1998)
4. *Happy to Be Here* (Oh Boy Records, 2000)
5. *New Connection* (Oh Boy Records, 2002)
6. *East Nashville Skyline* (Oh Boy Records, 2004)
7. *That Was Me: The Best of Todd Snider 1994–1998* (Universal Music Company, 2005)
8. *The Devil You Know* (Hip-O Records, 2006)
9. *Peace, Love and Anarchy* (Oh Boy Records, 2007)
10. *Cheatham Street Warehouse* (Aimless Records, streaming only, 2007)
11. *Peace Queer* (Aimless Records, 2008)
12. *The Excitement Plan* (Yep Roc Records, 2009)
13. *Time as We Know It: The Songs of Jerry Jeff Walker* (Aimless Records, 2012)
14. *Agnostic Hymns & Stoner Fables* (Aimless Records, 2012)
15. *Eastside Bulldog* (Aimless Records, 2016)
16. *Cash Cabin Sessions, Vol. 3* (Aimless Records, 2019)
17. *The First Agnostic Church of Hope and Wonder* (Aimless Records, 2021)
18. *Crank It, We're Doomed* (Aimless Records, 2023)

* See toddsnider.net for information on all of Snider's remade studio albums, which he recorded at the Purple Building for his Aimless Records.

Live Todd Snider Albums

1. *Near Truths and Hotel Rooms* (Oh Boy Records, 2003)
2. *Live at Grimey's Nashville* (Next Door Records, 2007)
3. *Todd Snider Live: The Storyteller* (Aimless Records, 2012)
4. *Live: Return of the Storyteller* (Aimless Records, 2022)

Forty Essential Todd Snider Songs

1. "Play a Train Song," *East Nashville Skyline*, 2004
2. "Just Like Old Times," *The Devil You Know*, 2006
3. "Doublewide Blues," *Near Truths and Hotel Rooms*, 2003
4. "Can't Complain," *Viva Satellite*, 1998
5. "Tension," *Todd Snider Live: The Storyteller*, 2014
6. "Cheatham Street Warehouse," *Cheatham Street Warehouse*, 2015

7. "Conservative Christian, Right-Wing Republican, Straight, White, American Males," *East Nashville Skyline*, 2004

8. "East Nashville Skyline," *Todd Snider Live: The Storyteller*, 2014

9. "Easy Money," *Songs for the Daily Planet*, 1994

10. "D. B. Cooper," *Happy to Be Here*, 2000

11. "The Devil You Know," *Todd Snider Live: The Storyteller*, 2014

12. "The Ballad of the Kingsmen," *Todd Snider Live: The Storyteller*, 2014

13. "Tillamook County Jail," *East Nashville Skyline*, 2004

14. "Greencastle Blues," *The Excitement Plan*, 2009

15. "The Ballad of the Devil's Backbone Tavern," *Happy to Be Here*, 2000

16. "Looking for a Job," *The Devil You Know*, 2006

17. "Long Year," *Happy to Be Here*," 2000

18. "Talking Seattle Grunge Rock Blues," *Songs for the Daily Planet*, 1994

19 "Beer Run," *New Connection*, 2002

20. "Age Like Wine," *East Nashville Skyline*, 2004

2.1 "Happy New Year/All That Matters (Reprise)," *Live at Grimey's Nashville*, 2007

22. "Statistician's Blues," *New Connection*, 2002

23. "Iron Mike's Main Man's Last Request," *East Nashville Skyline*, 2004

24. "Side Show Blues," *Step Right Up*, 1996

25. "If Tomorrow Never Comes," *The Devil You Know*, 2006

26. "Stuck on the Corner," *Todd Snider Live: The Storyteller*, 2014

27. "Rose City," *New Connection*, 2002

28. "Alright Guy," *Songs for the Daily Planet*, 1994

29. "Waco Moon," *Near Truths and Hotel Rooms*, 2002

30. "Like a Force of Nature," *Cash Cabin Sessions, Vol. 3*, 2019

31. "Broke," *Near Truths and Hotel Rooms*, 2003

32. "In Between Jobs" *Agnostic Hymns & Stoner Fables*, 2012

33. "From a Rooftop," *Peace, Love and Anarchy*, 2007

34. "In the Beginning," *Agnostic Hymns & Stoner Fables*, 2012

35. "Nashville," *East Nashville Skyline*, 2004

36. "Brenda," *Agnostic Hymns & Stoner Fables*, 2012

37. "Blues on Banjo," *Cash Cabin Sessions, Vol. 3*, 2019

38. "Forty Five Miles," *Todd Snider Live: The Storyteller*, 2012

39. "Hey Pretty Boy," *East Nashville Bulldog*, 2016

40. "Trouble," *Songs for the Daily Planet*, 1994

Twenty Essential Todd Snider Cover Songs

1. "Don't It Make You Wanna Dance" (Rusty Weir), *Todd Snider Live: The Storyteller*, 2011

2. "Fortunate Son" (John Fogerty), *Peace Queer*, 2008

3. "Oh Boy!" (Buddy Holly) with Joe Ely, *Not Fade Away: Remembering Buddy Holly*, 1996

4. "Corpus Christi Bay" (Robert Earl Keen), *The Excitement Plan*, 2009

5. "L. A. Freeway" (Guy Clark) with the Band of Heathens, *Remote Transmissions*, 2022

6. "Mr. Bojangles" (Jerry Jeff Walker), *Time as We Know It: The Songs of Jerry Jeff Walker*, 2012

7. "Good News Blues" (Billy Joe Shaver), *East Nashville Skyline*, 2004

8. "Take It as It Comes" (Bobby Rambo), *Time as We Know It: The Songs of Jerry Jeff Walker*, 2012

9. "A Boy Named Sue" (Shel Silverstein), *Twistable Turnable Man: A Musical Tribute to the Songs of Shel Silverstein*, 2010

10. "Alcohol and Pills" (Fred Eaglesmith), *East Nashville Skyline*, 2004

11. "Crooked Piece of Time" (John Prine) with John Prine, *New Connection*, 2002

12. "Sangria Wine" (Jerry Jeff Walker), *Time as We Know It: The Songs of Jerry Jeff Walker*, 2012

13. "Enjoy Yourself" (Herbert Magdison, Carr Sigman), *East Nashville Skyline*, 2004

14. "Pissin' in the Wind" (Jerry Jeff Walker), *Time as We Know It: The Songs of Jerry Jeff Walker*, 2012

15. "The Songwriter" (Kent Finlay), *Cheatham Street Warehouse*, 2015

16. "Betty Was Black (And Willie Was White)" (The Bis-Quits), *Happy to Be Here*, 2000

17. "I've Lived Some Songs" ("I've Written Some Life") (Kent Finlay), *Cheatham Street Warehouse*, 2015

18. "Little Bird" (Jerry Jeff Walker), *Time as We Know It: The Songs of Jerry Jeff Walker*, 2012

19. "West Nashville Grand Ballroom Gown" (Jimmy Buffett), *Agnostic Hymns & Stoner Fables*, 2012

20. "Hill Country," (Kent Finlay), *Cheatham Street Warehouse*, 2015

Twenty Essential Songs Written or Cowritten by Todd Snider and Recorded by Others

1. Jack Ingram, "Airways Motel" (written with Jack Ingram and Tom Littlefield), *Livin' or Dyin'*, 1997

2. Robert Earl Keen, "Play a Train Song," *Ready for Confetti*, 2011

3. Yonder Mountain String Band, "East Nashville Easter" (written with Jeff Austin), *Yonder Mountain String Band*, 2006

4. Loretta Lynn with Elvis Costello, "Everything It Takes" (written with Loretta Lynn), *Full Circle*, 2016

5. Jack Ingram, "Barbie Doll" (written with Jack Ingram), *Hey You*, 1999

6. Mark Chesnutt, "Trouble," *Wings*, 1995

7. Tom Jones, "Talking Reality Television Blues," *Surrounded by Time*, 2021

8. Jerry Jeff Walker, "Alright Guy," *Gonzo Stew*, 2001

9. Jack Ingram, "Feel Like I'm Falling in Love" (written with Jack Ingram), *Hey You*, 1999

10. Billy Joe Shaver, "Deja Blues" (written with Billy Joe Shaver), *Freedom's Child*, 2002

11. Will Kimbrough, "Cape Henry" (written with Will Kimbrough), *Godsend (unreleased songs 1994–2002)*, 2006

12. Gary Allan, "Alright Guy," *Alight Guy*, 2001

13. Billy Joe Shaver, "The Real Deal" (written with Billy Joe Shaver), *The Real Deal*, 2005

14. Jason and the Scorchers, "This Town Isn't Keeping You Down" (written with Jason Rigenberg), *Midnight Roads & Stages Seen*, 1998

15. Cross Canadian Ragweed, "Late Last Night," *Garage*, 2005

16. Corb Lund, "Age Like Wine," *Songs My Friends Wrote*, 2022

17. Jack Ingram, "Easy As 1, 2, 3 (Part II)" (written with Jack Ingram), *This Is It*, 2007

18. Cross Canadian Ragweed, "I Believe You," *Mission California*, 2007

19. Jason Rigenberg, "James Dean's Car" (written with Jason Rigenberg), *All Over Creation*, 2002

20. Will Kimbrough, "Horseshoe Lake" (written with Will Kimbrough), *EP*, 2007

Index

In fond memory of the late, great Wrecks of Honor:

Jeff Austin

Neal Casal

Kent Finlay

Nanci Griffith

Col. Bruce Hampton

Cowboy Jim

Skip Kenneth Francis "Play a fuckin' train song" Litz

Bob Mercer

Mike Mitchell

John Prine

Billy Joe Shaver

Eddy Shaver

Eddie Van Halen and the Eddie Van Halen Band

Jerry Jeff Walker

Michael "Moondawg" Webb